William Henry Seward
and the Secession Crisis

D1564075

$20.00

941231

William Henry Seward and the Secession Crisis

The Effort to Prevent Civil War

LAWRENCE M. DENTON

To: Mason-Dixon CWRT,

Keepers of the faith,

Larry Denton

June '10

McFarland & Company, Inc., Publishers
Jefferson, North Carolina, and London

LIBRARY OF CONGRESS CATALOGUING-IN-PUBLICATION DATA

Denton, Lawrence M.
    William Henry Seward and the secession crisis : the effort
to prevent civil war / Lawrence M. Denton.
        p.   cm.
    Includes bibliographical references and index.

    ISBN 978-0-7864-4428-1
    softcover : 50# alkaline paper ∞

    1. Seward, William Henry, 1801–1872.   2. Seward,
William Henry, 1801–1872 — Political and social views.
3. Political leadership — United States — Case studies.
4. Legislators — United States — Biography.   5. United
States. Congress. Senate — Biography.   6. Presidential
candidates — United States — Biography.   7. Governors —
New York (State) — Biography.   8. Secession — United States.
9. United States — Politics and government — 1849–1861.
10. United States — History — Civil War, 1861–1865 — Causes.
I. Title.
E415.9.S4D46   2009
328.73'092 — dc22   2009020565
[B]

British Library cataloguing data are available

Cover image: Seward bust, Seward House, Auburn, New York

Manufactured in the United States of America

McFarland & Company, Inc., Publishers
  Box 611, Jefferson, North Carolina 28640
    www.mcfarlandpub.com

CONTENTS

To the memory of James Edward Bayne (1879–1955)
of Baynesville, Maryland.

*The son of a Civil War veteran, and my maternal
grandfather, who introduced me to the war.*

PREFACE AND
ACKNOWLEDGMENTS

This work presents the remarkable effort of William Henry Seward to find a peaceful solution to the secession crisis. Seward, called Henry by his family and close friends, is the principal subject; Abraham Lincoln is discussed also. I came to "know" Henry Seward during the 1980s while completing research on a book about the secession crisis in Maryland, *A Southern Star for Maryland*. Data and correspondence from the antebellum period constantly referenced this man. Contemporaries raved about his capabilities and his character. Although there were other antebellum political leaders of real stature, John J. Crittenden, Stephen A. Douglas, and Jefferson Davis, for instance, it was Seward who was ranked second to none for his outstanding reputation as a political leader *and* his true visionary nature. Throughout the world, he was a very well known and highly respected politician. What actions did William Henry Seward take during the secession winter to avert war? How close did he come to success? Could Seward, had he been president-elect, have prevented the Civil War?

William Henry Seward and the Secession Crisis posits answers to these questions.

***

Some may contend it is presumptuous to suggest Seward could have made a difference, that he could have accomplished something Lincoln could not. I look at Seward's actions not only from the view of historical evidence, but from the background of a working Washington insider who experienced the world of real politics for some twenty-five years. In analyzing the secession drama, I have attempted to balance a mixture of secondary sources, views of distinguished experts, with pertinent primary source material from actual participants. The contemporary viewpoint, the opinions of those who interacted with Henry Seward and Abraham Lincoln firsthand, will be highlighted. Pulitzer Prize winners David Donald and Doris Kearns Goodwin influenced me greatly, as did the distinguished historians William W. Freehling and Daniel W. Crofts, surely two of the nation's top secession crisis experts.

I am deeply indebted to three reviewers who helped through the early stages of the manuscript: Robert I. Cottom, Edward L. McDill, and Peter A. Wisbey. Their many helpful comments early on framed the work; also, their encouragement kept me going through some dark moments when loose ends seemed to rule. In addition, I am indebted to Peter, executive director of the Seward House, for permitting me access to the Seward family photograph collection and to permit publishing some of the photographs in this work, several seen in these pages have not been previously published.

Daniel C. Toomey, author and publisher of over a dozen Civil War books, offered valuable suggestions on the third draft as did Barbara B. Lamb. However, no one is more worthy of my deep appreciation than Professor Daniel W. Crofts. Dan not only offered insightful comments on what was supposed to be the final (third) draft, but gave me many substantive suggestions about what needed re–doing. I had resisted a fourth draft until Dan interceded. The fourth draft was ably edited by Therese Boyd who also assisted in final manuscript preparation. Ted Alexander offered thoughtful comments on this draft as well. Also deserving special mention is John R. Riina, authors' representative, who taught me the ropes of publishing. Recognizing the many comments and suggestions from the above reviewers, to whom I owe lasting appreciation, I take full responsibility for all that is presented here, including the errors that inevitably creep into every book.

In addition, I am grateful to many who offered assistance during the research phase of this work. At Washington College in Chestertown, Maryland, I owe thanks to Ruth C. Shoge, now director of the Miller Library, to David Dudek, electronic resources librarian (who coincidently hails from Auburn, New York) and to my research assistant, April Hill, class of 2003. At the University of Rochester, I am indebted to Mary M. Huth, assistant director, Rare Books and Special Collections in the Rush Rhees Library, for her valuable suggestions and for permission to publish letters from the William Henry Seward Papers and the Thurlow Weed Papers housed at Rhees. Also, Mary introduced me to a graduate student in the department of history at Rochester, now Dr. Tara McCarthy, who transcribed a large number of letters from the Seward Papers and Weed Papers (in spite of his brilliance, Henry Seward had atrocious handwriting). I am indebted to Tara for her hard work.

Special mention must be made regarding Professor Glyndon G. Van Deusen, former chairman of the department of history at the University of Rochester and an outstanding 19th century American historian. Dr. Van Deusen died at the age of 89 on April 8, 1987. His books on Seward and Weed helped inspire this work. *Thurlow Weed: Wizard of the Lobby* still ranks as the seminal work on Weed. His widely praised biography *William Henry Seward* is the best of its kind. His eulogy included these words from a long-time colleague: "Glyndon Van Deusen was a dramatic and inspiring teacher who brought reason to complex issues and problems." His books did also.

I am also grateful to family and friends who gave encouragement and offered suggestions during the years taken to produce this book, including Robert D. Barton, grandson of historian William E. Barton who is cited in these pages, David G. Burton, Philip D. Caraci, Mark D. Garrett for helping me through several computer glitches, Johanna McDill, William S. Myers, Ron and Betsy Sapp, and finally, Edward R. Thieler, who assisted in many ways. Lastly, a special debt is owed my wife, Susan, whose steadfast support never wavered.

Lawrence M. Denton
Oxford, Maryland
Summer 2009

INTRODUCTION

It is too easy for historians to merely ratify the past and suggest what
happened had to happen.— Gabor S. Boritt

William Henry Seward was the most recognized, the most adroit, and
the most visionary politician of the antebellum era — small in stature but
larger than life. Abraham Lincoln, almost by happenstance (he referred to
himself as the "accidental instrument"), was elected president of the United
States on November 6, 1860, largely through the efforts of Henry Seward.
From the time of Lincoln's election until the time of his death, he and Seward
were so intriguingly connected (Seward almost died from a would-be assas-
sin's knife attack the same night Lincoln was shot), it is difficult, at times, to
separate cause and effect in their relationship.

In the spring of 1860 Henry Seward, recognized as the nation's leading
Republican, was the odds-on favorite to receive the Republican Party nomination for president of the United States. Although his fortunes were undone
by the unexpected nomination of Abraham Lincoln at the Chicago convention, nevertheless he played *the* pivotal role in getting Lincoln elected. During the secession crisis over the winter of 1860–61 (the secession winter),
Seward was everywhere. While his early activities were somewhat clandestine, he was openly talked about by this newspaper and that newspaper in
virtually every section of the country. Contemporary reports suggest the
nation's leadership, not only in politics but in business, commerce, finance
and trade looked to him to find a solution to the unfolding crisis. As states
in the lower South began to withdraw from the Union, it can be argued Henry
Seward — not President James Buchanan or President-elect Abraham Lincoln — took charge of efforts to find a workable solution to the crisis in the
nation's capital. To be sure, other leaders took an active role too, John J. Crittenden, Stephen A. Douglas and Charles Francis Adams, to name a few, but
it was Seward who dominated. This book has as its focus Seward's herculean
work to avert war. The epilogue discusses how Seward, as president-elect and
then president, could have prevented the Civil War.

***

Immediately after the Civil War, the information gathered and documented by historians came for the most part from actual participants in the conflict. This early history appears in the *Official Records of the War of the Rebellion*, and numerous publications by authors who witnessed events, much of it published before the end of the nineteenth century. While emotions were still high both Southerners and Northerners sought to justify the war from their respective positions. Some of these authors knew Abraham Lincoln personally. John G. Nicolay and John Hay, Lincoln's personal secretaries, published a ten-volume work, *Abraham Lincoln: A History*, in the late 1880s. William H. Herndon, Lincoln's long-time law partner in Springfield, added his first-person account, *Herndon's Lincoln: The True Story of a Great Life*, and Ward H. Lamon, Lincoln's bodyguard, using sources obtained from Herndon, published *The Life of Abraham Lincoln*. These works, widely read and debated, painted a unique picture of the martyred Lincoln, who probably has been written about more than any other historical figure. For any author, "the main problem with studying Lincoln is not finding sources, but choosing which sources to follow."[1] On the other hand, William Henry Seward, Lincoln's closest advisor and one who played such an important role during this time, has received very little attention — when compared to Lincoln, virtually none.

During the research effort culminating in this work, I have been influenced by two works from the mid–twentieth century. David M. Potter's *Lincoln and His Party in the Secession Crisis* sparked the first premise leading to the genesis of this book with his famous quote about Lincoln, "He was far more fit to *become* than to *be* President" (italics mine).[2] William Henry Seward, with his vast political experience and intimate knowledge of Washington, thought he was fit to *be* president. In 1958 Richard N. Current published his acclaimed work, *The Lincoln Nobody Knows*, in which he stated, "Abraham Lincoln, despite the wealth of words written by him and about him, remains in many ways a mysterious man."[3] Perhaps no one truly knows why Lincoln made the decision which led to war; he seemed genuinely troubled, perhaps confused. One fact is clear: Abraham Lincoln did not know the nation's political leaders, either North or South, *at the time he was making the momentous decision*. On the other hand, William Henry Seward knew virtually everyone who mattered in Washington, on both sides— Jefferson Davis was his neighbor and friend.

I have also found much inspiration in four more recent works. Daniel W. Crofts's *Reluctant Confederates* chronicles the daily work of William Henry Seward as he tried to forge a relationship with upper South Unionists during the secession winter.[4] Seward led the effort to promote conciliatory policies toward the South, which, despite Lincoln's clandestine opposition, aided in building a new "Union Party" in the upper South. This emerging party, dominated by nonslaveholders and political moderates, commanded a solid, if not overwhelming, majority and thereby held the potential to avert war, at least in the eyes of Henry Seward.

The penetrating biography *Lincoln*, by David Donald, is perhaps the most insightful work on Lincoln ever written. Donald documents the "bungling Lincoln" as the crisis hour approached: "Lincoln needed all the help he could get because, as he freely admitted, later, when he became President 'he was entirely ignorant not only of the duties, but of the manner of doing the business' in the executive office. He tried to do everything himself."[5] William Henry Seward, a political leader steeped in the affairs of Washington, sought to take charge of the Lincoln administration as the moment of crisis approached.

In the recently published *Team of Rivals,* Doris Kearns Goodwin covers some of the same ground as this work and uses many of the same sources for Seward (as there are so few).[6] *Team of Rivals* presents a broad perspective on Lincoln and his three principal advisors (Henry Seward the most important), from his nomination for the presidency to the end of the war. Goodwin concludes Seward was a very good man, Lincoln the great one. This is a Seward-centric work more narrowly focused, from the time he lost the nomination through the first few weeks of the Lincoln administration. During the secession crisis, a Seward-centric story presents Lincoln as a very good man, Seward the great one.

Finally, for the serious student of the Civil War the new volume 2 (2007) of William W. Freehling's *The Road to Disunion* will surely become a must read text regarding the secession crisis.[7] It is hard to imagine anyone producing a more thorough analysis of the period between 1854 and 1861. Freehling's treatment of the lower South as the moment of decision arrived is riveting. He captures the happenstance of history, both with individuals and events. Sometimes only a day or two or even a few hours could have changed the outcome of a debate or the reaction of a crowd or a key vote. Could William Henry Seward, with the nation's foremost political boss, Thurlow Weed, at his side, have pushed events along in a different direction had he been president-elect?

***

William Henry Seward is an often maligned and certainly neglected giant of America's storied past. Abraham Lincoln, a true giant, must be discussed because his actions and inactions during the secession winter and early weeks of the new administration affected Seward so deeply. Some historians have analyzed the shortcomings of Lincoln as a new president; some even suggest he was one of the least qualified persons ever to assume the presidency.

This work will propose that William Henry Seward was one of the best qualified persons ever to seek the presidency, discuss how he almost prevented war as secretary of state, and finally in the epilogue speculate on what he could have accomplished had he been president-elect and then president.[8]

Henry Seward has received little attention over the century and a half since he strutted and fretted his hour upon the stage. In fact, many have dismissed Seward out of hand for statements he made in two speeches, saying the remarks branded him a radical. Although he would come to regret those words, Henry Seward was not a radical. Seward, first and foremost, was a practical politician. He was the ultimate Washington insider — a man who wielded immense power in early 1861, for as secretary of state-designate many thought he would be the controlling voice in the new administration. As president-elect, he would have commanded even more power, and thus the perspective of power politics could have taken new shape as the crisis escalated from the bluff stage to real secession.

***

The Civil War is our nation's ultimate tragedy. Nothing comes close to matching it in scope, in devastation, and in pure and total horror. At least 620,000 men were killed, some in the most brutal ways imaginable. Thousands of innocent civilians were killed or wounded (including many slaves), thousands of families destroyed, the economy of one-third of the nation wrecked for half a century. Virtually every family in the country during 1861–65 experienced the utter agony of war with killed or maimed or lost loved ones.

Drew Faust, in her riveting new book *This Republic of Suffering*, chronicles the impact death and dying had on the American people. The governments in both North and South were utterly unprepared for a war of the scope and magnitude that evolved. Americans of all political persuasions were stunned beyond belief. Faust notes hauntingly, "As war continued inexorably onward and as death tolls mounted ever higher, soldiers on both sides reported how difficult it became to believe that the slaughter was purposeful and that their sacrifice had meaning."[9]

Even more hauntingly, Gabor Boritt, long-time leader of the Gettysburg Civil War Institute, ponders whether Abraham Lincoln himself was stunned beyond belief too. "Had Lincoln admitted to himself that a colossal war would be the price of freedom, he might have been paralyzed. Could he have squarely faced ... a future that would require, in the calculations of David Potter, 'the life of one soldier, either Rebel or Yank, for every six slaves who were freed'?"[10]

If the above numbers were applied to today's population, they would produce these astounding figures: over 6,000,000 killed, tens of thousands of civilians killed or wounded and families destroyed, and hundreds of billions of dollars in economic loss. If one adds together the losses from all the terrible tragedies that have struck America—from wars to natural disasters to terrorism — Civil War casualties and economic loss dwarf all of the rest.

Finally a comment regarding the Lincoln legend, a legend that has grown decade after decade until this president has become larger than life. Don Fehrenbacher remarked, "Lincoln's symbolic importance transcends his own life and time. He has been abstracted from history to serve as the representative American, and as a consequence, much of the nation's self–image is visible in the image of Abraham Lincoln that successive generations have fashioned."[11] Of course, Abraham Lincoln was the quintessential self–made man; he is what all hope our country represents. The Lincoln legend, however, created after the war and after his tragic death, often is spun to justify the Civil War and the catastrophic period of Reconstruction that followed. And there is little question Abraham Lincoln made the decision that began war. Doris Goodwin comments, "Without the march of events that led to the Civil War, Lincoln still would have been a good man, but most likely would never have been publicly recognized as a great man."[12]

Could the Civil War have been prevented with a different leader? Of course, this is *the* great unknown. But there was one man on the scene in 1860 with the vision and political experience necessary to avert war — William Henry Seward of Auburn, New York, the nation's leading Republican and the man who was driven to saving the nation without war.

1

LUCK OF THE DRAW

Thus did one-term Congressman Abraham Lincoln — out of elected
office for a dozen years — snatch the nomination from William H.
("Mr. Republican") Seward. — Webb Garrison

This book begins at the Wigwam in Chicago, Illinois, on Wednesday,
May 16, 1860.

Illinois Republicans, at the urging of Abraham Lincoln and others, had
pressured the National Republican leadership to hold the Republican Party's
1860 presidential nominating convention in Chicago. The other site in play
was St. Louis, but the National Committee voted for Chicago with one of Lincoln's friends, Norman Judd, casting the deciding vote. In 1860 the Old Northwest was the fastest growing section of the nation and many residents felt it
was time for national recognition. Chicago, robust despite its youth, "rapidly expanding and bragging of its importance," was the region's "most prom-
ising metropolis." The largest grain center in the world and the railroad hub
of the new Northwest, Chicago's vast internal improvements put it "at least
a quarter of a century in advance of her sister cities. In gayety and fashion
she is entitled to rank a number one."[1] Even at this early stage in its development, Chicago was vying to compete with the great cities of the East.

A nominating convention in Chicago turned out to be a masterful stroke
of good fortune for Abraham Lincoln. Illinois Republicans constructed a large
building to house the convention, the first structure ever built for the sole
purpose of holding a political meeting, and nicknamed it the Wigwam. Delegates from twenty-four states and three territories assembled to choose the
Republican Party's presidential and vice-presidential candidates for the 1860
election and to adopt a party platform. In the mid–nineteenth century, candidates did not personally campaign for the presidency, but had leading men
in each state, city, and town represent them during the campaign. Likewise,
at the nominating conventions, the candidates rarely appeared but had managers or advisors do the work of securing their nomination.

William Henry Seward, the former governor of New York and the leading Republican in the U.S. Senate, was the well-known favorite. Most delegates felt Seward would secure the nomination on the very first ballot.
Historian Frederic Bancroft, who interacted with many of the conference
attendees, recorded the following:

> The fact that Seward had been prominent so long; that for a decade he had
> had no rival in the opinion of the progressive people of the North; that he
> had been in perfect harmony with the changing tendencies, first of the best
> Whigs and then of the best Republicans— these furnished opportunities for
> dangerous attacks upon him. Notwithstanding the numerous objections—
> some sincere but many specious— Seward was still the favorite of a very large
> majority of the Republican voters and politicians.[2]

Across the land his extraordinary reputation as a politician was known by all;
in fact, some Democrats considered him to be the best qualified candidate in
the field because he was so "beloved by all classes," so "enterprising and patriotic," so "dauntless and intrepid." Indeed, many Republican newspaper editors felt Seward "was held to be the representative man of his party, and who,
by his commanding talents and eminent public services, has so largely contributed to the development of its principles."[3] Even in Lincoln's home state
of Illinois, especially in the north, Seward was the leading candidate and
widely expected to receive the nomination.[4] By the spring of 1860, many in
the North referred to him as "Mr. Republican."

Other leading men mentioned for the top spot on the ticket included
Edward Bates of Missouri, Simon Cameron of Pennsylvania, Salmon P. Chase
of Ohio, and a host of other less favored men such as William L. Dayton of
New Jersey, Abraham Lincoln of Illinois, and John McLean of Ohio. Lincoln
had some support because of his challenge to Stephen Douglas in the Illinois
Senate race of 1858 but was mostly considered for the second spot on the
ticket as a result of his showing for that spot at the 1856 convention. For the
most part, however, Lincoln was not very well known by delegates: "Yet so
obscure was Lincoln in certain circles before his nomination that some pun-
dits had not included his name on their lists of seven or a dozen or even
twenty-one potential candidates. Several newspapers spelled his first name
Abram."[5] Abraham Lincoln would be considered a long shot by any standard.

Lincoln and his Illinois friends devised a clever strategy to offset the
Seward advantage— they promoted Lincoln as the best second choice if
Seward did not receive the nomination early and then worked feverishly to
keep Seward from getting the nomination on the first ballot. Lincoln had one
real advantage— he was so unknown few opposed him outright. Most other
candidates had, over the years, offended one faction of the Republican Party
or another. Lincoln, because he was so new to the national scene, was

untainted. As early as March 1860 he had defined his strategy: "I suppose I am not the first choice of a very great many.... Our policy, then, is to give no offence to others—leave them in a mood to come to us, if they shall be compelled to give up their first love."[6] As it turned out, this strategy, with the help of New York's Horace Greeley and some others, worked to near perfection.

At the opening of the convention on May 16, the New York delegation, headed by the best-known political boss of the era, Thurlow Weed (affectionately dubbed "The Dictator" by New Yorkers), felt very confident about their candidate, Henry Seward. They had come to Chicago in a special thirteen-car train with plenty of money to pass around and an unlimited amount of liquor. "By trading legislative charters to build city railroads for campaign contributions, Weed had assembled what one observer called 'oceans of money,' a campaign chest worth several hundred thousand dollars."[7] Weed had made the customary deals with key state delegations (promises of cabinet appointments, jobs as patronage, government contracts to supporters) and the situation looked fully under control. Weed felt very confident the Republicans would win the election outright, stating he "had no doubt of the nomination of his friend" and felt strongly that "if Douglas [the leading Democratic candidate] should be put aside for a southern man, Seward's election would be certain" because the election would then "be fought on the question of extending or protecting slavery."[8]

Dressed in their fashionable New York clothes, staying at the best hotel, the New Yorkers had a confident air. They firmly believed Henry Seward had earned the nomination and many felt a vast majority of the nation's Republicans favored him; contemporary evidence suggested they were right. The words of one convention participant rang loudly for Seward:

> Governor Seward had a strong and peculiar claim to the highest reward which Republicans could bestow. His whole term of service in the United States Senate has been signalized by toils and sacrifices, amid rancor and persecution, political and social, such as no other statesman in this country has ever experienced. His fidelity to freedom in the darkest hours, his boldness in exposing and denouncing misgovernment ... he has stood up in his place, and dared to do whatever each crisis demanded.[9]

Henry Seward was regarded as a true statesmen and a man of real vision; even one Democratic paper conceded ,"We have recognized the genius and leadership of the man."[10]

Most of Seward's opponents thought he could not be defeated, his former political partner turned bitter rival Horace Greeley, powerful editor of the *New York Tribune*, among them. Seward, Weed and Greeley, political allies for decades, had had a major political falling out in 1855 (Greeley claimed they would not support him for political office), but Weed thought he had the Greeley situation fully under control.

> As the convention approached, overconfidence reigned in the Seward camp
> and poor judgment set in. Despite Weed's generally keen political intuition,
> he failed to anticipate the damage Seward would suffer as a consequence of a
> rift with Horace Greeley.... At some point that spring [1860], Weed had a
> long talk with Greeley and came away with the mistaken conviction that
> Greeley was "all right," that despite his editorial support for Bates, he would
> not oppose Seward at the convention.[11]

Weed had been a major player in the formation of the Republican Party in
New York State and in the nation as well. He knew his man deserved the
nomination. Others in the New York delegation felt likewise. On the morning of May 18, William Evarts, chairman of the New York State delegation,
wired Seward, assuring him that "everything indicates your nomination today
sure."[12]

Horace Greeley, still bitter from the 1855 rejection, had come to Chicago
in a carefully planned effort to derail the Seward nomination. He "wrangled"
a seat with the Oregon delegation (as he was not welcomed by his own New
York contingent) and his "early appearance ... at Chicago was an evil omen
to the followers of Seward." The "irrepressibles" (the term used to denote
Seward followers) were concerned "when they learned that he was staying at
the Tremont House, where the Bates and the Lincoln men had their respective headquarters, and that he was making it his first aim to defeat Seward."[13]
Still, early in the convention Greeley thought Seward looked undefeatable
and on May 17, the day of the first scheduled ballot, he wired home to the
Tribune staff, "The conviction is that the opposition to Governor Seward cannot be concentrated on any other candidate, and that he will be nominated."[14]

Lincoln's Illinois campaign team, headed by the 300-pound Judge David
Davis and including Norman Judd, Leonard Swett, Jesse K. Dubois, and a few
others, had different ideas. Davis had been working nonstop behind the scenes
to implement the plan to promote Lincoln as the best second choice if Seward
did not win the nomination early. Davis, with some effort, had managed to
get all of the Illinois delegation committed to Lincoln and he felt other serious support from the Northwest might crystallize as well, especially from
Indiana. Davis and his friends loved to play the game of politics and they laid
plans for a surprise on May 18, assuming Seward did not win on the first ballot. Their home-field advantage included Norman Judd, one of Lincoln's
closet advisors, acting as floor manager for the convention. Their plan was to
use the location, "every feature of which was favorable to Lincoln," to influence delegates to vote for their candidate.[15]

First, Davis met with the key lower North delegations of Pennsylvania,
Indiana, and New Jersey, urging support on the second ballot for Lincoln. His
"basic strategy was of necessity a stop-Seward stratagem" for he knew "if this
failed, Weed would stampede the convention." Cleverly, Davis instructed his

men to cooperate with "the delegations for Cameron, Dayton, Bates" and to push "in innumerable colloquies that Seward could not carry" the lower Northern states. In the 1856 presidential election the Republicans had lost Pennsylvania, New Jersey, Indiana, and Illinois, and many of the delegates surely realized they needed to carry most of these states to win the 1860 election.

Davis had his men point to Seward's (inaccurate) reputation as a "radical" and then caution that this supposed radicalism would make it difficult for the Republicans to win the lower North states, which were more conservative. Norman Judd's suggestion "that a 'quiet combination' against Seward could stop him ... [had] met with tacit agreement." Davis used Horace Greeley, not only a prominent New Yorker, but one the delegates thought was still close to Seward, to counter Weed's influence by whispering to delegates the same message — Seward's radicalism would not enable him to carry the lower North states.[16] As Weed's men would leave a delegation, Greeley would slip in to deliver his anti–Seward remarks.

Davis and Judd were shrewd politicians and no doubt made some offers to counter Weed, certainly to the Pennsylvanians where there is good evidence Davis promised a cabinet post to Simon Cameron (political boss of Pennsylvania and its senior senator) in exchange for Pennsylvania's vote on the second ballot for Lincoln. Caleb Smith, head of Indiana's Republican Party, was wooed as well. Lincoln's team approached some members of the Ohio delegation who were not enthusiastic about their state's favorite son, Salmon P. Chase, to plead for support of Lincoln after the first ballot. They undoubtedly promised something to the powerful Blair family of St. Louis, if their favorite son, Edward Bates, faded, for both Frank Sr. and Jr. swung votes to Lincoln on the critical third ballot. They pleaded with delegates to consider Lincoln as the next best choice — the candidate with no enemies — and constantly trumpeted Seward as the radical, unable to carry the lower North in the general election.

The lower North was certainly critical to Lincoln's nomination, but what about the upper South? William Freehling's insightful summation "when the Blairs swerved to help Lincoln's nomination" is stunning. Frank Blair Jr. had brought to the convention a southern presidential candidate, Edward Bates, who received forty-eight votes on the first ballot, as many as Cameron and Chase. Amazingly, ninety delegates from the South were eligible to vote at the Republican convention, about 20 percent of the total — this from the supposedly most anti–Republican region of the nation. On the first ballot all of Missouri's vote went to Bates, likewise all of Delaware's, and most of Maryland's (controlled by Frank Blair Sr.'s son, Montgomery). On the second ballot Lincoln received but twenty-nine Southern votes. But then, "on the third ballot, where Lincoln squeaked to victory," the Blairs "switched Maryland's delegation from Bates to Lincoln, giving the Railsplitter 42 southern votes (almost half of the South's total and 18 percent of Lincoln's tally)."[17] No doubt, Frank Blair Sr., a political boss who rivaled Thurlow Weed, would "expect compensation."

Davis left no stone unturned and had his young supporters, led by Ward Hill Lamon, arrange to have counterfeit tickets printed and handed out to Chicago friends who were told to arrive at the Wigwam early, essentially packing the house with Lincoln people. "The Wigwam had been well advertised and the populace, in tourist spirit, was anxious to look at it.... Never before had such a meeting been held in a building specially built for its use; never before had the general public been admitted wholesale."[18] Judd, knowing the critical role Pennsylvania would play in the voting and acting in his capacity as floor manager, pulled off a classic political stunt by placing the New York delegation at one end of the Wigwam with the Pennsylvania delegation at the other end, the Illinois and other delegations between the two. A host of Lincoln delegates and Westerners thus could obstruct movement between the fashionably dressed New Yorkers and the Pennsylvanians, whom Weed was trying throughout the day to shore up. The stage was set for a home-field surprise.

Happenstance or luck often plays a part in historical events. The first ballot was put off a day because the printer failed to deliver tally sheets. Davis was delighted, if not implicated in the delay, for it gave his team much needed time to maneuver during the night of May 17, which they used to the utmost. On the morning of the eighteenth, the Seward men were still very confident as they marched, a thousand strong, from their hotel to the Wigwam, where "they asked the opposition to suggest some one for second place."[19] They had every right to be confident as most newspapers across the nation, Democratic and Republican, felt Seward would receive the nomination. While there were no polling organizations in 1860, most voters in the North most likely favored Seward for the nomination because he was by far the most recognized name in the field. And many delegates said afterwards that if the first ballot had been taken on May 17, as scheduled, Seward would have been nominated.

Surprisingly, after a night of heavy drinking and "negotiations," Seward did not receive the nomination on the day-delayed first ballot. Equally surprising, Abraham Lincoln placed second—173 votes for Seward, 102 for Lincoln, 233 needed to win. The Lincoln plan was in motion. Indiana had come around on the first ballot casting all thirteen votes for Lincoln and providing much needed momentum. Judge Davis and his team continued to meet with the delegation from Pennsylvania to push even harder the idea Seward was not strong in their state, a state almost all Republicans thought they must carry to win. Also, they canvassed wavering individuals in other state delegations, asking that they vote for Lincoln on the second ballot as the next best hope to Seward, again promoting the idea of Lincoln as the untainted candidate and Seward the too-radical candidate. Chase, Bates, and the other candidates seemed to dim and a two-way race quickly took shape. Weed was still very confident of success as he assumed the large block of Pennsylvania votes would go to Seward on the second ballot (over fifty), putting him within a few votes of the nomination.

* * *

As previously noted, often the course of history hinges on some strange occurrence, or happenstance, or luck — in this case the lack of a meeting between two powerful political bosses. Simon Cameron, the leader of Pennsylvania Republicans, had been a strong Seward supporter throughout 1859 and into the spring of 1860.

> Early in April, [Cameron] told Seward that he wanted to see Weed and would meet him at any time appointed by the latter, either in Washington or in Philadelphia [Cameron was likely looking for a formal commitment of a high place in Seward's cabinet]. But in the weeks that followed Weed and Cameron could not get together. For this failure both men seem to have been responsible, although years later Cameron was reported to have said that if Weed had gone to Chicago by way of Harrisburg, Seward would have been nominated.[20]

Indeed, Weed thought he had a firm commitment from Cameron to deliver the Pennsylvania vote to Seward on the second ballot in return for a place in Seward's cabinet. Another explanation for Pennsylvania's defection could be that Andrew Curtin, soon to be governor and a growing rival to Cameron in the state, sought to have his supporters desert Seward to demonstrate his newfound political clout, that he could rival Cameron. In any event, Weed's "Pennsylvania commitment" slipped away.

If Pennsylvania's vote had swung to Seward on the second ballot, there can be little doubt Seward would have received the Republican Party's presidential nomination in 1860. Leonard Swett, a key member of Lincoln's campaign team, recalled the fateful night of May 17:

> The chance lay in Pennsylvania, which had, as I remember, fifty four votes. The Seward men were laboring with delegates from that State, and so were friends of Mr. Lincoln, and both were hopeful; but in the small hours of Friday morning, in a room of the Tremont house, two of Mr. Lincoln's friends and two of Mr. Cameron's being present, our arguments prevailed, and the Cameron men agreed to come to us on the second ballot. They did so right nobly and gave us forty-eight votes. This, with other accessions, was a blow in the centre which disorganized the forces of our great opponent.[21]

So the events of May 1860 unfolded, and doomed Henry Seward to a subordinate role in our nation's history, perhaps for lack of a simply conversation.

***

David Davis struck a deal here and a deal there and the second ballot saw Seward gain but eleven votes while Lincoln gained an astonishing seventy-nine, putting him just three votes shy of Seward. The great momentum for Lincoln on the second ballot had come from Pennsylvania, just as Indiana had provided it on the first ballot. Stunned, Weed immediately sent messenger after messenger to the Pennsylvanians asking what was going on and pleading for change on the now-critical third ballot. But Judd's delegation placement now worked its magic as the crowded floor — with delegates drinking, smoking, shouting, boisterous at every turn — obstructed the ebb and flow of Weed's deal-making. His messengers did not return in a timely manner and panic began to set in with the New Yorkers. The Blairs, always seeking to rival Weed and his powerful New York clan, sensed the momentum switch. On the third ballot, the nearly 10,000 spectators in the Wigwam, almost all Lincoln supporters— many admitted with bogus tickets— roared with every additional vote for Lincoln, creating the impression of an irresistible tide. Weed was beside himself— this was not how he planned the event. After the third ballot, Lincoln was just two votes shy of the nomination. Weed frantically pleaded for support from various delegations, but to no avail as the turmoil (and noise) in the Wigwam was out of control. When the chairman of the Ohio delegation stood up and, in a dramatic moment, asked to be recognized, and then switched four votes to Lincoln, the Wigwam exploded with a deafening roar. Horace Greeley, who indeed had worked tirelessly with the Lincoln men in the "stop Seward" movement, was described, "a beaming smile, a smile of unspeakable triumph" spread across his face "as he sat amid the Oregon delegation."[22]

A few days after he returned from the convention, Henry Jarvis Raymond, founder and erudite editor of the *New York Times* (and a solid Seward man), exposed Greeley's role at the convention in a blistering editorial:

> In an open letter, dated at Auburn, and doubtless written with Seward's full knowledge, Raymond charged Greeley with being the chief cause of Seward's defeat, and with having plotted it in a way that was both deceitful and dishonorable. Announcing what had taken place six years before, he declared that Greeley in his recent acts was "deliberately wreaking the long-hoarded revenge of a disappointed office-seeker."

Greeley answered with an equally stinging editorial the next day and demanded his 1854 letter to Seward be returned — it was and Greeley published it in its entirety in the *Tribune* as did the *Times* and several other papers.

Some have downplayed Greeley's role in Seward's defeat. But in New York "the public was amazed, and took sides with great feeling for a time";

even opponents of Seward were amazed "for many persons believed that but for Greeley's persistent hostility Seward would have obtained the great ambition of his life."[23] Whether Greeley was truly instrumental in Seward's defeat can still be debated, but contemporaries felt the hubbub raised in the press prevented Greeley, a short time later, from receiving the nod from the New York Legislature to replace Seward in the U.S. Senate. David Davis, ever the shrewd politician, had used Greeley repeatedly to plant the seeds of Seward's radicalism and supposed weakness in lower North states.

Seward's followers were heartbroken. Many felt the Republican operatives at Chicago had betrayed Seward and the majority of Republican voters in the country as well. They felt Lincoln was simply not the candidate of choice.

> One of the striking features of this convention was the fact that Seward was sincerely regarded by the scheming politicians, the general public, a very large portion of the truest antislavery men, and the most cultured Republicans, as their best representative.... Lincoln's nomination was the triumph of availability and local enthusiasm, assisted by unexpected circumstances [Greeley and trickery], over great merit and still greater popularity.[24]

Thurlow Weed took the defeat hardest as it was on him "the blow fell with greatest effect." Overcome with emotion, "he lost his habitual prudence and stoical self–possession, and gave way, at first, to angry words and tears."[25] Weed felt Lincoln "had been shouted into nomination by leather-lunged sons of the prairies against the thoughtful protests of the men of sane and mature judgment."[26] The overconfident New Yorkers accepted defeat bitterly for many reasons; surely one was the image of their man, the nation's leading Republican, being turned away by the party that owed him so much.

Why did Lincoln win? Many have examined the issues and drawn conclusions that range across the board. Surely the site played a significant role, as did the delay in balloting, as did Horace Greeley and Simon Cameron. Lincoln's team out dueled the New Yorkers, whose arrogance and overconfidence added to the end result. Trickery, a common tactic in mid–nineteenth-century politics, was employed more successfully by the Lincoln team. Bates recorded in his diary, "Some of my friends who attended the convention assure me that the nomination of Mr. Lincoln took every body by surprise: That it was brought about by accident or trick, by which my pledged friends had to vote against me."[27]

Illinois Republicans were divided in their support for Lincoln. William E. Barton, a Lincoln biographer and long-time Chicago minister, observed, "Illinois Republicans ... wanted to see Lincoln receive a good hearty complimentary vote, but did not wish to see him nominated." Barton noted some Lincoln newspapers "feared rather than hoped for his nomination." Even "the *Chicago Press and Tribune*, which for the honor of Illinois, and for its sincere regard for Lincoln, had been running his name at its column-head since February, as its candidate for the presidency, but at heart deeply concerned lest Lincoln should draw votes from Seward and weaken the Republican prospects for success."[28] While modern historians have debunked some of these views, those closest to the scene must be given some weight.

Some suggest there were lofty ideals at work. "[I]t is clear that when opportunity called, Lincoln was best prepared to answer the call" and he won as "the result of his character and life experiences."[29] But when one considers the noisy, smoke-filled Wigwam, with many of the delegates drinking or drunk, with the gallery packed with screaming Illinois Lincoln supporters, with promises and money flowing freely, it seems improbable that loftiness was at work. Many factors contributed to Lincoln's success, but if one is forced to choose a single factor, luck or happenstance would seem to win out.

Abraham Lincoln would not forget the work of his managers at the convention or of those who offered support as Seward dimmed. David Davis would be rewarded with an appointment to the U.S. Supreme Court. Norman Judd received an ambassadorship. Ward Hill Lamon became marshal of Washington, D.C. Whether David Davis made formal promises of rewards for votes cannot be fully verified, but Caleb Smith of Indiana became secretary of the interior, Simon Cameron of Pennsylvania became secretary of war, and Montgomery Blair of Maryland became postmaster general. And Horace Greeley, he would be given unlimited access to the White House as the Lincoln presidency began, becoming the envy of the nation's press corps.

So the relatively unknown Abraham Lincoln received the Republican Party nomination for president of the United States. Hannibal Hamlin of Maine, an early New England Lincoln supporter, received the nomination for vice president. But how could this relatively unknown, this "untested and untried" politician from the Northwest win the presidential election that was controlled by the Electoral College votes of the populous states of the Northeast?

***

Some brief background on the presidential election of 1860. First, it was the most unusual presidential election in the nation's history, and still is.

> Occasionally in the first eighty-odd years of the Republic a presidential election had been held with three serious candidates. This usually resulted in some abnormality, and once the House of Representatives even had to choose the president. But in 1860, as established political parties shattered and attempted to reform, there appeared four serious candidates backed by four serious parties to divide the electorate in different ways.[30]

The four parties were the Southern Democratic Party, the Northern Democratic Party, the Constitutional Union Party, and the Republican Party.

The Democratic Party broke apart at its convention in Charleston that spring; two factions reconvened in Baltimore (a third in Richmond) a bit later and formed two distinct parties. The Southern wing established the Southern Democratic Party and nominated the vice president of the United States, John C. Breckinridge of Kentucky, as their candidate. The Southern Democrats were first and foremost states' rights men. They believed the federal government derived its powers from the sovereign states as defined in the Constitution. They believed it was the federal government's responsibility to protect slavery wherever it existed. They were opposed to limiting the expansion of slavery and believed the North was trampling on Southern rights by proposing it. They would appeal to slave-owning Southerners and those of a more conservative bent. In the election, Breckinridge would not win a majority of Southern votes (45 percent Breckinridge to 55 percent all others), but he carried ten of the fourteen Southern states in the all-important Electoral College.

The Northern wing of the party formed the Northern Democratic Party and nominated Stephen A. Douglas of Illinois as their candidate. Douglas was one of the best-known politicians in the country and their platform was one of his making, essentially one opposed to congressional interference with slavery, support of Supreme Court decisions on slavery, and support of Douglas's doctrine of popular sovereignty for determining slavery in the territories. They portrayed themselves as a party of moderation and had won the presidency in 1856 with this same theme. Douglas did very well nationally, polling 29 percent of the popular vote, the second highest number. But he lost every Northern state to Lincoln, except New Jersey, and won only Missouri in the South. Douglas came in last in the Electoral College, despite his impressive numbers in the popular vote.

Former Southern Whigs (and some in the North as well) formed a new party, the Constitutional Union Party. This was deemed the party of "old conservatives" and, indeed, they attempted to avoid all sectional hostility by proposing to preserve the Union and the Constitution "as it was." They avoided mention of the slavery issue, appealing to American patriotism for votes. They nominated John Bell, head of the former Whig Party in Tennessee, for president. Surprisingly for a political party established just for this contest, they did remarkably well. Not so surprisingly, they attracted the votes of most of the South's nonslaveholders, as their appeal was to moderate Southerners. Bell narrowly lost the popular vote in the South to Breckinridge (45 percent to 40 percent), carrying only three states— Kentucky, Tennessee and Virginia. He lost closely in Louisiana (45 percent to 40 percent), Maryland (46 percent to 45 percent) and North Carolina (50 percent to 47 percent). Despite increasing sectional hostility, these numbers demonstrated strong anti–Southern Democrat (and antislaveholder) political strength in the South.

The Republican Party, composed of former Northern Whigs, antislavery Democrats, Free Soilers, and a hodgepodge of other splinter groups, nominated Abraham Lincoln of Illinois, as documented. The party's platform was one of challenging Southern (and Democratic) interests. They opposed the extension of slavery in the territories, they opposed Douglas's concept of popular sovereignty, and they favored a stronger federal government, essentially rebuking the states'-rights doctrine of the Southern Democrats. Many Republicans viewed themselves as moderates, but that was not how they were viewed by many Southerners who focused on the extreme abolitionist element in the party. Some of the more radical Southern Democrats threatened to promote secession if this sectional party of supposed extremists won the election.

In the election, the Republican juggernaut was in full stride as Lincoln swept the North, he split the New Jersey vote. While he won just over 39 percent of the popular vote nationwide, he polled 54 percent of the Northern vote, rolling up a huge majority in the Electoral College (see table on page 202). Students of the Electoral College process know it is a winner-take-all contest. Thus, if the popular vote in Pennsylvania goes to any candidate by just one vote, that candidate receives all of the Electoral College votes for the state. This explains the anomalies, for instance, where Douglas received 29 percent of the popular vote but just 4 percent of the Electoral College vote. (See table on page 202.)

***

How did the Republicans win such a landslide in the Electoral College? Who was responsible for the stunning victory? A look at Henry Seward during the campaign tells a good part of the story.

Henry Seward was devastated by his defeat in Chicago, and so were his friends. He was the nation's leading Republican and a man widely regarded as presidential timber, yet something had gone terribly wrong at the convention. His friends found "a very great surprise and disappointment" in the result and attributed it "to a number of causes, notably the course of Horace Greeley." The reasons for his defeat mattered little to him, but the loss was one of profound disappointment.[31] For a few days, Seward remained out of the public eye but soon regained his bearings, including his marvelous sense of humor, and began to appear in public. In late May he returned to the Senate to complete his term. Surprisingly, he was consoled by many Senate leaders, including "old foes like Jefferson Davis and James Mason" who "seemed genuine in their expressions of sympathy."[32]

Rumors circulated Seward would retire from public life at the end of his term, but many leaders in the nation's capital felt he would be indispensable in guiding the Republican Party and managing affairs in Washington during the Lincoln administration.

Two prominent members of the House, Charles Francis Adams and Israel
Washburn, called at his Washington home.... The two men urged him to
remain an active Republican leader, for they were alarmed lest, with Lincoln
at the helm, the party might lose direction. Seward listened to them and,
much to their relief, appeared to be receptive.[33]

As summer came to an end, Seward was urged by Republican Party leaders to take an active part in the campaign that was foundering badly; little
enthusiasm for Lincoln or the Republicans had emerged. Lincoln knew he had
to have Seward's active support for Seward was Mr. Republican, not only the
leading spokesmen of the party but its most well known leader. Business, commerce, and finance leaders in New York — at least those who opposed the
Democratic machine — also urged him to get involved. So with Weed's encouragement and support, Seward decided to take an active part in the presidential canvas. He was a politician first and foremost and did not want the new
administration to fall into the hands of the wrong people (the radical Republicans). He made a tour of New England on behalf of the party and then a
truly triumphant four-week tour of the West (today's Midwest). Seward's
entourage included Charles Francis Adams Sr. (President John Quincy's son
and heir to the Adams family political legacy), Adam's son, Charles Francis
Jr., Seward's daughter Fanny, one of her friends and a few others. Seward
made a dozen major speeches in which his vision for America was extolled —
economic development and prosperity, a role for everyone (including immigrants), "land for the landless," and one including Alaska and maybe even
Canada. His speeches were rife with "moderation and peace" and optimism.

Democrats and Republicans and folks with no particular political affiliation came to see him. His entourage was astounded. "Adams found Seward
a delightful traveling companion but wondered how he found time to prepare 'the really remarkable speeches' he delivered during the campaign swing."
Seward wowed his audiences as "the majority of [his] addresses were visionary evocations of the greatness that lay ahead for a united America. His tone
was so nonpartisan that at some stops he entirely neglected to mention the
Lincoln-Hamlin ticket."[34] A judge traveling on the same boat with Seward
remarked, "Gov. Seward, you are doing more for Lincoln's election than any
hundred men in the United States." In Chicago, over 200,000 people turned
out to hear America's visionary — the largest crowd ever to see a single politician in the state of Illinois. Many of his contemporaries thought it was the
greatest political tour in the history of the nation. Even the discriminating
senator Charles Sumner, who was never easy to impress, expressed utter
amazement: "I know nothing like such a succession of speeches by any American," he said.[35]

What was it about Henry Seward that commanded the attention of so
many Democrats and independents? Why did rank-and-file Republicans find

him so engaging? Why did people from all walks of life travel miles and miles to hear him speak?

Part of the answer lies in the Whig Party that he and Weed helped establish in the 1840s. The party appealed to the rising middle class, it appealed to those who owned property (or wanted to), it appealed to the "self–made man." The Whig Party "stood for growth, for development, for progress" and opportunity for all. The party also "attracted many of the wealthiest and best-educated members of society," and it "appealed to young men who aspired to get ahead."[36] Seward's vision for America was to use government to foster economic growth — through government-financed internal improvements, through giving land to settlers in the West, through a central bank that would be less prone to political tampering, though a protective tariff to encourage American manufactures. Seward's vision for the nation was what enthralled Northerners in 1860 (and Southerners who opposed the slavocracy as well), and it was what drew so many to hear him, irrespective of party affiliation.

Many contemporaries felt Seward's extraordinary fall campaign secured the election for the Republicans.

> At every stop, Seward was met with "cannons, brass bands, and processions." ... Fifty thousand people gathered to hear Seward speak in Detroit, and the fervor only increased as his tour moved west. Thousands waited past midnight for the arrival of his train in Kalamazoo.... In St. Paul, Minnesota, a correspondent reported, Seward's arrival was "a day ever memorable in the political history of our State." Early in the morning, the streets were "alive with people — the pioneer, the backwoodsmen, the trapper, the hunter, the trader from the Red River." ... It often appeared "the whole population of the surrounding country had turned out to greet him."[37]

William Henry Seward was the most popular politician in the North that fall — and Republicans hailed him as the great benefactor of the party. Democrats and others listened as well, including many moderate Southerners.

On return to his home in Auburn, New York, the exhausted Seward had little rest. After attending a state dinner at Governor Morgan's house in Albany for the prince of Wales, who was making a trip through America incognito, Seward launched a tour of New York State. The Republican leadership was concerned the opposition might be successful in its fusion efforts (the political move to combine all Republican opposition into one ticket) and all knew New York's thirty-five Electoral College votes were needed to win the election outright. Seward's exhaustion turned to illness and friends urged him to slow down. He would not. As an exclamation point to his efforts, four days before the election, he delivered a rousing speech at New York City's Palace Garden. Heavily Democratic New York City turned out in record numbers to hear their former governor, and the reception was enthusiastic beyond any expectation. "The crowd was so great that benches were smashed in the crush, and there were overflow meetings ... [his] speech was interrupted repeatedly by cheers and applause, and at its conclusion there was a deafening ovation." Many New Yorkers felt Governor Seward had saved the state for the Republican Party with this speech at the garden, playing "no inconsiderable part in holding the fusion ticket's New York City majority to 30,000, which was wiped out by the enormous Republican vote upstate."[38] Henry Seward's incredible effort that fall made *the* difference in the election; without his efforts Abraham Lincoln could very well have lost the election.

But what was Governor Seward about? Political insiders knew full well Seward and Weed would not go into action without "a cause." With Seward (and Weed) on the move in the campaign, talk was rife about the role Seward might play in the new administration if the Republicans won. The press knew Weed had visited Lincoln in Springfield shortly after his nomination (they talked about campaign strategy for sure, but what else, they pondered). They did not know of the secret meeting Weed had had with Judge Davis in August. Undoubtedly, Weed laid the groundwork for Seward to play a significant if not dominant role in the new administration during these discussions.

Seward shortly after ending his second term as governor of New York, the young, handsome "John F. Kennedy" of his generation (Seward House, Auburn, New York).

> He [Charles Francis Adams] cautiously recorded in his diary that, from the tenor of Seward's conversation, it looked as though the New Yorker expected to wield considerable influence in the Lincoln administration. Adams was not the only one saying this, the *New York Herald* was declaring openly that the Senator from New York had dreams of being the real President of the United States.[39]

***

Could Henry Seward have won the presidential election of 1860 had he been the Republican candidate? Obviously, any analysis is speculative. But a careful review of the numbers leads to the following judgment.

First, the Republican Party was on the rise in 1860. In the state elections that fall in Pennsylvania and Indiana — lower North states that were thought to be "toss-ups" in the upcoming presidential election and ones the Republicans had lost in the 1856 presidential election — the Republicans scored impressive victories.

> The returns — which would be closely paralleled in the general election a month later — showed that the Republicans by disavowing immigration restrictions had succeeded in holding on to a fair share of the foreign-born vote, especially among younger, Protestant voters ... and they proved that despite Lincoln's personal lack of interest, the Wide-Awake clubs, with their frequent meetings, organized drills, and processions, stimulated immense enthusiasm on the part of younger voters, many of whom cast their first ballots in this election.[40]

Although Seward, because of his support for immigrants, would have lost some of the former Know Nothing vote that was an important part of the Republican base, his enthusiastic support for the Wide-Awakes and his appeal to disgruntled Democrats would likely have offset it.

In the Northwest — Wisconsin, Minnesota, Iowa, and Michigan — huge increases in population were occurring due largely to free land provided by the Homestead Act. And the people migrating there were mostly immigrants or people from upstate New York or Ohio — and for some reason they became Republicans. "The politicians, if aware of this (and there is little contemporary evidence that they were), had no reason to know that these people, their children, and their children's children in northern Illinois and southern Wisconsin and in the areas of Indiana, Michigan, Iowa and Minnesota (all settled about the same time) would be Republican until death or depression."[41] These "death or depression" Republicans would surely have supported the well-known and hugely popular Henry Seward — and Seward would have done better with foreign-born voters, especially the Germans who truly loved him.

Second, the Democratic Party was badly split and neither side, Northern or Southern, could carry enough states to win in the Electoral College. The Constitutional Union Party would further split the Electoral College vote as their strength was in the border states. Thus, it was the Northern states, with their substantial majority in the Electoral College, which held the key to winning the election. "The electoral vote in 1860 totaled 303. The fifteen slave states had 120, and the eighteen free states 183. Therefore, 152 votes were needed for election."[42] A state-by-state analysis on the vote in the North can be found in the appendix.

It can be argued the majority of Republican votes were party votes, that is, anti–Democratic votes or antislavery votes or reformists votes or whatever. They were *not* votes for Abraham Lincoln per se, simply because the vast majority of voters did not know him at all. As William Freehling has demonstrated, nineteenth-century voters were fiercely loyal to their parties, some 90 percent voting the party line irrespective of circumstances. "Northern Republicans were particularly consistent nineteenth-century partisans."[43] Although some have argued Seward was too weak in Indiana and Illinois and may have lost those states in the general election, even if he had lost both of them (unlikely with Weed in control of a Seward campaign), he still would have won in the Electoral College. The Republican juggernaut was in full swing in the presidential election of 1860 and with Henry Seward's popularity and name recognition (any political scientist will speak to its importance) he would have vaulted into the White House.

Finally, the tools Seward would have had at his disposal had he been the presidential nominee cannot be overlooked. It was Seward who had the political organization, it was Seward who had direct access to New York money (and let no mistake be made, the vast majority of political money in the country in 1860 resided in New York State), and it was Seward's "visionary evocations" that captured the attention of the press. The incomparable Thurlow Weed cannot be underestimated either. Not only would he have been at Seward's side, planning strategy, but his Herculean efforts, with his life-long friend at the top of the ticket, would have been extraordinary — New York money and influence would have covered the country in unimaginable ways.

In the fall of 1860 Seward's contemporaries regarded him as the greatest American statesmen. His popularity throughout the North was unmatched. When he spoke, as noted earlier, often the crowds were filled with people from different political parties. In fact, sometimes the political clubs from the different parties would join forces to organize a Seward event. Local and state officials, irrespective of party affiliation, would welcome him. These people reacted to Seward's appeals with unbounded enthusiasm.[44] Most in these pumped-up crowds would have voted for Seward on Election Day, 1860, and he would have won the election handily.

But who had the right set of political assets to deal with the sectional crisis during the secession winter of 1860–61 — indeed, who had the credentials to *be* president on March 4, 1861? A brief look at the backgrounds of William Henry Seward and Abraham Lincoln will provide some answers.

2

TO *BE* PRESIDENT

He [Lincoln] was far more fit to become than to be President.
— David M. Potter

Immediately after the presidential election in November 1860, the nation began to fall apart. Within days of Lincoln's election, South Carolina began to make plans to call a state convention to consider seceding from the Union, other states of the lower South were in turmoil. While there have been no perfect presidents (and certainly no perfect politicians), it is fair to raise this question: Could a political leader with a different background have kept the nation from disintegrating?

Abraham Lincoln

Abraham Lincoln is so well known that little review of his background is needed other than for comparison with Henry Seward, whose background is largely unknown. By the spring of 1860, Abraham Lincoln was becoming known on the national political landscape, although his political background was not overly impressive. He had served several terms in the Illinois legislature and one term in the U.S. House of Representatives (the Thirtieth Congress, which began in December 1847). He had an unsuccessful run for the Senate in 1855, a disappointing quest for nomination as vice president on the Republican ticket in 1856, and, of course, the 1858 Illinois Senate race with Stephen A. Douglas, which was not successful either.

Abraham Lincoln was the quintessential self-made man. His father and stepmother were poor farmers living in near wilderness. Young Abe, along with the other household children, had to work the farm and hunt wild game merely to survive. Manual labor and long hours of rough, tough work were all he knew as a young man. His early life on the frontier in truly crude surroundings was simply hard and dirty. At twenty-one he left the family to start life on his own. He knew only one thing — he did not want to follow in his father's footsteps. During the next ten years "he tried nearly every other kind of work the frontier offered: carpenter, riverboat man, store clerk, soldier, merchant, postmaster, surveyor, lawyer, politician." He read books constantly, studied law, "and by the time he was thirty the direction of his career was firmly established."[1] Abraham Lincoln was going to be a lawyer.

Lincoln pursued a career in law because of his interest in language — and because it offered him a way out of the hard life he had endured, "the short and simple annals of the poor," as he stated in a campaign biography. Although he had little formal education, essentially self-taught, he was very bright and through constant effort mastered grammar and the subtleties of language.

> Lincoln's real interest was in the structure and use of language, and he decided that he needed to learn grammar. Samuel Kirkham's *English Grammar* was considered the best guide, and when Lincoln learned that a farmer named John C. Vance had a copy, he willingly walked the six miles into the country to get it. He set himself systematically to master this detailed text, committing large segments to memory.[2]

Lincoln had the facility to memorize and over the course of his career he committed much to memory. As he began to practice law, his interest in politics deepened and reached its pre–1860 apex in the Senate contest with Stephen Douglas.

That Senate race provided Lincoln much-needed national exposure because the debates captured the attention of the national press and were reported widely. Douglas was a national political figure and Lincoln, by standing up and successfully debating him, became identified as a national figure also. The newly formed Republican Party, too much identified with radical abolitionists, had a new face in Lincoln, albeit one from the Northwest. Lincoln espoused a more moderate or conservative point of view on slavery; that is, he favored limiting the expansion of the institution, not eliminating slavery where it already existed. Indeed, some of the radical liberals of the North had denounced Lincoln as too conservative when "Wendell Phillips even went so far as to call Lincoln 'the Slave Hound of Illinois' because he refused to advocate repeal of the fugitive slave law."[3] The Republicans found growing strength in the Northwest partly because of their support for the Homestead Act, which permitted the government to give land to settlers. As previously mentioned, most folks who immigrated to the region, for reasons that are still not fully understood, became Republicans.

Lincoln developed a reputation as a dynamic political speaker. He had honed his oratorical skills as a lawyer on the judicial circuit in Illinois and was in much demand. He made numerous speeches across the state during the 1850s and in early October 1854, at the Illinois State Fair in Springfield, he delivered a rousing response to Douglas's defense of the Kansas-Nebraska Act. Lincoln tied the wrong of slavery—"there can be no moral right in connection with one man's making a slave of another"—to the wrong of the extension of slavery provided by the Kansas-Nebraska Act. This speech and others received state and sometimes regional coverage in the press, but rarely national coverage.

On the evening of June 16, 1858, at the statehouse in Springfield, Lincoln gave his acceptance speech to the Republican State Convention that had earlier in the day nominated him for the U.S. Senate. Borrowing from the Bible, Lincoln delivered the speech that included the statement, "a house divided against itself cannot stand."[4] It was a denunciation of the spread of slavery and an attack on Stephen Douglas as the architect of slavery's expansion. Republican newspapers across the North gave it some coverage. Newspapers in the South viewed it as the embodiment of Republican radicalism, some even to suggest war would be declared on the South if that party were to ascend to national leadership.

In addition to his speech-making reputation, Lincoln grew in prominence as a lawyer. During the 1850s he developed one of the largest law practices in Sangamon County, Illinois. He regularly appeared before the Illinois Supreme Court as well as the U.S. Circuit and District courts. He did a good business in the local circuit courts, where he traveled extensively twice a year with other lawyers and a judge (David Davis) to argue cases at county courthouses across the state. Lincoln became known as a highly competent if not masterly lawyer and one with impeccable integrity; he was referred to as "Honest Abe." More important, toward the end of the decade he came to represent the expanding railroad interests, notably the Illinois Central Railroad, which greatly increased his prestige (and income). Lincoln had made it to the big leagues as a lawyer and was so recognized in the Northwest, but not in the more prestigious East.

His legal practice kept him in the public eye in Illinois and in constant contact with leading men in the state. When a group of editors met in early 1856 to plan for the upcoming presidential election, Lincoln was invited and attended as the only non-journalist. This group of "anti–Nebraska editors" would expand and become the nucleus of the Republican Party in Illinois, where Lincoln became a conspicuous and active player. On May 29, when the Republican Party was created, it was Abraham Lincoln who delivered the keynote address establishing the motto of the party, "Liberty and Union, now and forever, one and inseparable." Lincoln was becoming known to the leadership of the emerging Republican Party, certainly known as one of the leaders of Republicans in Illinois.

Finally, in 1859 and early 1860, Lincoln began to broaden his exposure by speaking at various venues outside Illinois. He spoke in Ohio to counter the Democratic Party and Stephen Douglas, who continued to promote popular sovereignty. He launched a tour of Iowa, Indiana, Wisconsin, and Minnesota, where he developed the premise that slave labor would compete with white laborers in the territories. "[I]t is due to yourselves as voters, as owners of the new territories, that you shall keep those territories free, in the best condition for all such gallant sons as may choose to go there."[5] These speeches were received warmly. In February 1860 he spoke in New York City at the invitation of the Young Republicans at Cooper Union. Lincoln's speech, carefully researched for a sophisticated Eastern audience, presented the Republican view as a moderate one, again emphasizing the conservative point to exclude the spread of slavery while protecting slavery where it already existed. He said, "Let us have faith that right makes might, and in that faith, let us, to the end, dare to do our duty as we understand it."[6] The speech was a resounding success, carried by many of the most prominent New York papers. Lincoln also had his photograph taken by the inimitable Matthew Brady. The picture was not only flattering, it was so widely distributed during the campaign that some argue it greatly helped him get elected. He went on to give talks in Massachusetts, Rhode Island, New Hampshire, and Connecticut using the same theme. This Eastern trip put Lincoln on the national stage as a politician to note, but not one to rival the sophisticates of the Eastern establishment.

Did this background qualify Abraham Lincoln to *be* president of the United States? As mentioned, Lincoln was a highly respected and highly paid Illinois attorney. He had some political experience at the state level but very limited experience at the national level. He was a captivating speaker, a great storyteller, a consummate jokester and he had a "something" about him that endeared him to many.[7] Although self-educated and not well read by Eastern standards, he was an accomplished writer who wrote with great precision and clarity of expression, even though his spelling at times was atrocious. Above all, Lincoln was a highly ambitious politician. Herndon, his young law partner, noted that "his ambition was a little engine that knew no rest. Politics were his life and his ambition, his motive power."[8] His physical appearance was something to behold. At the Cooper Union, George Haven Putman recorded Lincoln's appearance:

> The long, ungainly figure, upon which hung cloths that, while new for the trip, were evidently the work of an unskilled tailor; the large feet; the clumsy hands ... the long, gaunt head capped by a shock of hair that seemed not to have been thoroughly brushed out ... made a picture which did not fit in with New York's conception of a finished statesman.[9]

He spoke with a twang, often used homespun words—"git" for "get"—leading some to characterized him as a crude, unsophisticated backwoodsmen, friends and foe alike.

While Abraham Lincoln may not have met the Eastern establishment view of a finished statesman, he certainly had many attributes to be a good president. Again, he was a captivating public speaker. His speeches would begin in a high-pitched, almost squeaky tone, but his voice would warm to the effort and end with a smooth and mellow pitch, adding to the effectiveness of the delivery. Second, he captivated the press. He loved to tell stories and often entertained crowds of all sizes with jokes and tall tales. The press loved Lincoln's storytelling because he almost always provided good copy. In fact, some did more than love it, some made money out of it. "Newsmen picked up this facet of his life and some wrote about it.... Printers and publishers saw an opportunity, and so they began putting out little books such as *The Humors of Uncle Abe* and *Old Abe's Jokes*."[10] He was also highly intelligent with a keen mind. He knew how to play with words. Some even considered him the best writer ever to occupy the White House. "He must rank as the most gifted writer among American statesmen of all time. Of the other Presidents, only Thomas Jefferson and Woodrow Wilson could be compared with him in powers of literary self-expression, and surely at his best he surpassed them both."[11] Finally, he was crafty and sly, some contemporaries described him as downright shrewd.

All in all, Abraham Lincoln had the "right stuff" to *become* a very good politician at the national level. But was he prepared to *be* president on March 4, 1861?

Several aspects of Lincoln's background would prove problematic as the nation began to disintegrate after his election. During the winter of 1860–61, seven states of the lower South seceded from the Union. The eight states of the upper South rejected secession decisively but looked to Washington for a compromise proposal on slavery expansion to solve the crisis. At first, the crisis was purely political — so political experience to deal with the unprecedented event of secession was sorely needed.

Abraham Lincoln had little Washington experience. As mentioned, he had served one term in the U.S. House on Representatives, beginning in December 1847, but had had little contact with the Washington establishment for over a decade. He personally knew very few of the key players who participated in the great Washington struggles of the 1850s, either Northern men or Southern men (Stephen Douglas the obvious exception). Edward Hale, another early twentieth-century historian who had interviewed many of the participants, summarized the view many had of Lincoln's lack of experience: "It nowhere appears that there was the wide-spread feeling of confidence in the ability of Lincoln ... He was, indeed, almost an unknown quantity, for though he had sat in the state legislature and in Congress, it had not been for long, and his service had done little to establish public confidence in him."[12] Republican Party delegates returning home from the Chicago convention were often strongly rebuked for having "nominated for the presidency of the United States a man of almost no experience in national political affairs."[13] Abraham Lincoln was simply unknown to the vast majority of movers and shakers in the nation's capital — and it was this group that held the key to keeping the nation from war.

This lack of Washington experience was part of the reason Lincoln misread Southern Unionists during the secession winter. Southern Unionists, the vast majority in the upper South, were quite strongly pro–Union (and even more so anti-secessionist) but needed the Washington establishment to understand their pro–Union views were "conditional," that is, requiring a compromise on the extension of slavery. Although he was born in Kentucky and had a Southern wife (and some critics claimed he was a Southern man), Lincoln did not reach out to these Southern moderates after his election. He viewed their pro–Union stance as "unconditional" and thought most Southerners would not support secession if the time came to choose. He had few face-to-face meetings with Southern Unionists, corresponded with only a handful, and therefore had no sense of their passion for finding an acceptable compromise to sell to their constituents. He was not part of the contentious debates during the fifties and could not see the reasoning of Southern Unionists' calls for compromise. These former Whigs and anti-secession Democrats began to assume power as elections to consider secession in the upper South were producing huge pro–Union (and anti-secession) majorities. By February, Maryland, Virginia, North Carolina, Kentucky, Tennessee, and Missouri had swung decidedly against the secessionists — and it was this group of Unionists that needed to be understood and cultivated. In both the North and the South, in fact, moderates "outnumbered the antagonistic minorities." They represented "an undoubted majority of Americans" who "preferred that the center hold and expected it to do so. Widespread surprise and astonishment thus greeted its sudden collapse in mid–April 1861."[14]

Washington experience (or inexperience) had a personal touch. In an era when there were no telephones or radio or television or really any way to rapidly interact (the telegraph was too new and too unreliable), personal interactions were of greatest importance for the politician. Lincoln certainly knew this from his experience in Illinois. In 1860 Washington was known for its hosts and hostesses as the town was a constant party when Congress was in session. Hardly a day would go by when some senator or congressman or diplomat or senior military officer did not hold a dinner or social function. And it was at these social functions where much of the preparatory work of the government took place, where politicians could informally offer an idea or a proposal. Important, too, it was at these social functions where wavering colleagues or even opponents could be convinced to vote on some piece of legislation. Friend and foe alike got to know one another. Some of the most experienced Washington politicians would develop almost a sixth sense, an ability "to read" an opponent during face-to-face encounters. During the secession winter, when face-to-face interactions meant so much, when "reading" an opponent was so important, Abraham Lincoln was stuck in Springfield, Illinois, surrounded by hordes of gawking folks from all walks of life.

Another aspect of Lincoln's background was his inexperience in management. He had none. Nor did he have confidence enough in anyone who had experience to call on for advice. As David Donald notes, he tried to do everything himself. He had managed a small country store, had organized men in his military service, had participated in state government organizations, but, for the most part, his professional experience consisted of running a two-person law firm. Lincoln was not unique in this facet of background as some of his predecessors had little experience in managing large organizations when they took office either, but few were as isolated and lacking in experienced people around them as this president. And sadly for Lincoln (and the nation), he was confronted with a country "falling apart" on day one of his administration — he had no time to learn the ropes before momentous decisions were upon him. The White House, the center of political activity for any administration, required management. The bureaucracy, including the all-important military, required management. His daily activities required management. All of this would require competent staff, or at least a few people who knew what to do. John Nicolay and John Hay, his two principal assistants, did not have such background. Lincoln, as he freely admitted afterwards, did not know what to do when he took office, and no one chose to show him, although some offered advice.

As Lincoln began his presidency, his White House was similar to many others, for at the beginning of most administrations the White House is to some degree in disarray. But this chief executive thought he needed to interact with everyone, stating they "don't want much and don't get but little, and I must see them." As unbelievable as it sounds today, in 1861 security was not viewed as a major concern. The White House was open to all and one merely had to stand in line at the front door to get an interview with the president. And stand in line they did; often at the beginning of a work day there would be hundreds waiting to see the president, office-seekers, people with petitions of one kind or another, those with various grievances to express, those who merely wanted to shake his hand. Initially his staff did not screen visitors and the place was overwhelmed. "[W]e scarcely have time to eat or sleep," observed John Nicolay.[15] This White House was total chaos.

Still another aspect of background was Abraham Lincoln's persona — his public face. People just did not know what to make of him when they first encountered this physically awkward, badly-clothed man who spoke with a twang. Abraham Lincoln was a true original. Contemporaries found him impossible to read. Even Washington sophisticates like Henry Seward and Charles Francis Adams misinterpreted his motives early on. While he was the consummate entertainer (one who often was the center of attention at public gatherings), loved a good joke, and had many friends, he seemed to have trouble developing deep or confidential friendships. Some suggest he had few if any truly close friends or confidants: "views of Lincoln's contemporaries ... said that during his entire life he formed an intimate friendship with only one person — Joshua Speed — who was five years his junior."

But Lincoln did have close relationships with his secretaries, John Nicolay and especially John Hay, and with Ward Lamon, Elmer Ellsworth, Edward Baker, and a few others (Sandburg maintained he had a "confidential relationship" with the elder Frank Blair, for instance). And Lincoln was known for mentoring young men as well. A more telling point is the observation that "in most cases, Lincoln seemed to erect a barrier between himself and persons with whom he frequently was in contact."[16] He did not share his feelings easily with associates. Still other contemporaries who knew him well said he would be out of touch at certain times, that he was truly mysterious. Joshua Shenk writes, "Of all the paradoxes of Lincoln's life, none is more powerful than the man who would come to be known throughout the world ... was deeply mysterious to the people who knew him best," noting Herndon's observation that "he was a hidden man and wished to keep his own secrets."[17] In the early days of his administration, when the nation teetered on the brink of war, Lincoln was misunderstood by too many.

His persona also included periods of moodiness, if not depression, for which he was widely known. And this moodiness added to the complexity and uncertainty during these early days in office. Donald documents Lincoln practicing law in Springfield:

> Some days he would arrive at the office in a cheerful mood, but then, as Herndon recorded, he might fall into "a sad terribly gloomy state — pick up a pen — sit down by the table and write a moment or two and then become abstracted." Resting his chin on the palm of his left hand, he would sit for hours in silence staring vacantly at the windows. Other days he was so depressed that he did not even speak to Herndon when he entered the office.[18]

When Lincoln was on the circuit traveling around Illinois with Judge Davis and other lawyers, they "noticed his unpredictable moodiness.... Awakening suddenly, Lincoln jumped out of bed, 'put some wood on the fire, and then sat in front of it, moodily, dejectedly, in a most somber and gloomy spell, till the breakfast bell rang.'"[19] His moodiness sometimes led to long periods of pure silence.

His friends were fascinated by his enigmatic silences. Herndon, after sharing an office with him for more than sixteen years, concluded that he was ... the "most shut-mouthed" man who ever lived.... David Davis wrote, "I knew the man so well; he was the most reticent, secretive man I ever saw or expect to see."[20]

When Abraham Lincoln took office on March 4, 1861, the lower South had seceded from the Union—nothing, absolutely nothing, like that had ever happened before. On March 5, Washington (and the nation) was crying out for a leader who knew what to do (or at least act that way), but to use David Donald's words, what they got was a "reticent, secretive man."

In addition to Lincoln's own persona and moodiness, his wife, Mary Todd, added another layer of complexity to the White House. Her behavior was truly remarkable. A "friendly" biographer called her an "emotionally unstable girl," her contemporaries called her "slightly insane." How deeply troubled she was can be argued by others, the most recent and perhaps the definitive work on her concludes, "signs of her mental illness began long before her 1875 commitment ... [in] Mary's early life, one can discern early manifestations of Manic-Depressive Illness (now called Bipolar Disorder)...."[21] In any event, at times her outlandish behavior proved a true burden to the new president. She opposed several of his Cabinet appointments (especially Seward and Chase); she sought to influence the president on patronage appointments (some evidence suggests she took bribes); she spent lavishly on herself and on the White House, creating huge debt for the new president at a most inauspicious moment; at times she dressed inappropriately creating public uproar; she embarrassed her husband with public temper tantrums—all in all her behavior was just outrageous for a first lady. In the early, critical days of his administration, Lincoln had to spend precious time and emotional energy dealing with a wife who sometimes was simply out of control, or as Herndon put it, Lincoln "had to do things which he knew were out of place in order to keep his wife's fingers out of his hair."[22] One Lincoln author summarizes, "Mary Lincoln had never been a national darling, and after she left the White House she became something of a national villain."[23]

Finally, there was Lincoln's habit where he used stories or jokes to parry difficult inquiries. Many times "the listeners—his victims—seldom realized the stalling function of his stories." On other occasions he used stories to illustrate a point, and with still others "the real object was to distract his callers, deflect them from the purpose of their visit, and ease them, laughing, out the door."[24] Some did not enjoy this aspect of Lincoln's persona, some were offended, and even others felt it bizarre, as did his second secretary of war, Edwin Stanton. Sometimes Lincoln's use of humor, especially in very difficult or tense situations, added an additional complexity and did not help clarify his positions. As will be documented in the next four chapters,

Henry Seward (and most others) had real trouble reading Lincoln during these critical early days of his administration, a situation that surely complicated efforts to avert war.

***

An objective look at Abraham Lincoln as he assumed the presidency is a study of great strengths intermingled with great weaknesses as "even Lincoln's most ardent supporters recognize that he abounds with contradictions." Lincoln, a man of high moral stature, was at the same time a shameless politician. He was an intellectual but ignored Darwin and Spencer. Lincoln, the quintessential self-made man who had sprung from the most humble origins, was ambitious to a fault.[25] A great public speaker, a captivating personality, a great writer, crafty and sly — he had all the ingredients required for greatness in a politician. Yet, he was moody, secretive, had few close friends, and was decidedly inexperienced. He had no kitchen cabinet and often went down the decision path alone, or as Herndon observed, "Lincoln never had a confidant, and therefore never unbosomed himself to others."[26] On balance, Potter's conclusion seems about right: Lincoln was "far more fit to *become* than to *be* President."

William Henry Seward

By the spring of 1860, Henry Seward had become the leading Republican in the eyes of the nation. A former Whig, he had associated himself with the Republican Party to counter the Democrats and re-ignite the Whig agenda, including support for government-financed internal improvements (like the transcontinental railroad), a strong central bank, promoting expansion of the West (through free land provided by the Homestead Act), and controlling the spread of slavery. After having served as one of the youngest members of the New York State Senate, he was elected twice governor of New York at an early age. It was in this capacity that he honed his political and administrative skills in managing the most populous and, economically speaking, most important state in the Union. Now completing his second six-year term in the U.S. Senate, where he demonstrated remarkable skill in promoting legislation and championing the new Republican agenda, he had become the dominant force in a badly confused Washington. In addition, he had traveled extensively in Western Europe, the center of political, financial and military power in the world, and was regarded there as an American head of state.

Contemporaries regarded Henry Seward as not only a true statesman, but a true visionary. After the deaths of Daniel Webster, Henry Clay and

John C. Calhoun, Seward stepped in to fill the void and became one of the political giants of his day. Seward's vision for America was a continental empire driven by "peaceful colonizations" with an ever-growing assortment of government-funded internal improvements to expand economic development and foster "the building up and multiplying of republican institutions."[27] An America driven by economic opportunity for all and expanding over the entire continent had no place for slavery, in his view. Maintaining and strengthening the Union was key to all achievement — even the elimination of slavery. For Seward the Union was the bedrock of his American vision. During the secession winter, he came to believe a compromise on slavery expansion was necessary to preserve the Union — preservation of the Union first, elimination of slavery second became his guiding principle.

***

Henry Seward came from a well-to-do, close-knit family. Samuel Seward, his father, had been a physician, judge, farmer and land speculator and, as with most landowners in the region, owned slaves to work the family farm. Henry was very well educated, having graduated from Union College with Phi Beta Kappa honors at nineteen. He began legal studies in his hometown with a well-known lawyer and completed them in New York City. He was admitted to the New York bar at twenty-one. He married the daughter of Auburn, New York, Judge Elijah Miller, Frances, lived in Judge Miller's house (the judge was a widower), and joined his law firm. While practicing law in Auburn, he became involved in a new political movement, the Anti-Masons, which would eventually combine with other anti–Democratic political elements to become the Whig Party. Seward, like many bright young men of his day, was a reformer at heart. The Anti-Masons, with their avowed interest in reform, were a natural attraction for the young Seward, who had truly become smitten with politics. In 1824, by accident, he met a rising young newspaperman working in Rochester, New York — Thurlow Weed — and they began a correspondence on political issues of mutual interest.

***

Thurlow Weed, four years older than Henry Seward, was in the process of starting a newspaper in Rochester when they met. Like Lincoln (and so many others of his day) Weed was self-educated. He got into the newspaper business from his work as a printer. Weed's newspaper effort was being financed by a wealthy Anti-Mason, so he moved it to Albany, the state capital. When he found that Henry Seward was also interested in reform, a natural friendship began. Weed, another Anti-Mason, was part of the rapidly growing middle class, many of whom became anti–Democrats because of the big money and corruption of New York's Regency (the name of the Democ-

ratic political machine in the state). He even looked the part of a rising political boss "in the prime of life, and a commanding figure, his large and com-
pact frame indicated his great vigor, ... [H]is strongly marked face with its
deep eyes set under shaggy brows, its prominent nose ... a firm line of mouth
beneath, and the high forehead ... marked him as a leader, one who was accustomed to the exercise of power."[28] Weed was elected to the state legislature,
where he became fascinated by the Regency and studied its organization carefully.

Weed took a leadership role in the formation of the Whig Party. As one
of the founders of the party in New York State, he systematically maneuvered
his way into key positions and built a reputation as an astute politician. By
the mid–1830s he was the undisputed leader of the party. Shortly thereafter,
the Whig Party gained power in New York and Weed, although thoroughly
distrustful of the Democratic organization, set about creating a political
organization of his own — one that in time would rival the Regency. Using
the Regency as a model, he made patronage appointments and awarded government contracts to friends in building a statewide political organization of
like-minded individuals. In 1834 he managed to have the young Henry
Seward, who by then was regarded as a rising star, nominated for governor.
Although Seward would not be successful on this first try, Weed did it again
in 1837, this time successfully, as the Whigs carried one house of the legislature and won the gubernatorial race.

Weed did not care much about elective office but truly relished the role
of political boss. In time he would become a true superstar in the business.
He used editorials in his paper, the *Albany Evening Journal*, continually and
effectively to promote his political views. Henry Seward's popular appeal and
Thurlow Weed's political acumen meshed quite nicely and the Seward-Weed
"machine" was born. During the 1840s and 1850s the machine steadily
increased its reach in the state (and the nation) by building the Whig Party.
"In 1855, Greeley, who certainly was not prejudiced in Weed's favor, called
him a giant in ability and ranked him as 'the greatest man we have left."
Weed dominated politics in New York State and commanded great respect at
the national level. "His power was as extraordinary as Seward's popularity."[29]

By 1860 no one in America had more political power than Thurlow Weed.
One of his leading contemporaries, Samuel Bowles, visited with Weed at
Albany in February 1860 and wrote, "He is a great man — one of the most
remarkable men of our time — one whom I had rather have had such an interview with than with any President of our day and generation."[30] Weed went
to Chicago as leader of the New York delegation to manage the campaign for
Henry Seward's nomination for president. The New York delegates "had
hinted to this man and that man supposed to wield some influence, that if
he would throw that influence for Seward, he might, in case of success, count

upon proper 'recognition.'" The delegates had "spent money freely and let everybody understand that there was a great lot more to spend." And "among these men Thurlow Weed moved as a great captain, with ceaseless activity and noiseless step, receiving their reports and giving new instructions."[31] Lincoln biographer William E. Barton called Weed "one of the ablest politicians America has ever known."[32] For Thurlow Weed, the great failure of his long and distinguished political career was not securing the presidential nomination for his lifelong friend, Henry Seward.

***

Thurlow Weed, political boss of New York State (some say the nation), was the life-long political partner of Seward. Weed knew how to make government work by "blending" politics with business (Seward House, Auburn, New York).

The year 1830 found Seward, at the age of twenty-nine, delivering a major report at the Anti-Masons' first national convention. Articulate and highly intelligent, he quickly became known as a young politician to watch. In the fall of 1830 Weed, becoming more and more impressed with the young Seward, helped him get elected to the New York State Senate as an Anti-Mason. Seward rapidly learned the ropes from his Anti-Masonic colleagues, including Millard Fillmore. As Seward began to develop a deep friendship with Weed he discovered that Weed was not so much interested in political office as in becoming a political powerbroker. Weed saw in Seward a person of like political interest with a keen mind and remarkable energy, a young man with "unmistakable evidences of stern integrity, earnest patriotism, and unswerving fidelity," and one with "a rare capacity for intellectual labor ... an industry which never tired and required no relaxation."[33] Henry Seward was a political prodigy in the making, Weed recognized the potential instinctively.

In 1833 Seward's father asked Henry to accompany him on a six-month tour of Europe. Samuel Seward was well-to-do, a multimillionaire by today's standards, and paid for the entire trip. Henry Seward made a deal with Weed to send him letters of his experiences and Weed agreed to publish them in his newspaper. Samuel and young Henry spent time in England, where they went to the House of Commons, and then on to Ireland and Scotland. They crossed the English Channel to Holland and in Paris visited the famed Marquis de Lafayette as well as the Chamber of Deputies. Trips to Germany and Switzerland rounded out the voyage. Henry gained much from this trip, not only a first-hand knowledge of European governments but, through Weed's efforts in publishing his letters, name recognition to western New York State's rapidly growing population. The trip added to Seward's growing reputation in the region and established him as an urbane man, for "while Lincoln, Chase, and Bates would never visit the Old World, Seward, at the age of thirty-two, mingled comfortably with members of Parliament and received invitations to elegant receptions and dinner parties throughout Europe."[34]

In the fall of 1834 Weed helped Seward (who had just turned thirty-three) get the Whig Party's nomination for governor. The Whigs, a new party, were still a minority in New York State and were running against the powerful Regency and its incumbent governor, William Marcy. Despite his youth (and the Democratic attack on same) Seward ran well in the western part of the state, losing statewide by a mere 11,000 votes. Seward came across to the electorate as a man of reason, a reformer of the first rank, and one who could stand up to the Democrats despite his youth. He was a captivating speaker — a genuine charmer — and folks just liked him. Although the loss was heartfelt, William Henry Seward was now a name all in New York State recognized.

In 1837, again with Thurlow Weed as chief promoter, Seward once more placed his name in contention for the Whig nomination for governor. Weed did his magic at the Whig convention and Seward won the nomination again. New York State was the biggest prize for any political party in the non-presidential election year of 1838. Everyone was focused on the race for "the Whig Party's national development coincided with its growth in New York State, and nationally as well as locally it was conservative in character."[35] The gubernatorial race in New York turned into a spirited campaign in which the Democrats were blamed for the "Panic of 1837" (a significant economic downturn) and, as usual, accused of corruption. Weed, now firmly established as the New York Whigs' political boss, pulled the various party elements together and thirty-seven-year-old Seward won by over 10,000 votes, becoming one of the youngest ever elected governor. The Whigs, both in New York State and nationally, were elated. Seward was besieged with congratulatory messages from across the country. Here was a handsome, bright, charming young man who could run with the best of the seasoned politicians—the John F. Kennedy of his generation.

Prior to the Civil War, state governments had more power (and were more important to the citizens) than the federal government in Washington. The real work of running the nation, everything from improving roads to financing local projects to education to legal reform, was done at the state level. Most Americans experienced the federal government only through the postal service. Thus when Henry Seward took control of the government of New York State, he was one of the most powerful figures in America. Governor of New York was viewed at the time as one of the more prestigious political posts in the nation, ranking close to president of the United States, certainly more important than vice president. The inaugural address of the governor of New York "received much of the national attention that is reserved today for a president's inaugural address."[36]

Weed took control of the governor-elect, immediately finding Seward a house to rent, stocking it with food

AUBURN UNION EXTRA.

WELCOME

TO

SEWARD

BY THE

Military & Citizens,

WITH BELLS, ARTILLERY &c.

On Friday Dec. 30, at 3 o'clock P. M.

Gov. Seward has arrived in the City

of New York, and is to-day enjoying the hospitalities of that city, tendered him by the Mayor and Common Council.

He will reach Auburn to-morrow at 3 o'clock P. M., when his fellow citizens here will have the pleasure of bidding him Welcome Home.

P. S. The Teachers and Pupils of

the Public Schools, and the Ladies, will arrange themselves to receive him in Exchange Street.

The handbill announcing the welcome home celebration for Seward after his highly successful trip to Europe. Seward was treated on both continents as a head of state in total contrast to Abraham Lincoln who, at this time, was not widely known or respected anywhere but central Illinois (Department of Rare Books and Special Collections, University of Rochester, Rochester, New York).

and wine, even selecting his inaugural outfit. Weed "met with hundreds of office seekers, eventually selecting every member of the governor's cabinet."[37] Seward had over 1,500 political appointments to make, an expanding and complex bureaucracy to run, and a tangled web of politics to manage with the state Senate under Democratic control. Seward learned quickly and proved himself equal to the task of running the largest state government in the country. He oversaw the improvement in numerous public works, public schools were put in the hands of elected boards, legal reform was instituted, more humane treatment of the insane was championed, repeal of racially discriminatory voter eligibility requirements were promoted, and a major overhaul of the badly run state prison system was completed.

The Auburn State Prison. Seward championed prison reform, demanding more humane treatment for prisoners when it was not popular to do so — the mark of a true visionary (Seward House, Auburn, New York).

Seward also demonstrated he had the "right stuff" by often championing causes that were not popular. He pushed for the rights of immigrants, especially the rowdy (and at times unpopular) Irish, in an attempt to attract traditional Democrats to the Whig Party. He made a deal with Bishop John Hughes of New York City whereby he proposed state monies for support of Catholic schools, again an attempt to attract traditional Democrats. He took up the cause of the Oneidas Indians in their fight to control their ancestral lands. On at least three occasions he made national headlines by standing for the "right" under tremendous political pressure to do otherwise. First, in a famous land-rent dispute in the western part of the state, he backed down gun-carrying farmers with the state militia. The farmers attempted to take the law into their own hands by chasing state sheriffs out of the territory who were trying to serve legal notices on them for refusing to pay their rent. A conciliator by temperament, he adroitly found a way to appease the farmers by making a promise to adjudicate their grievances with the state legislature. Second, he tackled the increasingly touchy issue of slavery by refusing to send back to Virginia for trial three New York seamen who had attempted to smuggle a slave out of Norfolk. This resulted in the legislature passing his law to guarantee fugitive slaves a trial by jury. Finally, he skillfully managed the McLeod affair, in which a Canadian, Alexander McLeod, was arrested by New York authorities and charged with murder. Although he received no support from Daniel Webster, secretary of state in Washington, Seward resolved the dispute skillfully by letting the Canadian government know, informally, that he would pardon McLeod and return him to Canada if he were convicted.

In addition to running the executive office of the state, Seward and Weed put in place a statewide Whig Party organization that would successfully challenge the Democrats for nearly two decades. Seward and Weed used political jobs, state government contracts, and political influence to utmost advantage (awarding government contracts to political friends was a widely accepted practice in the nineteenth century) "to broaden the Whig Party beyond its base of merchants, industrialists, and prosperous farmers." In addition, Weed raised money for a new weekly newspaper in an effort "to appeal to the masses of workingmen, who had generally voted Democratic since Andrew Jackson's day." Weed appointed Horace Greeley editor and "the new partisan weekly became an instant success, eventually evolving into the powerful *New York Tribune*." This began the famous Seward-Weed-Greeley combination which "for nearly a quarter of a century ... collaborated to build support first for the Whigs and, later on, for the Republicans. For much of that time, the three were like brothers."[38]

Despite the failure of some of his programs, especially those responsible for increasing the state's indebtedness, in 1840 Seward was re-elected to a second term as governor, albeit with a smaller majority. His often-courageous but unpopular stands on issues had cost him more votes than it gained, especially his support for Catholics. However, in 1841 Seward announced he would not seek a third two-year term as governor. He had had a grueling four years, his personal finances were in sad shape, and he had tired of the often-trivial politics found at the state-government level. Although he had made his share of enemies (and mistakes), his announcement drew real expressions of gratitude and real testimonials from business, finance and education leaders from across the state and nation.

The governor of New York was thrust into national political discussions because the state had more Electoral College votes than any other and because it was so powerful in commerce, finance, and trade. During his two terms as governor, Seward handled this national spotlight flawlessly (with Weed's help, of course) and emerged from the governorship firmly established as a political figure of national stature at forty-one. Seward had gained hands-on experience not only managing a large government bureaucracy, but also dealing with the powerful elites in business and finance, centered in New York City. His experience as governor provided Henry Seward, a conciliator by temperament, the perfect background to save the nation from war.

Seward returned to Auburn and for the balance of the decade devoted his time to his law practice, restoring his finances, and spending more time with wife Frances and his children. It was a good time for Seward. His law practice flourished (as everyone wanted to be represented by the former governor) and within a few years he was able to pay off all his debts. He was kept in the state and national eye by his defense of William Freeman, a local black man who had murdered a white farmer and his family, on grounds of insanity. While this was an extremely

> In the days when William H. Seward was Governor of the State, it was commonly supposed that Thurlow Weed had an undue influence over him. He happened to be traveling one night in the stage in one of the southwestern counties where he was little known. The passengers, not recognizing him, were commenting quite freely on some of the Governor's measures. After listening awhile, he controverted their statements. They answered him by asking, "Who are you that you happen to know more about these matters than we?" He answered frankly, "Well, gentlemen, I am the person on whose measures you have been commenting so freely!" "What! You Governor Seward? Likely story! Quite a joke! Yoh, hoh, hoh!" "Well, gentlemen, at the next place where we stop (about sunrise) I am well acquainted with the hotel-keeper, and although he differs in party views, he will say who I am." When they reached the place they asked, as he stepped from the stage, if he was "William H. Seward, Governor of the State of New York?" The landlord answered with an arch smile, "There is no doubt that you are William H Seward—but I rather think that Thurlow Weed is at present the Governor of the State of New York!"

An article that appeared in an Auburn newspaper as the young Seward first assumed the governorship of New York State (Seward House, Auburn, New York).

unpopular move with the locals, Seward felt Freeman was insane and that defending him pro bono was the right thing to do. Seward was a man of high principle and at no time in his long career was it more evident than with the Freeman case. During this time Seward never strayed far from politics, clearly his first love.

The 1840s also found Seward lecturing throughout the state, commenting on one issue or another as Whigs in the region asked him to speak. He took a trip to Washington, where he advised the New York delegation on several matters, and then met other key national leaders. In the presidential election of 1848 the Whig Party nominated Zachary Taylor for president and Seward's former colleague in the state senate, Millard Fillmore, for vice president, and they won. During the campaign Seward had toured New York State in support of the ticket and went to New England to stump. In one of those fateful moments in time, Seward shared the platform (and a hotel room) in Boston with Abraham Lincoln. This was the first meeting of the two men who would play such an important role in the nation's future — they would not meet again for thirteen years.

Rapid economic growth continued to spur the rise of the Whig Party in New York State. The statistics for New York are truly impressive, between 1790 and 1850:

- [T]he state's population had increased ninefold ... with 3,000,000 inhabitants in 1850, it outranked in numbers any other state in the Union;
- There were 2345 miles of railroad in operation within its borders in 1854, roads that carried millions of passengers and close to a million tons of freight;
- 1,288,000 tons of shipping were registered, enrolled and licensed at New York port alone in 1855, nearly five times the amount entered in 1815, and over twice that of rival Boston.[39]

Seward and Weed participated in this rapid economic growth and used the economic planks in the Whig agenda to attract new members to the party, substantially increasing the party's base. Weed was just phenomenal as he "moved resolutely and at ease amidst this teeming economic life." More important, he became "a political power in a country and in a state where business and politics were becoming ever more closely and inextricably intertwined."[40] Weed knew how to mix business and politics and his efforts paid off handsomely when the November election saw the Whig Party returned to power in New York. Hamilton Fish, a Whig, was elected governor and both houses in the legislature went to the Whigs as well. This was especially fortuitous for Henry Seward because in the mid-nineteenth century U.S. senators were elected by their state legislatures. The term of John Dix, senior senator from New York, was set to expire in 1849.

Weed was determined to have a voice in Washington to bolster his grow-ing influence there. He carefully laid plans to fill the role with his close friend and colleague, Henry Seward, who was anxious to return to politics. With his customary zeal, Weed worked the state legislature, maneuvering this del-egate and that delegate. Seward was elected by a landslide, 121 to 32. When Congress was set to convene, Weed arranged for Seward to be received with some fanfare in the nation's capital. Even President Zachary Taylor (who felt Weed had been instrumental in his election) put out the welcome mat for the freshman senator from New York State. For Seward was not just another local politician coming to Washington, this was the former governor of New York, a man closely connected to the business and financial power structure of the country and a man who had run an organization as big as the Washington bureaucracy. Seward swept into the capital where his "charm, persuasive logic and untiring perseverance were employed to the full." Weed saw that he met the right people and Seward "cultivated the genial brother of the President, Colonel J. P. Taylor, and was all amiability and charm with the Colonel's wife." The colonel's wife was not only "a forceful and spirited lady" but she brought Seward "into the social circle that revolved about Old Zack."[41] Quickly Seward outranked many senior senators in influence — he was years ahead of his freshmen colleagues, Democrats Jefferson Davis of Mississippi and Stephen Douglas of Illinois. He preferred to be called "governor."

Seward was an experienced politician, one who was known throughout the country, and his auspicious arrival in Washington was noticed by all. "Probably no man ever yet appeared for the first time in Congress so widely known and so warmly appreciated," declared the *New York Tribune* after his election. Seward arrived with "an aura of celebrity, even notoriety."[42] It is fair to say he even outranked Vice President Millard Fillmore. On March 11 Seward delivered his first speech, to a packed gallery in the Senate, opposing legislation introduced by Henry Clay proposing a compromise on the slav-ery issue. It was an extraordinary effort for a freshmen senator. He not only opposed the compromise offered by the venerable Clay, but took a pronounced antislavery stand as well. The speech "was independent and courageous" and Seward "spoke as a leader rather than as a supporter of the President, a fact that his enemies promptly noticed." He even "differed openly and repeatedly with Webster," another venerable member of the Senate.[43] But the speech achieved immortality when Seward said "there is a *higher law* than the Con-stitution." Although those eight words would live forever, in the speech Seward was trying "to remind his audience that there was Caesar's law and there was God's law" and "man's law drew its sanction" from God's law.[44] Widely circulated in both North and South (tens of thousands of copies were printed), the speech was too radical for the time and Seward's enthusiasm was tempered when he received a sharp note from Weed: "Your speech ... sent me to bed with a heavy heart" and "a restless night and an anxious day have not relieved my apprehensions." Seward was much troubled for he "recognized that his mentor's political instincts were usually better than his own."[45] Seward immediately began a campaign using his undeniable charm and conciliatory nature to assuage moderates of both North and South.

At this time, Weed also was active in the nation's capital as "he approached the President through Colonel Taylor and devoted himself to a gentle but earnest course of tutelage in the matter of appointments." Weed had played a decisive role in Taylor's election indeed and now sought the rewards for "the President, already impressed by Seward and doubtless remembering the part Weed had played in his own elevation, was ripe for instruction." His efforts paid off for "in an astonishing short space of time the word went out to the Treasury and Post Office ... that fodder should be provided for those deserving Whigs who had borne the heat and burden of the day."[46] Weed had become a prime mover and shaker at the national level, constantly driven by his pragmatic approach to politics, which was always to seek the practical result, always opt for accomplishment over political opportunism.

In late June Seward delivered his second major speech, again to a packed Senate chamber. He addressed mankind's right to liberty and justice: "Equal justice always excites fear, and therefore always gives offence, otherwise its ways would be smooth and its sway universal. The abstractions of human rights are the only permanent foundations of society. It is by referring to them that men determine what is established because it is RIGHT, in order to uphold it forever...." He called for the federal government to restrict the spread of slavery and empower the common man. It was a speech "that a Northern laboring man, as well as a Southern Negro or poor white, could read with the feeling that he had found a champion."[47] Seward had a way with words and folks flocked to hear him, not because he was a spell-binding orator with booming voice or charismatic style, but because "his manner was that of a philosopher rather than an orator."[48] Seward's boundless stream of ideas attracted the public wherever he went in the North; in the South, moderates read his speeches with deep interest, slaveholders with deep distrust. Seward's words touched Americans of the antebellum era like few others.

In July of 1850 Zachary Taylor died suddenly (after eating spoiled food) and Millard Fillmore assumed the presidency. This was a severe blow to Seward and Weed (Fillmore, a conservative Whig, had become estranged from them) for now Fillmore would have the upper hand both in New York State, with patronage appointments and government contracts, and nationally, with regard to programs and plans. Seward suddenly found himself without influence at the White House. His star in Washington dimmed. As 1851 dawned, Seward found time to assess, reflect, and mend fences and strengthen contacts in the nation's capital. But his public popularity in the capital never waned and when word of a Seward speech in the Senate leaked out, large crowds always appeared.

In 1852 Henry Seward promoted the candidacy of Gen. Winfield Scott (in a rare disagreement with Weed) at the Whig nominating convention and Scott won the nomination. The election, however, was a complete debacle, and the Whigs lost badly to the Democrats. Franklin Pierce of New Hampshire became president. The election marked the end of the Whig Party. Northern and Southern factions, already on shaky ground over slavery, were confronted by new factions driven by the "ethnocultural issues" of temperance and nativism. "Zealous drys mounted a crusade to enact prohibition laws" that ripped the Whigs apart in several Northern states, and the nativist movement, an anti–Catholic and anti-immigrant coalition, suddenly gained real power in the mid–Atlantic states.[49] By 1854 two new political parties were emerging from the shattered Whigs. First, the nativists formed the American Party (Horace Greeley called them Know Nothings because many members would say "I know nothing" when asked about their bigotry). Second, abolitionists, Free Soilers, and others would form the Republican Party, whose central thrust was to oppose slavery. Seward, although clearly a liberal in his day, was not an abolitionist, and as the leading proponent of immigrant rights was as strongly opposed to the Know Nothings as any Whig could be. He viewed these new parties as splinter groups who were too radical and not prone to compromise; his own instincts were "those of a mainstream politician."[50] Again, Seward was a conciliator by temperament and although a bit of an idealist, he recognized more than most that the democratic process required compromise: moderation carried the day in Washington as he had learned first-hand in his days as governor in Albany.

Seward's mainstream instincts and his dislike of radicals certainly played a major role in the dissolution of the famous Seward-Weed-Greeley political partnership in the fall of 1854. Horace Greeley, editor of one of the most widely read newspapers in America, had become a true eccentric. An odd duck, he was a radical who would take up just about any strange cause that came along, including support for communal living, vegetarianism, and temperance (in the mid-nineteenth century these were considered wildly radical concepts). Seward and Weed distrusted radicals. Weed confided to an old friend "reformers were apt to be erratic." He referred to temperance folks as "queer chaps" and felt "many freethinkers were just plain crazy."[51] Seward felt much the same way and as a result he and Weed became much more closely aligned with the political moderate Henry Jarvis Raymond, of the *New York Times*, a paper that was beginning to rival Greeley's *Tribune*. Greeley sent a letter to Seward in November ending their partnership. Many feel he parted company with Seward and Weed over their failure to support him for political office, but from Seward's point of view Greeley's radicalism was a key issue. Seward did not want to be associated closely with radicals— whether abolitionists, temperance folks, or Southern "fire-eaters"— he viewed them as the no-compromise types who posed the greatest threat to democracy and his beloved Union.[52]

The year 1854 also saw Stephen Douglas introduce the Kansas-Nebraska Act in the Congress. If enacted, the act would essentially repeal the Compromise of 1850, which banned slavery north of Missouri. In addition it proposed that settlers of the new territories of the West determine whether slavery should exist or not by vote, this principle became known as "popular sovereignty." Seward felt passage of the act would re-ignite the extension of slavery question and open the acrimonious slavery debate once again. He led the opposition. In a dramatic speech on the Senate floor Seward warned that the bill opened the conflict "between conservatism and progress, between truth and error, between right and wrong."[53] But complex political intrigues were at play and Seward's efforts failed, the act passed the Senate by a wide margin. And, as Seward predicted, passage of the act opened the gates of anti-slavery public opinion in the North and new, active groups of "anti–Nebraska" folks sprang up in every state.

Seward's first term was set to expire in 1855 and the disarray in the Whig Party nationally and in New York in particular would prove problematic. Nativism was on the rise in New York (primarily as a reaction to the often-rowdy Irish Catholics), and many in this group opposed Seward. Many Whig conservatives from the old Fillmore camp could not be counted in Seward's camp and, of course, disheartened Democrats could not be counted on either. The relationship between Seward and Weed was going through some strain but, undaunted, Weed launched a "Re-elect Seward" campaign in the legislature. He focused on Seward's growing national reputation and his leadership of the moderate antislavery forces in Washington. Weed, by putting together a coalition of antislavery Whigs and anti–Nebraska legislators, succeeded, but not without real difficulty. In the final vote, however, Seward won a second term handily.

On his return to Washington, Seward rented a large home and moved the family there, but Frances was not happy. A short time later she returned to Auburn (supposedly because of one of her frequent illnesses) and Seward made an important personal move. He asked his son Fred to become his legislative assistant, but in a move that would have more impact in the nation's capital, he asked Fred's wife, Anna, to serve as his full-time hostess. Both Fred and Anna agreed. Anna was an attractive and quite polished young lady and quickly established Seward as one of the leading hosts in the city. Dinner parties were so essential during this time because it was a moment when opponents could interact informally without the pressure of peer review. "After a

Fred and Anna Seward, circa 1864. Fred served as Seward's assistant at the State Department, and Anna served as his hostess. She was described as "sophisticated and charming" (Seward House, Auburn, New York).

second dessert of apples, nuts, and prunes, the ladies would retire, leaving the men to talk politics over brandy and cigars. Henry loved to talk and so did his guests. An evening at the Sewards was rarely dull."[54] Many of his dinner guests were Southern Whigs who would come to hold the balance of power as the nation moved to crisis point; but even with prominent Southern Democrats "Seward took special pains to cultivate pleasant relations" for, "unlike Sumner and others, he had no prejudices against slave-holders [after all, his father had been one]. He was at one time very friendly with Jefferson Davis."[55] His reputation as a leading host, and his friendly relations with Southerners, would later offer real opportunities to resolve contentious issues during the secession winter, as moderates sought to hold the country together. Again for emphasis, in mid-nineteenth century politics, personal encounters, the face-to-face discussions, were all-important.

A clear example of Seward's mainstream political views can be found in the "Sumner affair." Charles Sumner, radical Republican senator from Massachusetts, was widely known for his intemperate speech. In May 1856 he delivered a speech in the Senate characterized "as one of the most ugly speeches ever delivered in the Senate of the United States." Sumner, once again, bitterly attacked slave owners, but this time he insulted a Senate colleague, the respected Sen. Andrew P. Butler of South Carolina, in a most rude way. Preston Brooks, a congressman from South Carolina and relative of Butler's, took the comments as an insult to his family. He entered the Senate chamber and physically attacked Sumner with a cane a day or so later. Seward was appalled and "deplored the assault on his colleague"; however, he "felt that Sumner had provoked it," which was a view shared by many Northern moderates. Former senator Robert Winthrop wrote that "he deplored Brook's assault" but "hoped never again to read a speech in the Senate as distasteful as Sumner's." Winthrop ended his statement with a remarkable tribute to Henry Seward: "Would that every member of the Senate, in his discussions, would take counsel of your distinguished colleague [Seward], whose speeches are not more remarkable for ability than for decorum, good temper (and) good taste."[56] Seward had become the consummate Washington politician and was so recognized by his contemporaries throughout the North, and moderates in the South as well.

As the 1856 presidential election neared, the Republicans began to think of Seward as their leading candidate. He was clearly Washington's leader of antislavery forces. And he and Weed had been instrumental in building the Republican Party. "John Bigelow declared that Thurlow Weed was 'the only Whig in the state with enough wisdom to see the practicality of fusing the free soil elements of the state's old parties into a new organization, and influential and able enough to bring his own partisans into the combination."[57] As a result, Weed held great power in the new party and could have pushed Seward to the forefront. But he was not convinced the time was right as this would be the Republican Party's first try at national office. Seward had great support at the Republican nominating convention, "When Sen. Henry Wilson, in a speech, suggested the possibility of nominating 'the foremost statesman of America, William H. Seward,' the convention broke into its greatest ovation yet."[58] In the end, Seward would withhold his name, the Republicans would nominate John Fremont, and they would lose the election to Democrat James Buchanan of Pennsylvania.

The 1856 nominating convention convinced Seward that he could (and should) become president, and he and Weed began to work on it at every point. "During the next four years, Seward kept himself in the public eye. He called for a transatlantic telegraph cable, a transcontinental railroad, river and harbor improvements, free homesteads, a protective tariff, and the expansion of American commerce in the Pacific"— truly the stuff of a political visionary.[59]

No discussion of William Henry Seward is complete without mention of "irrepressible conflict," a phrase that has identified him to many students of the period. During the fall of 1857 and spring of 1858, Seward had developed a theme in his talks that spoke of two economic systems in the country, one based on slave labor and one based on free labor. Seward felt the two systems could not exist together in the long run. Campaigning for Republicans in the fall of 1858, playing to an antislavery crowd in Rochester, he gave a rousing speech that truly caught the nation's attention.

> Shall I tell you what this collision means? They who think that it is accidental, unnecessary, the work of interested or fanatical agitators, and therefore ephemeral, mistake the case altogether. It is an *irrepressible conflict* between opposing and enduring forces, and it means that the United States must and will, sooner or later, become either entirely a slave-holding nation or entirely a free-labor nation.[60]

The speech was given wide press. It electrified the North, and the South as well. Moderates in both sections of the country were surprised by its radical nature, Weed included.

Interestingly, Abraham Lincoln earlier in the same year had given his "house divided" speech and was on very similar ground with "a house divided against itself cannot stand." Some historians have concluded that Seward's speech permanently identified him as a radical, but his past actions (as well as his future ones) identified him with the moderate antislavery forces. "Historians have explained this pattern of actions in various ways ... but the greater weight of authority leans to the view, well expressed by Allan Nevins, that Seward's radicalism was more rhetorical than real and that his compromising tendencies by the end of the 1850s marked the emergence of his 'natural conservatism.'"[61] Every politician blunders along the way and the *irrepressible speech* was one of Seward's worse, for the speech was just too radical. Later he conceded, as one historian wrote, "if heaven would forgive him for stringing together two high sounding words, he would never do it again."[62]

During 1859 Seward and Weed began to lay the groundwork for Seward's presidential nomination at the upcoming Republican convention scheduled for May 1860. The "Dictator" set about the work with his customary zeal. He sent financial help to Republican organizations (and some politicians) in key states, he lined up newspapers to begin a "Nominate Seward" campaign (Raymond's *New York Times* was one of the leaders), and he personally used his influence to parry some of the criticism leveled at Seward, especially from former Know Nothings. Weed, most influential Republicans, and even many antislavery Democrats thought Seward was due the nomination.

With his campaign in good hands, Seward, with Weed's concurrence, set off on an extended trip to Europe in May 1859. His send-off in New York Harbor was sufficient for a president-elect and his reception in Europe likewise. In London he was entertained by Lord Palmerston and Lord John Russell, two of Britain's most influential leaders. "He attended the opening of Parliament and was made an honorary member of the Reform Club." Queen Victoria was so anxious to meet him she arranged for a "private presentation." He traveled to France and Italy, where the pope "expressed appreciation for [his] attitude toward Catholics and wished him well in his hopes for 'higher advancement.'"[63] Importantly, European governments, more enlightened than most anywhere else, led efforts to eliminate slavery peacefully during the previous decades— and they had been successful. Seward studied these programs carefully. Returning to New York in late December to a 100-gun salute, he seemed to be recognized as a head of state on both continents. Seward had differences with the British though for sometimes he spoke too freely which caused the staid British to react negatively, as they were wont to do with former colonists.

Early 1860 saw Weed and Seward shoring up the nomination. Weed continued to work newspapers in key states, sound out former Know Nothings as possible running mates (in an effort to soften nativists opposition to Seward), and send money (or promises thereof) to key state delegations. Weed arranged for Seward to visit Simon Cameron, political boss of Pennsylvania and its senior U.S. senator, where he received a very warm reception. Seward reported, "He [Cameron] brought the whole legislature ... to see me, feasted them gloriously, and they were in the main so generous as to embarrass me."[64] On February 29 Seward made a major speech to the usual packed Senate gallery, intending to identify himself firmly as a moderate. He urged admission of Kansas as a free state, deplored John Brown and his fanatical followers, and sought to reassure the nation on the question of disunion. "Those who seek to awaken the terrors of disunion ... have too hastily con-

Seward, in hat, sitting with the captain of the *Wayanda* in July 1864. He sailed to Europe in the spring of 1859 on such a ship to meet with leaders of European governments, partly to discuss their successful programs to eliminate slavery (Seward House, Auburn, New York).

sidered the conditions under which they are to make their attempt. Who
believes that a Republican administration and Congress could practice tyranny
under a Constitution which interposes so many checks as ours?"[65] Henry
Seward had the ear of the North for sure (and even some in the South). "[T]he
speech produced deafening applause in the galleries and widespread praise
in the press. Reprinted in pamphlet form, more than half a million copies
were circulated throughout the country."[66] Barton noted, even "those who
loved him least listened with respect when he spoke."[67] William Henry Seward
was ready to embark on his quest for the presidency.

So the stage was set for his nomination and Henry Seward left Washington in early May for his home at Auburn, fully confident he would not
return to the U.S. Senate.

***

Was William Henry Seward the best candidate for the Republicans? Did his
background qualify him to *be* president of the United States?

Like Lincoln, Henry Seward was a most ambitious politician and like
Lincoln also there were those who truly liked him and those who did not.
Seward had made mistakes: he had angered nativists by supporting Catholics
and immigrants; he had supported government-financed internal improvements and a strong central bank, which angered antislavery Democrats coming into the party; and, at times, his incautious use of speech had aligned him
with the radicals angering the more conservative former Whigs in the party.
Many radical Southern Democrats simply could not tolerate him. He was not
a great orator because his voice did not project well. And sometimes he could
be too free with his private conversation, especially in after-dinner conversations. But in contrast to Abraham Lincoln, Henry Seward had three aspects
of background that prepared him to *be* a good (if not great) president on
Inauguration Day

First and foremost, Henry Seward was an exceptionally experienced
politician. To repeat for emphasis, he began political life as one of the youngest
members of the New York State Senate. He was elected governor of New York
at the age of thirty-seven. He was reelected to a second term and likely would
have been elected to a third term had he so desired. He had been elected twice
to the U.S. Senate by the legislature of New York, the most populous and
wealthiest state in the Union. Entering Washington as a freshman senator,
he was quickly recognized as a major player. Here was the former governor
of New York, one of the most prestigious political posts in the land, taking a
seat in the U.S. Senate. Unlike other junior senators he had immediate access
to the president and other key leaders of the Washington establishment, such
as Gen. Winfield Scott, commander of the Army.

Few, if any, politicians of his era arrived in Washington with a better background. His speeches were carefully written and usually circulated widely for their cultured and urbane prose, with several of his speeches printed in quantities of 50,000 or more. In fact, "the speeches of no political orator of the period were so popular and effective, or attained so high an average of excellence" as those of Seward. He was a true visionary, imaginative but practical, whose "political wisdom and sound judgment" was reflected in most of his work.[68] Henry Seward became such an extraordinarily popular politician because his ideas for the country, such as expansion of the empire, economic growth spurred by government-financed internal improvements, opportunity for all, resonated with Americans of his day. The "American dream" of that era — what drew people from the world over to risk their lives to get here — was the opportunity to achieve wealth, to experience freedom of choice (religious and otherwise), and to be free from the domineering aristocrats of the Old World.

Most of Seward's contemporaries identified him as a moderate or mainstream politician (the "higher law" and "irrepressible conflict" speeches the exception). He learned to seek compromise and was recognized as a conciliator of real merit. He was constantly sought as a speaker and, even more important, was constantly sought for advice by colleagues of different political persuasions. He knew the major Washington players first-hand — he was a friend of Jefferson Davis, Stephen Douglas, John J. Crittenden, Charles Francis Adams, and a host of other congressional leaders. He was known by virtually everyone who counted in Washington, from senior clerks in the bureaucracy to lobbyists to newspapermen. Seward loved politics, but more critical to the nation's future, he was an extremely able politician, recognized as one of high moral fiber. While most other politicians engaged in acrimonious debate that often ended in personal attack, not so Henry Seward. He would not interrupt a colleague with annoying questions or engage in contentious discourse. On the contrary, Seward often acted "in the capacity of a peacemaker" when angry confrontations between senators occurred.[69] Friend and foe alike regarded Seward as the consummate politician. He had earned their respect, if not admiration.

Henry Seward also knew how to run a government. His two terms as governor of New York had taught him the ropes of managing a bureaucracy, essentially how to play the game of government. He had honed his managerial skills in a state with a bureaucracy that was nearly as large as that in Washington. He knew the importance of close advisors, and he knew how to use them effectively. New York was not only the most populous state in the nation, but it was the center of trade and commerce and the center of banking and finance for the country. Seward, with Weed's help, had had to learn how to deal with the financial elites of the nation — from all parties. Most important, he had learned how to make government work, when to stand firm and when to compromise. To manage New York State was close to managing the country in mid-nineteenth-century America.

And from the perspective of power politics, Seward had a well-run political organization at his disposal. By 1860 Thurlow Weed was *the* political boss of the nation, rivaled by the Blairs in the West, but few others. Weed had hundreds, if not thousands, of political contacts throughout the nation — men who were former Whigs, fellow newspaper editors, powerful business leaders. And Weed knew how to mingle business with politics, he knew how to make a government run. Seward, although not a machine politician and often uncomfortable with the underside of politics, was well aware of Weed's activities. On Inauguration Day — March 4, 1861— Henry Seward was probably the one person in the nation who had the experience and wherewithal to take charge and run the country from that day forward. And on that particular day in the early spring of 1861, after seven states had seceded from the Union, with war or peace hanging precariously, taking charge at once was precisely what was required.

A third enduring asset was Seward's personality. Friendly, with a great sense of humor, he was truly a likable fellow, most folks liked to be around him as he was "courteous, outgoing and genial." He made friends easily, even those with whom he had political differences. "Shortly after Louisiana's Judah P. Benjamin finished excoriating Seward and his allies on the Senate floor, Seward buttonholed him in the aisle. 'Benjamin,' he remarked, 'give me a cigar, and when your speech is printed send me a copy.'" His Washington neighbor and Senate colleague Jefferson Davis was a good friend, in spite of being on the opposite side of many political issues.

> One January, Varina Davis became critically ill after giving birth. The city was in the grip of a snowstorm, and word reached Seward that Mrs. Davis's nurse was unable to reach her through the blizzard.... [Seward] ordered his own carriage brought out and, after several mishaps, the nurse was conveyed to the Davis home. Later, when Seward learned that his Mississippi colleague was in danger of losing an eye to an infection, he became a regular visitor to the Davis home. "There was an earnest, tender interest in his manner which was unmistakably genuine," Varina Davis wrote. [70]

Seward loved to entertain and he was very good at it, especially with daughter-in-law Anna acting as hostess. In Washington, where opportunities to mingle informally were so important at mid-century, Seward was at his best — he was a master at small group conversation with debating skills second to none. Even with those who disliked his political views he scored impressively.

> Mr. Seward was anxious to enter the "charmed circle" of southern social life, from which, as a black Republican, he was rigidly excluded. Doctor Gwin [senator from California] with considerable trepidation, he afterwards con-

fessed, invited him to a large dinner party at his house, where nearly all guests were southern Senators—among them, Toombs, Hunter, Mason, and Breckinridge—and their wives. Mrs. Gwin, afraid to assign him to any of the lady guests, herself took Mr. Seward in to dinner. Mr. Seward, by his brilliant and interesting conversation, soon dissipated the chilliness his presence had caused, and turned into a great success what Doctor Gwin had feared would prove a dismal failure.[71]

Seward never held a grudge and reciprocated invitations from Southerners. "After Mississippi's 'Hangman' Foote had threatened to 'currycomb' him in one exchange on the floor, Foote was astonished to receive an invitation from Seward to a dinner of terrapin, fried oysters, and roast duck."[72] Seward was a true charmer and had the capacity to influence friends (and foes) over a good cigar and a good glass of brandy. He was a Washington natural.

In addition to his social skills, Seward was regarded by everyone as well educated, well read, and well traveled—truly an urbane man. He possessed a keen mind, he seemed always out in front of the pack, and many contemporaries viewed him as *the* true visionary of his time. Highly cultured Southern gentlemen regarded him as a peer, one with whom they could debate honorably, even when differences were sharp. Henry Seward had a background matched by few others in the nation's capital.[73] When Southern Whigs and anti-secession Democrats sought advice and counsel during the secession winter, when they looked for someone with intellectual depth and true vision to align Southern moderates with Northern moderates, they reached out to Henry Seward. In the view of these moderates or mainstream politicians, "higher law" and "irrepressible conflict" aside, he was *the* man to turn to as the crisis hour approached. When Henry Seward is examined closely, when the views of his contemporaries are collated and condensed, he emerges at the top of the class of presidential timber. On March 4, 1861, Henry Seward was qualified to *be* president.

***

After the election returns confirmed Lincoln as the choice, the nation tumbled into utter chaos. In every city and town in the South, meetings were hastily organized to discuss what to do. Several states, with stunning quickness, moved to withdraw from the Union. In the North, too, confusion reigned as folks began to realize a purely sectional party had gained the presidency, which could cause the nation to disintegrate. Everyone looked for someone to take the lead. It was not President Buchanan or President-elect Lincoln who stepped forward, it was William Henry Seward. Let us look at Henry in action.

3

HENRY TAKES CHARGE

I will try to save freedom and my country.— William Henry Seward,
in a letter to his wife, late December, 1860

The secession winter of 1860–61 found the nation mired in its greatest
political crisis — seven states in the lower South seceded from the Union after
the election of Abraham Lincoln. No one knew what to do. We can only speculate what a message about preservation of the Union with the simplicity and
power of the Gettysburg Address might have accomplished as the nation
drifted toward war.

But if the crisis was to be resolved, and the Union restored, it would take
a leader with extraordinary political experience — and extraordinary vision
as well. The time for debate had ended, it was time for bold action. On Inauguration Day, March 4, 1861, the nation needed a leader who could take charge
immediately.

***

On Inauguration Day, Henry Seward, eight years senior to Lincoln, was highly
qualified by any standard to be president, whereas Lincoln had marginal
qualifications. David Donald speculates about Abraham Lincoln:

> Perhaps it is too cynical to say that a statesman is a politician who succeeds
> in getting himself elected President. Still, but for his election in 1860, Lin-
> coln's name would appear in our history books as that of a minor Illinois
> politician who unsuccessfully debated Stephen Douglas. And had the Presi-
> dent been defeated in 1864, he would be written off as one of the great fail-
> ures of the American political system — the man who let his country drift
> into civil war, presided aimlessly over a graft-ridden administration, con-
> ducted an incompetent and ineffectual attempt to subjugate the Southern
> states, and after four years was returned by the people to the obscurity that
> he so richly deserved.[1]

Of course, Abraham Lincoln, despite numerous obstacles, was elected president in 1860, and again in 1864. All politicians need some good fortune to

succeed and Abraham Lincoln had his fair share, as his nomination in May and election in November 1860 demonstrate.

Abraham Lincoln often referred to his meager qualifications— some say his self-deprecating style was deliberate ruse. For instance, after his election in November, he told an Illinois friend he would rather have had a term in the Senate, where he felt he could do more good. In New York at the time of his Cooper Institute speech in the spring of 1860, he said when responding to a friend who had asked about his personal financial condition, "I have the cottage at Springfield and about $3,000 in money. If they make me Vice-President with Seward, as some say they will, I hope I shall be able to increase it to $20,000."[2] In early May 1860, Lincoln told Anson S. Miller of Rockford: "Judge, if I had the making of the President, I would make Seward President."[3] How serious he was with these types of comments is still subject to question. But on his unfamiliarity with the presidency there is little question, for "as he freely admitted later when he became president, 'he was entirely ignorant not only of the duties, but of the manner of doing the business' in the executive office. He tried to do everything himself."[4]

Of course, Seward and most of his well-connected and influential friends thought the governor should be president. And many senior politicians in Washington, whether Democrat or Republican, regarded Seward as highly qualified to be president of the United States. He had run the bureaucracy of New York State successfully, he knew the Congress (both Democrats and Republicans) better than anyone, and he knew the Washington establishment — he knew how to make government work. The role Henry Seward played in getting Lincoln elected to the presidency was unprecedented. Seward, after rebounding from the bitter disappointment of Chicago, rallied the Republican Party for Lincoln in the fall of 1860; no one but Mr. Republican could have done it. Again, many of his contemporaries contended he played *the* pivotal role in getting Abraham Lincoln elected. "Aside from the torchlight processions of 'Wide-Awakes' in every northern city and village, Seward was the great feature of the Republican campaign."[5] It was Henry Seward who was asked to tour the nation to stump for Lincoln. It was Henry Seward who drew huge crowds wherever he went and created great excitement for the Republicans. And it was Henry Seward who connected with many Democrats and drew votes across party lines, especially in all-important New York City. After the election, Henry Seward was still the acknowledged leader of the Republican Party, irrespective of whether he was president-elect or not. As the post-election furor commenced, the Washington establishment did not turn to President James Buchanan or President-elect Abraham Lincoln, it was Henry Seward who was called to the front once more.

***

It was very late on Tuesday, November 6, 1860, when the telegraph in Springfield, Illinois, finally tapped out the crucial results from Pennsylvania and New York, assuring Abraham Lincoln he had won the presidency. Springfield erupted in celebration and Abraham Lincoln was caught up in the excitement. Throughout the North victory parties were numerous and enthusiastic, but in the South, great consternation arose. Henry Seward, exhausted from his months of campaigning, was at his home in Auburn on election eve. Knowing the role he had played in the canvass, he was gratified with the results. He had intended to return to Washington in January. But on Saturday, November 10, just four days after the election, the South Carolina legislature called for a state convention to meet on December 17 to consider seceding from the Union.

Throughout the lower South ardent secessionists began calling for immediate action. In the upper South, a different reaction set in as most felt Lincoln's election, in and of itself, was not reason for secession. Most favored staying in the Union, assuming some accommodation to Southern concerns could be worked out in Washington. In the North, moderates from all political parties began to realize that the election could result in a breakup of the Union, and many sought ways to diffuse the heated rhetoric.

Flush with victory, Abraham Lincoln was exuberant, and crowds descended on his small home to offer congratulations. But from the first moments of his presidential win, he was confronted with the real threat of secession. Many states had threatened secession in the past, but when South Carolina's two senators, James Chestnut Jr. and James H. Hammond, resigned their seats in the Senate on this same day, November 10, 1860, it seemed to portend something different. Henry Seward, the most well connected politician in Washington, was concerned, but not overly so. As events unfolded, leading politicians in the nation's capital asked Seward to return at once and take charge of the Washington scene. Among those asking was the country's political prince, Charles Francis Adams Sr. On Sunday, November 18, Seward wrote Thurlow Weed of his intentions:

> Three or even two months ago I thought that I might properly remain here until the end of the Holidays. But now especially since the Southern demonstrations I have supposed that my absence even a day from Washington after the beginning of the session would if not even wrong per se, be a cause of dissatisfaction somewhere — So I am calculating to reach the capitol on Saturday night before the session begins.[6]

Seward packed, bade his family goodbye, and set off for the capital, arriving on November 30. He wrote Weed immediately: "The Chief Justice will not resign, nor will he die if he can help it [here, tongue-in-cheek, he refers to Chief Justice Roger Brooke Taney, a Southerner]. I have seen nobody yet."[7] Seward was summoned to the capital because congressional leaders, and indeed many leading figures, considered him the political leader of the nation. And someone was desperately needed — because of the sudden threat of secession and the uncertainty it portended, the New York stock market crashed on November 12. Washington was in a state of near panic, and no one knew the president-elect, or more important, what he intended to do. Abraham Lincoln was immediately asked to make a statement regarding secession, something to clarify his position and sooth the country.

Characteristic of political campaigns of the era, Abraham Lincoln had said practically nothing during the campaign. But now citizens wanted to hear from the president-elect. What were his views regarding secession? What did he intend to do? On that fateful November 10, Lincoln wrote Truman Smith, "I could say nothing which I have not already said, and which is in print, and open for inspection of all."[8] But there was very little to inspect that was current (transcripts of the Lincoln-Douglas debates were in print and a few speeches), and certainly nothing that addressed the momentous question of disunion.

Henry Seward arrived in Washington to much fanfare. Immediately he began a series of meetings, informal discussions, and dinner conversations with leading Northern and Southern men. In discussions with his Washington neighbor, Jefferson Davis, he sensed the devastation Southerners felt regarding their political irrelevancy — the South seemed not to have mattered in this election. Indeed, as Daniel Crofts observes, had no Southerner cast a ballot, the result would have been the same. And it was this "political irrelevancy" that radical Southern secessionists were using to justify their calls for immediate secession. Henry Seward sensed the secession issue was much more advanced than he thought. His first assessment of the unfolding national crisis is found in his December 2 letter to Weed:

> S. Carolina is committed. Nothing held her from declaring + practicing secession. But her course as to Forts + Customs yet undetermined. Georgia will debate ... but she probably follows S.C. Florida will prevaricate. Mississippi + Alabama likely follow.... Look closely into the 5th Article of Constitution, you will see that Congress initially could only propose definite amendments to states, while it cant call a General Convention until requested by the State Legislatures.... I think the Southern members will be over cautious ... If we can keep peace and quiet until the decree of S.C. is pronounced the temper will then be favorable on both sides to conciliation.[9]

Henry Adams, son of Charles Francis Adams, was in Washington as a reporter for his hometown paper, the *Boston Daily Advertiser*. He came to know Seward very well (because his father was a close political associate and close personal friend) and was constantly in Seward's company during the secession winter, either at the Adams family home or at Seward's home or in the halls of Congress or elsewhere. Henry Adams was extremely well connected and, almost all agree, had a true insider's view of Washington. In a long series of letters, some published in the *Advertiser,* he recorded the scene from his unique perspective. As a result, historians frequently cite his letters as examples of "the state of affairs" in Washington during the secession winter. Young Adams described Seward initially as

> great; a perfect giant in all this howling.... He came up here last Tuesday evening and I heard him talk for the first time. Wednesday he came up to dinner and was absolutely grand. No one was there but the family, and he had all the talking to himself. I sat and watched the old fellow with his big nose and his wire hair and grizzly eyebrows and miserable dress, and listened to him rolling out his grand, broad ideas that would inspire a cow with statesmanship if she understood our language. There's no shake in him. He talks square up to the mark and something beyond it.[10]

Many leading figures recognized Henry Seward in the same way, he was "up to the mark and something beyond it."

By early December Seward was beginning to get a better feel for the situation in the nation — Northern moderates were blasting the abolitionists as irresponsible and calling for some type of compromise, Southern moderates were attacking the reckless anti–Union talk of the radical Southern Democrats and talking of reconciliation. So his early judgment was to bide time and offer calm, "the best policy ... was one of moderation, kindness, and reticence, in order to reconcile southerners to the incoming administration." Everyone looked to Seward for answers and, of course he had none at this early stage, "he did his best to scotch rumors; when they [politicians] asked him what he proposed to do, he told them that they would know when he knew himself."[11]

But as the moderates called for reconciliation, the radical Southern Democrats began to call for the formation of a "Southern nation," and the radical Republicans began to boast, "no compromise, come what may." Because of his constant face-to-face interactions with leaders from all sides, Seward was one of the first to realize the central issue — the radicals of both North and South, if unchecked, could drive the nation to war. He ended his December 3 letter to Thurlow Weed: "The Republican party to-day is as uncompromising as the Secessionists in South Carolina. A month hence each may come to think that moderation is wiser."[12]

As a result of his Washington deliberations, Seward felt he had to consult with Weed more closely than ever as things could rapidly spiral out of control, and he knew Weed's political instincts were second to none. In addition, Weed's network of national leaders (his former Whig colleagues and the many newspaper editors he was close to), men who could be called on to help stem the unfolding crisis, would surely be needed. Also at this time, Seward and the Dictator began to see the need for compromise and began to plan accordingly. Weed decided to take the lead in promoting ideas that could be controversial with Republicans (to protect Seward's standing in the party), using editorials in his *Albany Evening Journal*. The central thrust of the editorials was "that a secessionist movement was developing with great rapidity in the South; that secession meant war; and that the only way to stop both was by a compromise adjustment of Southern grievances."[13] Seward and Weed knew what was going on: Seward because of his daily interactions with Washington politicians; Weed, because of the scores of friends (his network) in the South. In addition, Weed was constantly interacting with New York's financiers and leading merchants, men who had many, many contacts in the South because of their business interests. If any team in the nation could understand the Southern mind, it was Henry Seward and Thurlow Weed.

Seward and Weed agreed to employ the strategy they had used successfully in the past; Weed would "float" Seward's ideas and proposals for a political solution in the *Albany Evening Journal*, and then they could judge reaction. As these two "saw shortly after the election that the Southerners were in earnest and that civil war and disunion were threatened," they knew public opinion in the North must be managed and felt this could be done by careful attention to the presentation of proposals for reconciliation.[14] Many in Washington, indeed many throughout the nation, had little idea of what was going on between Seward and Weed. In fact, "only gradually did the astute young Henry Adams discern that 'Weed's motions, compromises and all, had been feelers on Seward's part.'"[15] Weed also agreed to run interference for Seward with the president-elect. Weed would assume the role of point man with Lincoln and his team for the Seward-Weed machine.

Stephen Douglas, John J. Crittenden and a few other leaders also took leading roles in the compromise movement. But Douglas had lost much luster with his election defeat, was blamed by many for stirring up the slavery issue with his notion of popular sovereignty, his health was beginning to fail (he would be dead by June), and the Northern Democratic Party was badly divided. John J. Crittenden, although venerated and beloved by many, was old and lacked the vigor to lead a national effort. It was Seward, who many felt would be the controlling influence in the new administration, who held the key to success.[16]

During the second week of December, Seward suddenly left Washington and went to Albany to confer with Weed, but not about a political solution for the national crisis. He had received a letter from Lincoln, dated December 8, nominating him for secretary of state in the new administration.[17] Seward and Weed were expecting such an offer and now that it had come, work needed to be done. At Albany, they decided a conference with Lincoln was in order and Weed was dispatched to Springfield to begin negotiations on the role Seward would have in the new administration and to confer on other cabinet appointments. While Seward was in Albany, the secession crisis took a decided turn for the worse as seven Southern senators and twenty-three congressmen called for the establishment of a Southern Confederacy.

Weed stopped in Chicago to consult with David Davis and Leonard Swett, with whom he had had a secret meeting in August (reports suggest they had agreed on Seward as secretary of state in the event of Lincoln's election), and the three of them proceeded to Springfield to meet with Lincoln. Davis and Swett represented the moderate or conservative side of Lincoln's advisors and were clearly in sync with Weed. The meeting began on December 20 and they discussed cabinet appointments and a "Southern policy," including the need for compromise. Weed suggested two Southerners be appointed to cabinet posts and he recommended four outstanding Southern Unionists— John Minor Botts of Virginia, Balie Peyton of Tennessee, Henry Winter Davis of Maryland, and John A. Gilmer of North Carolina. He recommended Charles Francis Adams Sr. for secretary of the treasury. He strongly objected to the rumored appointments of Gideon Wells and Montgomery Blair, and especially Salmon Chase.

Weed then presented his views (and Seward's) on the need for a compromise to assuage the South. This was Seward's first "trial balloon" to determine his level of influence with the president-elect. It did *not* go well. Although Lincoln was interested in having a Southerner or two in the cabinet, they were not ones favored by Seward and Weed; he showed no interest in Adams. Nor was he impressed with Weed's arguments on compromise. "Lincoln read this editorial [Weed had published an editorial in his paper advocating compromise on the day he left for Springfield], but was far from convinced by Weed's arguments. The president-elect was not interested in compromise stating he was inflexible on any step that would promote the territorial expansion of slavery."[18] Lincoln countered Weed by giving him three resolutions for Seward to present to the senate. On this same day, the electrifying news of South Carolina's secession arrived in Springfield. The people were anguished; Lincoln appeared calm.

Meanwhile, Seward cooled his heels in Auburn. He was disappointed, but he had expected the news from South Carolina; he had predicted as much to Weed days earlier. He met Weed on his return from Illinois in Syracuse and rode with him on the railroad to Albany. Seward was not happy with Weed's report, but agreed to sponsor Lincoln's three proposals in the Senate. He was most unhappy with the rumored cabinet appointments (feeling Wells and Blair could obstruct his now-emerging plan for conciliation, and being strongly opposed to Chase, a known no-compromise radical). He pondered Lincoln's stance opposing compromise as he felt a flexible strategy might be the best course at this time, pending developments in the lower South. As he began to have extensive meetings with Southerners, Seward sensed the need for a conciliatory approach to strengthen moderate Southerners in their quest for political power.[19] He began to see Lincoln's "vow not to interfere with slavery where it existed" meant nothing to the South, for Southern leaders felt they already were guaranteed that "vow" by the Constitution.

A few days later Seward began to grapple with the horns of a dilemma. He was coming to believe a compromise on territorial expansion of slavery was the only way to save the Union and avert war: yet he felt the president-elect might not support it, and he knew forthrightly radical Republicans opposed any compromise. If he promoted compromise too vigorously, he could lose the support of the president-elect and divide his own party. And the vexing issue of the day was the uncertainty about the president-elect's position on secession, an uncertainty compounded daily by Lincoln's continued silence. By early December, Springfield had become a beehive of activity, "a political mecca." Visitors and mail descended on Lincoln in almost unimaginable numbers. His daily schedule was consumed by huge crowds of curious folks, office seekers, and newspapermen. The nation, meanwhile, was adrift, and anxiously awaited a statement.

The Seward family in the gardens of their Auburn home. Frances, although not in this picture, found her greatest happiness here. Left to right: Fred Seward; Lazette Warden; unidentified; William H. Seward; Anna Seward; unidentified child; unidentified woman (sitting); William H. Seward; William H. Seward III (little boy on ground); unidentified toddler (Seward House, Auburn, New York).

As the secession winter unfolded, Henry Seward's efforts to push a compromise through Congress, and in the process bring along Lincoln and enough Republicans, came to dominate every political move he made right up to April 15. Seward knew he had a unique responsibility at this moment in the nation's history. His "past no less than his present position in his party gave him special responsibilities and opportunities in such a crisis. Every one regarded him as the foremost Republican." Again it must be emphasized that most in Washington felt Seward was *the* man to solve the crisis, many thought he would be the "premier" in the new administration. "No one on his side of the Senate, and perhaps no one in either house, had such pleasant personal relations with the other members of Congress," one of the essential ingredients for finding a solution to the unfolding crisis. His "immovable calmness" when others were excited, coupled with his pre-eminence led many leading citizens to assume Seward had a solution in mind.[20] Abraham Lincoln's continued silence led many to believe he had no policy: President Buchanan was simply viewed as weak and ineffective.

Seward and Weed conferred again and decided it would be best not to respond to Lincoln's cabinet offer right away. Seward wanted to sound out other leading Republicans, but what he really wanted to do was begin laying the groundwork with his friends to oppose Lincoln's anti–Seward cabinet choices (especially Chase) and to press the president-elect on the need for compromise. While at Albany, Seward began to formulate his own plan for the political solution he knew he would be asked to propose upon his return to Washington. Seward, perhaps more than any other political leader in the nation, realized the minority position of the Republican Party. The party had received only 39 percent of the popular vote, and a clear majority of these voters were not abolitionists; they were not in favor of risking war to end slavery. So he began to think the Republicans had the responsibility to "alleviate the crisis."

In addition to his dominant position in Washington, Seward was in close touch with the New York City financial and commercial power structure. It must be remembered Seward came to know this powerful clan during his years as New York governor, and even though more than a few were Democrats, they had come to know and respect him — and now sought his advice regarding the pending crisis. And this group, whose business interest demanded, favored compromise with the South in December. "Southern planters financed their operations through New York banks, negotiated contracts with New York business agents, transported their crops on New York ships, insured them through New York City brokers and purchased equipment and household goods from New York City merchants."[21] August Belmont, the great New York financier and a leader of the compromise forces, was convinced slavery was not the only cause for the Republican win, but suggested many factors were at play, including the corruption and ineffectiveness of the current Democratic administration.

Seward set about developing a plan to save the nation, a three-pronged approach that included working out a compromise on territorial expansion acceptable to upper South Unionists, strengthening the compromise spirit in the North, and "gaining time during which he might arouse southern loyalty to the Union."[22] This third point, "gaining time" to arouse Southern loyalty, would become the centerpiece of his plan to save the nation as the secession winter moved along. "Seward ambiguously echoed Weed's view that Republicans no longer need to worry about the spread of slavery to the territories" and he began to push more and more the compromise on territorial expansion.[23]

As Seward was about to leave Auburn on December 21 for his return to Washington, he was desperate to confer with Weed. He sent a cryptic dispatch to him:

> I am fairly driven out of my retreat and can hold it no longer [friends in Auburn were constantly seeking his attention when he was at home]. The Kansas bill is set for Monday and it would be High Treason in existing circumstances to be absent. You will of course write me or let me know how and where I can meet you.[24]

Seward then left for New York City, where the highly prestigious New England Society was holding its annual meeting. When they learned of Seward's arrival they forced him to make an impromptu speech (everyone in the nation wanted to hear from him): he did, assuring them the nation would be preserved and secession would quickly die.

But just a week later the nation seemed ready to come apart. Major Anderson had moved his troops to Fort Sumter on December 27. The South Carolinians then took possession of the remaining Federal forts in Charleston Harbor. Buchanan's cabinet disintegrated over the incident, the Southern members saying Anderson broke the promise the administration had given the governor of South Carolina to not move troops, the Northern members of the cabinet saying Anderson had every right to protect his men and did the right thing. The North, patriotic zeal coming from everywhere, rallied to Anderson's support. President Buchanan seemed paralyzed. Douglas and Crittenden redoubled their efforts to promote compromise, Henry Seward knew the time was fast approaching when he would need to act aggressively. Weed sensed "the outburst of patriotic fervor" could be used to advantage.[25]

But this sudden burst of patriotic fervor soon cooled and Weed became decidedly disheartened by Lincoln's intransigence regarding cabinet appointments and especially a conciliatory policy. Tension in Washington was extremely high, Republicans in congress wavered first for a fight, then for peace. Something had to be done. Weed felt Seward was due more consideration from Lincoln for his extraordinary efforts in winning the election, he felt Davis and Swett had so committed in their August meeting with him. He advised Seward to take a stand.

In a confidential letter to Weed on the twenty-ninth, Seward described the situation in Washington:

> The Cabinet again in danger of explosion. The S.C. interest demands the withdrawal of Anderson and abandonment of the forts, also on sending of armaments for Southern forts. The President inclines to yield. But there is an explosion if he does [Seward had penetrated the Buchanan cabinet and was receiving daily reports on confidential meetings]. The plot is forming to seize the capital and the government.... I am writing you not from rumors but knowledge. I have written to L that he ought to anticipate and come here by 2nd ... to know his agents ... with whom I am to act, and they ought to be here to make preparations. You will be welcome enough here in a few days. The Border states or at least their representatives are getting anxious and more practicable. A suggestion by and by for a convention two years hence when the storm has subsided would I think be well received by them and settle them. But our own friends are not yet pushing for it. Don't communicate this to anybody.... It would break up my communications with important personages.[26]

Seward's correspondence with Weed was critical at this point. He needed to maintain his standing in the Republican Party while moving the nation toward compromise. Weed's advice and counsel were paramount; "Weed and Seward were 'never in closer communication' than during the secession winter; the two 'were working together like the two hands of one man.'"[27] Weed began working on his proposal for a convention of all states. Seward was working to near exhaustion. Bolstered by his rising status and overly confident he would be the real head of the incoming administration, Seward sent a letter, dated December 28, to Lincoln formally accepting the secretary of state post.

It is important to note that after South Carolina seceded and after the debacle produced by the Buchanan Administration trying to deal with it, Republican moderates in Washington began to see that if a compromise was not forthcoming, war was imminent. They were interacting, on a daily basis, with Union-loving Southerners who became more desperate each day. Abraham Lincoln, hopelessly isolated in Springfield, had little first-hand knowledge of the unfolding events, relying on intermittent and inadequate reports from his few friends. Even the off-maligned James Buchanan, because he was in Washington dealing with the protagonists, could see the need for compromise to avert war. David Donald notes, "Lincoln's stand [to oppose any compromise] also reflected his deeply held conviction that Unionists were in a large majority throughout the South and that, given time for tempers to cool, they would be able to defeat the secessionists conspirators."[28] But Lincoln seemed not to understand the compromisers needed a compromise.

During the last few days of December, the compromise movement stalled, then rebounded. On the twenty-eighth, the Senate Committee of Thirteen voted against the Crittenden Compromise, a plan to re-establish the Missouri Compromise line and a plan widely supported in both North and South. Seward had received strong letters from Lincoln opposing any compromise that permitted slavery expansion in the territories, so he decided not to risk a confrontation with the president-elect at this point. However, after consultation with moderate Republicans on the committee, Seward went ahead and suggested a plan to the Committee of Thirteen whereby the New Mexico Territory (the huge landmass south of the Missouri Compromise Line) would be admitted to the Union as a state without regard to slavery (in essence a slave state, as slavery already existed there), with the rest of the Western territory — the huge landmass north of New Mexico — remaining free. This became known as the New Mexico Plan and it sidestepped the slavery expansion issue in this indirect way.

Seward and Charles Francis Adams had begun to interact discreetly with an eye toward finding a compromise that would be acceptable to both Senate and House. They came very close to pulling off a compromise with the New Mexico Plan as it gained substantial support among moderates. In the House, this plan evolved into the Adams-Corwin proposal, "a proposal with two major points: first, a constitutional amendment affirming safety of slavery in the states, as already proposed by Seward to the Senate Committee of Thirteen, and second, admission of the New Mexico territory into the Union as a state."[29] Seward, the consummate Washington insider and widely known as a talented writer, likely was the author of this proposal for the House, which eventually gained enough support to pass.[30] Adams presented the plan to the House Committee of Thirty-Three were it was accepted. "Despite the surge of hard-line pressure, conciliation was moving forward, if only cautiously, among Republicans." In the Senate, Seward carried the day, "three days later two other Republicans joined Seward in supporting a variation of the New Mexico plan, raising brief hope of a genuine compromise proposal."[31]

Seward's strategic purpose for the New Mexico Plan was to divide the South and "it was a complete success." Charles Francis Adams Jr. recorded "by conciliating the Northern tier of Slave States, including Virginia especially; and, holding them loyal until the tide of reaction, setting in, should drive the seceding States into a false position from which they would ultimately be compelled to recede."[32] While some upper South Unionists did not feel this proposal was strong enough and some real selling would have had to be done, it was fairly close to a workable compromise. If Seward had just known Lincoln a bit better, if he could have had a one-on-one conversation with him, the secession crisis could have moved toward resolution by the end of January.[33]

Although Seward wrote Lincoln repeatedly at this time, he never laid out his Southern strategy for the president-elect, a strategy that included a compromise on territorial expansion to build Unionist strength in the upper South, so that secession could be contained in the lower South. As a result, he took a calculated risk of gigantic proportions by moving down the path toward compromise in the face of a president-elect who was reluctant to support any compromise on territorial expansion. Probably Seward felt he was not ignoring the views of the president-elect (if he fully understood them at all) but truly thought he could persuade Lincoln to see the wisdom of his move toward compromise when it became necessary. Seward was at his persuasive best in face-to-face encounters and always confident and headstrong. No doubt, he assumed he could manage the inexperienced Lincoln. In his mind, he was not only the leader of the Republican Party, but of the Washington establishment as well.

December turned out to be a month of real political transition in Washington. At the beginning of the month, most Republicans still held to the view that Southerners would not countenance secession — they still believed it was a "bluff" — and thus were in agreement with Lincoln to offer no compromise to the South. Then in the middle of the month a compromise movement swept the North with many Republicans taking part. But by the end of the month, after South Carolina had seceded and Mississippi, Florida, and Alabama rapidly moved toward secession, many moderate Republicans changed their view and began to oppose compromise. Ominously for Seward (and the nation), Abraham Lincoln abetted this rising opposition by privately and confidentially applying the breaks to the compromise movement. He "abandoned his policy of remaining inactive until his inauguration" and brought the vast influence of his position as president-elect to bear on congressional Republicans seeking compromise. He began to write private letter after letter to thwart the once growing sentiment for reconciliation.[34] Grimly he had told a visitor, "I will suffer death before I will consent or will advise my friend to consent to any concession or compromise."[35] The horns of Henry Seward's dilemma now became very sharp.

***

Across the nation, the New Year was rung in with considerable consternation but not overbearing gloom. Most citizens felt a compromise would be worked out in Washington and that the might of the federal government, even though South Carolina had seceded, could not be resisted by just one state, or even a few states. In Washington, Seward and Weed were in high gear while Lincoln remained in Springfield, struggling with cabinet appointments, seeing a host of visitors, and receiving sporadic reports from the nation's capital. Significantly, the mood in Washington seemed to change daily from tough stance to compromise and then back again. Also of significance, the debate had changed entirely from the extension of slavery to secession and how to deal with it. Public opinion in the North seemed to change daily too, first supporting Seward and Weed's compromise efforts, then against. Weed, tall, soft-spoken and a gifted manager, "content to work behind the scenes," was everywhere. As an editor of the first rank, his instinctive sense for public opinion was almost unique, and he began to see that public opinion needed to be managed more aggressively.[36]

While some historians downplay Weed's influence, his contemporaries regarded him as the most adroit political manager of his day. Even those who opposed him respected his skill. He was in touch with fellow newspaper editors from across the nation and he interacted constantly with New York's commercial and financial interests, again people who had endless contacts in the South. And he traveled to Washington routinely to meet with members of Congress. Weed clearly saw the possibility that public opinion could be moved toward a more advanced support of compromise.

> It was an indisputable fact at this time that the vote cast for Douglas, numbering 1,365,976, and that cast for Bell, numbering 590,631, and the vote for Breckinridge in the free States, numbering 284,422, making a total of 2,241,029, was unanimously in favor of a peaceful and reasonable settlement of all difficulties with any of the Southern States.... Thus the voice of the people of the country ... was overwhelmingly in favor of conciliation.[37]

Weed analyzed the numbers time and again.

In early January the compromise momentum began to build in the border states and, at times, it began to build again in the North. Republican opposition stiffened though as a result of lower South states seizing Federal property. Seward began to more openly promote a political strategy that included compromise on territorial expansion. Seward, Crittenden, Douglas and others had received letters by the hundreds endorsing compromise. They came from ordinary citizens and powerful interests,

> letters from Charles A. Davis, the iron manufacturer; from John Brodhead, railroad president; from Anthony B. Allen, farm machinery manufacturer; from A.A. Lawrence, Boston textile magnate; from Edward Everett and George T. Curtis; from Edwin Croswell, Albany printer; from August Belmont and Jay Gould, financiers; from Winfield Scott; from Governor Thomas Hicks of Maryland; from David Lord, distinguished lawyer; from James de Peyster Odgen and James W. Beckman, aristocratic New Yorkers; from Horatio Seymour and John Dix.

The common theme was compromise, and in spite of Republican resistance, the spirit seemed to be genuine. Weed began to see an opening to exploit.[38]

Besides New York financial barons, many of Seward's letters came from Southern Unionists, which reinforced his belief in the need for compromise. Southern Unionists, who strenuously urged compromise, pushed Seward toward conciliation at an ever-increasing pace. John Gilmer, leader of Southern Unionists in the House of Representatives (and the second Southerner to be offered a post in Lincoln's cabinet), spoke on the floor of the House:

> Why, sirs, do you think these ultra men [the radical secessionists] insist on what they call protection [protection of slave interests in the territories], because it is any value to them? ...They demand it because they think you will refuse it, and by your refusal, they hope the South will be inflamed to the extent of breaking up this government — the very thing the leaders desire.[39]

These Southern Unionists chafed under the extremism of the slavocracy and the radical secessionists. They "looked forward to the day when sensible men North and South would rescue political affairs from the agitators and fanatics who plagued both sections." Like Henry Seward, "they indiscriminately abhorred abolitionists and secessionists." And also like Seward, they "believed a majority of Americans" abhorred the extremists too and longed for the time when "moderates from all parts of the country could make common cause." To these Southern Unionists, there was no "irrepressible conflict."[40]

In fact, many Southern Unionists did not feel their future was tied to the Cotton Confederacy at all, concluding the economic interests of the two regions were "irreconcilably antagonistic" and "in direct collision." They felt the upper South was developing more along the lines of Pennsylvania and Ohio than Mississippi and Alabama. In addition, many Southern Unionists believed the slavocracy deliberately conspired to break up the Union for its own selfish reasons, to protect their wealth and, by intimidation of poor whites, their political power.[41] Seward became convinced a compromise could succeed and the nation saved by promoting Southern Unionism. By playing to this nonslaveholder outrage of the slavocracy (many Southern whites viewed plantations owners as rich, arrogant aristocrats), Seward felt the radicals (who represented a minority of Southerners) could be isolated.

The logic for compromise on territorial expansion of slavery was pushed by Judge John S. Watts, formerly a federal judge who had lived many years in New Mexico. Watts had briefed Congress on slavery expansion in the Western Territories and had won many converts by convincing them that "natural conditions" prevented the establishment of slavery in the West. He noted craftily "New Mexico already had a slave code and that she might choose to enter the Union as a slave state, but in a short time ... climate soil and geography would make her free." He emphasized how few slaves (only eleven) were in the entire territory.[42] For Seward, his more aggressive support for a compromise on territorial expansion increased his exposure to Lincoln and the radical Republicans, so a careful plan of execution became critical. Weed was consulted once more.

It must be emphasized again, that in spite of the calls in the press and the hundreds of letters he received urging compromise, Abraham Lincoln would not bend. His confidential letters to Republicans in the Congress were crystal clear. He told Congressman William Kellogg to "entertain no proposition for a compromise in regard to the extension of slavery. The instant you do, they have us under again; all our labor is lost, and sooner or later must be done over." He wrote much the same to Congressman E. B. Washburne, "prevent, as far as possible, any of our friends from demoralizing themselves, and our cause, by entertaining propositions for compromise of any sort, on 'slavery extension."[43] He sent the same message to Sen. Lyman Trumbull. While Lincoln had good reason to draw the line in the sand from where he sat in Springfield, he was not in tune with Seward and those trying to find a way to solve the national crisis in Washington.

And the national crisis was escalating rapidly again. January 9, 1861, was a bad day for the nation. President Buchanan had ordered the resupply of Fort Sumter, General Scott had planned to send a warship to fight its way in, if necessary, but a convoluted series of events ended with a merchant ship, *The Star of the West*, dispatched from New York Harbor with supplies. At the last minute Scott changed his mind, but his message to recall the mission arrived too late, and the message notifying Major Anderson supplies were on the way went astray. The South Carolinians were notified of the mission by Southerner Jacob Thompson just before he resigned his cabinet post in protest. As a result, the South Carolinians fired on the ship as it attempted to enter Charleston Harbor, Anderson having no idea what was going on did nothing, so the ship turned about and headed back to New York.[44] The entire incident approached comic opera — the Federal government was hopelessly unprepared for war.

On this same fateful day, Mississippi became the second state to secede. On January 10, Florida became the third state, followed by Alabama on the eleventh. As these lower South states seceded, the Democratic press in the North increased calls for conciliation and for the president-elect to make a statement to clarify his position on secession and to soothe the now highly tense nation. Lincoln had "waged one of the most laconic campaigns in history," he had said practically nothing, in fact, "not one campaign speech did he make; not one letter did he write." And now that states were seceding from the Union, everyone wanted to hear from him, but "he said not one word to reaffirm, much less to elaborate, his position."[45]

Radical Southern secessionists were using Lincoln as their pariah, but it was Henry Seward whom they truly feared. It was Seward who was reaching out to moderate Southerners, and it was Seward who stood in their way of sweeping public opinion to the secession cause in the upper South. A typical reaction to Seward from a radical Tennessee secessionist: "William H. Seward ... had the tact and skill 'to build up a large abolition party' in Tennessee and the border slave states. 'Soft language will be used ... kind words' ... money without measure will be used."[46] Seward was in the bull's-eye of secessionist anger, no doubt.

When Seward received the news that Virginia's Governor Letcher had called the legislature into special session to consider calling a state convention to consider secession, he felt great distress. As other such state conventions in the South had produced secession ordinances, he now redoubled his efforts with upper South Unionists to find a workable compromise. He was rapidly coming to believe that the border states controlled the future of the country. A leading Virginian corresponding with Seward "asserted that without the Border States 'the squad of traitors in the extreme South cannot exist'" and "another declared to him that the projects of the cotton-states 'cannot culminate without the aid of the border states." August Belmont stressed to Seward the need to isolate the lower South by conciliating the upper South for in "his opinion ... the states could not be brought back once they had formed a Confederacy with fifteen members [all of the slave states]."[47]

Seward knew what holding the upper South in the Union meant: in population, in geographic size, in wealth, in commerce and trade, the eight border states where slavery existed represented substantially more than the seven states of the lower South. If the border states remained in the Union, Seward and many others believed the lower South would be so small and so limited in resources it could be isolated and dealt with; Seward even felt that, in cooperation with border state unionists, there was a very good chance most of the lower South could be brought back into the Union peacefully at some future date. Many Southerners, secessionists and Unionists, bought "the familiar argument for secession which predicted that 'better terms' could be had by seceding, these terms being capable of interpretation in the sense of return to the Union."[48] Robert Barnwell Rhett, the "father of secession," thought so, too. His Charleston newspaper, the *Mercury*, editorialized that "the secession of the other states was not made in good faith, looking to permanent separation, but was merely a political scheme for forcing concessions from the North."[49]

With his Southern strategy now more firmly settled, Seward bent to the task of building support for it, with the centerpiece being the New Mexico Plan or something like it that he felt would keep the border South in the Union. "With an eye on the situation in Virginia, where he was working hard to bolster Union sentiment, Seward twice intimated to a Virginia friend that, in substance, he favored the Crittenden Compromise."[50] While only a few in the Republican Party were coming around to his point of view, Seward knew he must have the support of Abraham Lincoln. Unwisely, he still chose not to present his Southern strategy to the president-elect.

Seward became the leader of those favoring compromise because both Crittenden and Douglas, although very active, never seemed to carry enough clout. But he was not about to roll over to the radical secessionists in the lower South. He urged the Buchanan administration to stand firm with the seceded states and counseled colleagues in New York to prepare for any contingency. He supported the staunch Unionists Buchanan appointed to his cabinet after Southerners resigned, one of whom was Edwin M. Stanton. As a new member of Buchanan's cabinet, Stanton was desperate to share information about cabinet meetings, Buchanan's inadequacies and his bungling administration. He knew this would be breaking his oath of office, but felt the country's welfare depended on it. He reached out to several Washington insiders, but it was Henry Seward whom he saw as "the most powerful conduit for his information."[51] Through an intermediary, Peter Watson, Stanton sent Seward secret messages about what was going on in the Buchanan administration, and Seward responded with suggestions for action. Seward urged New York financiers to lend money to the government at favorable interest rates. Overconfident of his position as spokesmen for the Republican Party *and* the new administration, Seward moved ahead.

The total confusion reigning in the nation's capital at this time cannot be overlooked. Seward was as engulfed in it as anyone. Public opinion seemed to change almost daily, politicians likewise. In early January, Crittenden had proposed his compromise plan be put to a popular vote, thus putting Republicans in an extremely awkward position: if they opposed, it would be construed they opposed the democratic process; and if they accepted, it implied tacit approval of the compromise plan itself. Seward, realizing Lincoln had not been briefed on the popular vote initiative and dealing with radical Republican opposition to it, sought delay. He was walking a tightrope at this moment and "maintained a silence strange for the acknowledged spokesman of a triumphant party."[52] But that was about to change in a very big way.

With Lincoln's stiffening resolve against compromise as expressed in his private letters, all Republicans voted for postponement of debate on Crittenden's popular referendum initiative, in effect killing the effort to have the public vote on compromise. This was yet another tragic moment for the nation during the secession winter, as most contemporaries felt the plan would have been approved by a substantial majority of Americans if it had been put to the ballot. David Donald concludes, "in objecting to all compromise measures, Lincoln was out of step with the members of his party in Congress who were better informed about affairs in the South and more alarmed as threats of secession became reality."[53] Lincoln was not only out of step with Congress, but with the all-important financial class, for as mentioned, they had lent huge sums to Southerners and with their enormous stake in the Southern economy supported compromise overwhelmingly.

At this critical juncture, Abraham Lincoln seemed to be out of step with the vast majority of Americans. James Ford Rhodes, again one who had interviewed many actual participants, recorded his telling summary:

> No doubt can now exist, and but little could have existed in January 1861, that if it [the Crittenden Proposal] had been submitted to the people it would have carried the Northern States by a great majority; that it would have obtained the vote of almost every man in the border States; and that it would have received the preponderating voice of all the cotton States but South Carolina.[54]

And why was being out of step so important? George W. Summers, leader of Virginia's Unionists in the State Convention, wrote these prescient words, "If disunion once begins, none can foresee where it will end."[55] Henry Seward, the nation's political visionary, redoubled his efforts to find peace.

Another effort he quietly pushed was the Border State Plan, a plan similar to Crittenden's but with language drafted by upper South Unionists to attract moderate Republicans, and it had initially received some support from that quarter. The Border State Plan included a constitutional amendment to protect slavery where it already existed and re-establishment of the old Missouri Compromise line (slavery permitted south of the line, prohibited north of it), and did not address restrictions on slavery in territories to be acquired.[56] When brought to a vote in the House, it failed largely as a result of Abraham Lincoln's letters. A leading moderate Republican, Congressman James R. Hale of Pennsylvania, had written to the president-elect to urge aid for the "true and loyal men" of the South. Thurlow Weed had gone to Washington to assist the compromisers and worked strenuously to make it happen. It is reported he even drafted a letter for Leonard Swett to deliver to Lincoln stating the situation in the nation's capital was "steadily progressing from bad to worse" because Republicans refused to aid the loyal men of the South. Weed went so far as to support the Border State Plan in an editorial in his *Evening Journal*.

Part of the reason for Lincoln's intransigence was radical Republican opposition — they loudly opposed each and every compromise effort and bullied those who would not support them. A letter from Congressman E. B. Washburne of Illinois to Lincoln offers some evidence. He wrote "great commotion and excitement exist to-day in our ranks in regard to a compromise that is supposed to be hatching by the Weed-Seward dynasty. Weed is here and one great object now is to obtain your acquiescence in the scheme to sell out and degrade the republicans." Washburne warned Lincoln of a pending visit from Leonard Swett, who he believed was "acting under the direction of

Weed," seeking support for compromise and bluntly declared "if you waiver, our party is gone." Lincoln then sent a stern confidential letter to Hale, protesting against any "surrender to those we have beaten" sternly stating "it would be the end of us."[57] Contemporary reports do not support Lincoln's view that "it would be the end of us," as many Republicans throughout the North were moving toward some form of compromise.

The moment had now come for Seward to make his stand publicly. On January 11, he announced he would make a major address to the Senate the next day. By this time, most of the national press had given up on getting any statement out of Lincoln to calm the nation, so they naturally focused on Henry Seward, now known as the secretary of state-designate, for a plan to save the country. Northern public opinion wavered — on and off again — for and against compromise. Weed sent Seward an ominous note on the ninth: "The war spirit is rising and raging. The surer the war is, the safer the ground you propose to occupy."[58] The citizens of the nation's capital, always alert to major happenings in the Congress, heard of the upcoming speech immediately. And on that famous day, they turned out in huge numbers, over 2,000 packing the Senate chamber to hear Seward.[59] But not only did citizens come, almost all the senators and their wives and most of Buchanan's cabinet came too.

As Seward rose to speak, the chamber turned deathly quiet and all strained to hear every word. The speech was magnificent. He opened with "yet I think that as prayer brings us nearer to God, though it cannot move Him toward us, so there is healing and saving virtue in every word of devotion to the Union that is spoken, and in every sigh that its danger draws forth." He did not cast aspersion; he loftily spoke of the common threads that bond Americans. "We have, practically, only one language, one religion, one system of Government, and manners and customs common to all." He insisted "saving the Union" was paramount, with the South's best interest secured in the Union not out of it. Everything must be second to the Union. "Republicanism is subordinate to Union, as everything else is and ought to be," he implored. He called for conciliation, concession, and peace, ending, "Still my faith in the Constitution and in the Union abides, because my faith in the wisdom and virtue of the American people remains unshaken."[60]

It was one of the supreme moments in the history of the U.S. Senate, a captivating speech that prompted deafening applause at its conclusion. The reporter for the *Chicago Tribune* stated: "never in the history of the American Congress has there been witnessed so intense an anxiety to hear a speech."[61] Indeed, it was a great moment for Seward and the country. "It was a moving speech, and at times during its delivery more than one Senator bowed his head and wept."[62] Senator Jefferson Davis, even though Mississippi had seceded, attended out of respect for his old friend and neighbor.

Radical Republicans condemned the speech for its conciliatory tone, radical Southern Democrats declared it contained nothing new; but Seward's words resonated with many moderates and conservatives in both North and South. Upper South Unionists were impressed, although not wildly so, and the all-important New York financial community responded with enthusiasm. Abolitionists did not like it but were silenced by the great Quaker poet John Greenleaf Whittier, who wrote a poem, "To William H. Seward," praising Seward and his speech, which began "Statesman, I thank thee!" and ended "And the peacemaker be forever blest!" Indeed, Seward told Frances he had to remain in Washington for "it seems to me that if I am absent only three days, this Administration, the Congress, and the District would fall into consternation and despair. I am the only hopeful, calm conciliatory person here." Young Henry Adams thought the speech "inspired hope and confidence" and "that Seward had become 'virtually the ruler of the country.'" And "George William Curtis [editor of *Harper's Weekly*] thought Seward greater at that moment than ever before."[63]

In addition to widespread national acclaim for his speech, Seward's ego was further boosted by a letter from Lincoln dated January 12 commenting on his appointment as secretary of state: "I am happy to find scarcely any objection to it. I shall have trouble with every other Northern Cabinet appointment, so much so that I shall have to defer them as long as possible to avoid being teased to insanity to make changes."[64] Lincoln was besieged by delegation after delegation urging one cabinet appointee after another, but not so for Seward. Almost all agreed he should hold the ranking post in the new administration. On this day, Henry Seward was, indeed, the nation's leading Republican; perhaps Abraham Lincoln thought so too.

Although Seward's speech has been downplayed by many because it offered no specific plan for adjustment, it did set the stage for renewed efforts to reach compromise. Whether accidental or not, the speech coincided with the rise of unionism in the upper South. "Considering the actual conditions and what was most urgent at that time, there is reason to believe that this was as wise, as patriotic, and as important a speech as has ever been delivered within the walls of the Capitol.... To Seward, almost alone, belongs the credit of devising a *modus vivendi*."[65] And his temporary arrangement coincided with a rise of moderation in the North, some reaction against the radical liberals was taking place, for instance pro–Union moderates broke up an abolitionist meeting in Rochester, New York. Weed was most pleased and wrote, "Your speech is greatly more than I dared hope it would be — and my expectations were not small."[66]

Seward did what he could do in the speech, implying that a compromise would be worked out. As previously discussed and with characteristic shrewdness, he secretly promoted the New Mexico Plan in the Senate now firmly believing Republicans, to unite the nation, had to drop their opposition to compromise on territorial expansion of slavery. Bancroft noted that California, Minnesota, Oregon, and Kansas had been admitted to the Union as free states and in all the remaining territories of the West there were but twenty-four slaves. "There was no further danger from slavery, and the question of union or dissolution might well be given precedence."[67] Weed, ever the political operative, was always ready to come to Washington to promote compromise, but in those days it involved more than just travel time. Weed wrote Seward on the eighteenth, "If there be any reason for keeping me away from Washington I will gladly do so for the going involves me in a whirl-pool of Applications [political patronage jobs]."[68]

On January 19 Seward received a private letter from Abraham Lincoln, "Your recent speech is well received here; and, I think, is doing good all over the country."[69] On this same day, the Virginia legislature passed a measure calling for all states to convene in Washington to consider a plan to resolve the national crisis. This was dubbed the "Peace Conference." Historians have not been able to prove categorically whether Seward was behind this effort, but he desperately needed more time to work his magic with the border states. The House had just reported it was unable to agree on a compromise proposal (largely as a result of Lincoln's letters to House Republicans) and the Senate was also deadlocked. Given this compromise stalemate in Congress, Seward knew he needed more time to get Lincoln to reverse course. And a peace conference would fit his plans perfectly. He and others could then argue that while work on compromise was in process no state should consider secession. Seward saw a huge advantage in such a meeting. Sadly, Georgia became the fifth state to secede on this day, although there was much division in the state (over 40 percent voted against the measure).

The calling of the Peace Conference was classic Seward. Adroit and highly experienced, he was in daily contact with many Virginians, he relished clandestine approaches, and "it is singular that the one Virginia Unionist known to have had interviews with Seward was also the author of the Peace Convention plan [James Barbour]." Of course, this could be a coincidence, but Henry Adams, who was as close to Seward as anyone, said that prior to the election of delegates to the Virginia Convention: "Mr. Seward had caused another Convention to be summoned at Washington." This comment by Adams certainly seems to confirm Seward's involvement.[70]

Seward was likely at the forefront of the Peace Conference movement. His interactions with dozens of upper South Unionists—John Gilmer of North Carolina, Emerson Etheridge and Robert Hatton of Tennessee, Henry Winter Davis of Maryland and a host of Virginians—George Summers, John Baldwin, James and Alfred Barbour, W. D. Moss, John Pendleton, Joseph Segar, John Minor Botts, to name but a few—was second to none, but how he did it has never been fully documented. On January 27 Seward informed Lincoln "recent events have opened access for me to Union men in Virginia and other Southern States. Among others, Mr. James Barbour of the State of Virginia has visited me. He is a Democrat, but the master spirit of the Union party."[71] Seward now sought new ways to approach Lincoln on conciliation. In addition, he broadened his reach, and broadened the scope of effort for compromise as well.

This broadened scope included building alliances with other moderate leaders in the nation's capital. On January 18 Seward arranged a meeting with three key pro-compromise senators, moderate Republican James Dixon (of Connecticut), Stephen Douglas, and John J. Crittenden, in an effort to form a coalition of like-minded conciliators. Sometime later, Douglas said he had "reasons satisfactory to myself upon which to predicate ... firm hope that the Union will be preserved." He was asked on what basis he made such a statement, to which he replied that "Union men were holding consultations, and framing measures which it would be premature to reveal." Surely Douglas was negotiating with the Republican Party's Washington leader.[72] Again, in characteristic Seward style, he went about the business he knew best: politics. A few days later Douglas hosted a large dinner party where Seward delivered an enigmatic toast: "Away with all parties, all platforms of previous committals, and whatever else will stand in the way of restoration of the American Union!" and Crittenden responded so enthusiastically he shattered his wine glass.[73]

Rumors of this great nonpartisan alliance surfaced, even President Buchanan was informed. Upper South Unionists, through John Gilmer, were also made aware of the meetings. Much hope ensued but nothing ever came of it. "For reasons unknown, the whole scheme failed, but the attempt shows again the diversity of Seward's connections, the finesse of his dealings, and the extent of his assertions to reach some amicable settlement of the sectional crisis."[74] Seward used every opportunity to promote a coalition of moderate Northerners (nonabolitionists) and moderate Southerners (nonslaveholders) in his effort to isolate radicals in both the North and the South. Seward was a visionary.

On the nineteenth, Congressman William Kellogg, Illinois member of the House Committee of Thirty-Three (the committee formed by House leadership to find a way to resolve the crisis), and a friend of Lincoln but one inclined toward conciliation, began two days in Springfield conferring with the president-elect. Kellogg was sent to see Lincoln on behalf of the Seward-Adams coalition of moderate Republicans. His mission was to convince the president-elect a compromise on territorial expansion of slavery was now required to keep the border South states in the Union. Again, the hand of Seward was at work: sending a friend of Lincoln with long Illinois connections, letting someone better positioned do the work, not confronting Lincoln directly because, if unsuccessful, there would be no fallback position. Kellogg initially appeared to make some headway on compromise.

About this time, Weed was also scheduled to see Lincoln to once again promote compromise, to reinforce the views of Republican moderates and to reinforce, subtly, Kellogg as well. Weed and Seward were in constant contact coordinating their activities and Weed, of course, was in daily contact with newspaper editors across the country, especially those in New York. After the *New York Herald* unexpectedly broke the story of Kellogg's visit to Lincoln on the morning of January 20, Weed sent a hurried note to Seward: "When you see what appears in the Herald this morning you will, I am sure, approve my determination not to go to Springfield just now. With the whole thing in the newspapers, Mr. L. could not but to regard my visit as ill-timed."[75]

Seward responded to Weed's letter the next day with a long report on affairs in Washington. He agreed about Weed not going to Springfield, explained Cameron's appeal to him for a cabinet post, and told Weed he would support Cameron, largely because he was a moderate. He then took a poke at Lincoln: "Mr. L. has undertaken his Cabinet without consulting me. For the present I shall be content to leave the responsibility on his own broad shoulders." Next, he gave Weed his view going forward. "Every thing now depends on Lincoln's Inaugural. I shall write to him about that. Before I spoke not one utterance made for the Union elicited a response.... Since I spoke there have not been 400 persons in the galleries any day and every word for the Union brings a cheering response. Cheerfulness and Hope are now needful watch words."[76]

In regard to Seward's support for Simon Cameron, in addition to his need for a moderate in the cabinet, it is important to note Seward's magnanimousness. In spite of Cameron's dramatic turnaround at Chicago that cost Seward the presidential nomination, he typically forgave and forgot. Seward could shake off even the worse verbal assaults and maintain very cordial relationships with his harshest critics. This is in stark contrast to Abraham Lincoln who could not tolerate those who turned against him. Michael Burlingame suggests psychological factors were at play: "Lincoln seems to have displaced the repressed anger he felt for his parents onto political 'abandoners.' Those who would turn against him — the 'abandoners' — were the victims of [his] most heated and cruel outbursts."[77]

Kellogg returned from Springfield and gave Seward a very positive report and was "full of compromise." He told Southern Unionists that a compromise proposal was forthcoming and went so far as to introduce in the House amendments "encompassing the basic ideas of the Border State plan."[78] Kellogg's actions were viewed quite positively by moderates, even generating some excitement in the nation's capital. Kellogg, however, took liberties with the interview, being far in front of Lincoln on territorial extension. Lincoln, sensing Kellogg's over enthusiasm, a few days later wrote Seward about the Kellogg meeting, restating his firm opposition to any compromise on territorial extension; intriguingly, he concluded by saying he did not "care much about New Mexico, if further extension were hedged against." Seward and Adams were looking for any opening from Lincoln and they took this as support for their New Mexico plan. Later events would confirm Lincoln did not commit to compromise with this one statement, but for the moment it was enough assurance for Seward and Adams to move forward.

And they needed to move forward to counter the secessionist momentum building after six states in the lower South had withdrawn from the Union. On January 21, Jefferson Davis led five Southern senators as they bade farewell to their colleagues. It was a poignant moment. Jefferson Davis, "immaculately clothed, pale and thin," stood and delivered a short, heartfelt speech. "He uttered no reproaches," the speech was "dignified and impressive." As he finished, he sat down, "laid his face in his hands" and wept. Henry Seward consoled his long-time neighbor.[79]

Meanwhile, as a result of Seward's Washington maneuvers, John Gilmer, Emerson Etheridge, George Summers, and many other leaders of upper South Unionists were becoming more optimistic about a compromise to save the Union. As January came to a close, secessionism had been stopped cold in the upper South. Unionism was on the rise as the Border State proposal and the New Mexico Plan represented possible compromise solutions and the upcoming Peace Conference held real promise. In addition, legislatures of upper South states calling for national conventions of one kind or another to address the crisis were encouraging to a growing, but conditional, body of compromise supporters in the North. The efforts of Henry Seward factored into all.

As mentioned, the body of those favoring compromise in the North was led in part by the financial leaders of New York City. August Belmont was a conspicuous player as well as Moses H. Grinnell, John Jacob Astor, Jr., Hamilton Fish, William H. Aspinwall, James DeP. Ogden, and Richard M. Blatchford.[80] It is important to note some were even supporters of the Southern Democrats, in fact, many claimed New York City was "cotton dependent."[81] Alarmed by the financial condition of the city (and the nation), these business leaders, again many Democrats, pushed for compromise at every turn. New York City banks could be in real trouble, they reasoned, if Southerners repudiated their debts, which many predicted if secession was not reversed. New York City was in a state of near panic as bankruptcies exploded. Crop failures in Europe created a huge demand for American grain, which fortuitously staved off a depression during the secession winter.[82]

Seward and Weed were in constant contact during these tense days. Seward to Weed on the twenty-seventh:

Webb writes me, of course sympathetically, that Evarts (prominent New York lawyer and head of the state's delegation at the Republican Party nominating convention) is in danger that I ought to interfere for him directly and invoke Mr. Lincoln's interference. I feel all my objects to Mr. Evarts, and at the same time my judgment informs me that if unusual proceedings ought to be taken even in such a case you are the one to call on me for this. As to Mr Lincoln's interference of course I understand how awkward that would be. Do not however let me fall unjustly under ... on the one side or surprised interference on the other.[83]

They continued normal activities, an example of business as usual is Weed's brief note to Seward on January 22: "Can you get the Pacific Rail Bill back in committee and strengthen it with better names. Corning ought not to have been stricken out."[84] Seward and Weed were in action every day, they knew how to make government work.

And many were not convinced Abraham Lincoln knew how to make government work. The financial elites were still smarting from his reaction to the November financial panic. Lincoln refused to accept any responsibility for the financial crash on Wall Street and rather haughtily suggested the New York financial community "go to work and repair the mischief of their own making, and perhaps they will be less greedy to do the like again."[85] Not words that would inspire financial interests; in fact, some New York City power brokers, led by Mayor Fernando Wood, proposed having the city secede from the Union — becoming a free trade zone — in order to continue business with both the North and the South in the event secession became permanent.[86]

Ominously for Seward and the conciliators, reports from Springfield were not encouraging. On January 25 the *New York Herald* correspondent wrote, "It is evident that influences are now at work here to commit Mr. Lincoln on the Border State propositions; but he as yet manifests no signs of yielding." A few days later, an even more disheartening editorial appeared in the *Illinois State Journal* (a newspaper that had close ties to Lincoln's team): "Mr. Lincoln is not committed to the Border State Compromise, nor to any other. He stands immovably on the Chicago Platform, and he will neither acquiesce in, nor counsel his friends to acquiesce in, any compromise that surrenders one iota of it."[87] Seward and Weed, reading these reports, knew real work was still ahead.

Much of the moderate press in the country now jumped onto the compromise bandwagon. The *Louisville Journal* on January 28: "an adjustment will be agreed upon in a very few days"; the next day the *New York Tribune* (Greeley's paper and one that was in line with the radicals, not the compromisers) reported "a compromise on the basis of Mr. Crittenden's is sure to be carried through Congress either this week or next, provided a very few more Republicans can be got to enlist in the enterprise"; the *New York Times* (Raymond's paper, which did support the compromisers) commented on a rousing speech by Emerson Etheridge saying that "such men indeed deserve to be sustained in their unequal contest, by whatever of aid and support the North can give them"; and the *Boston Advertiser* praised upper South Unionists, emphasizing the need "to give them our aid in their gallant struggle." After a moving speech on the House floor by John Gilmer, who pleaded with Republicans to save the Union men of the border states, Seward remarked to a reporter, "Some compromise must be made to keep John A. Gilmer from being carried down by the secession tide." Significantly, the next day he wrote Lincoln his strongest letter yet urging compromise.[88]

Seward saw the rising tide of compromise spirit come from everywhere by late January. From Missouri Senator Polk came a petition from St. Louis urging passage of the Crittenden Compromise and "more than ninety-five sheets of foolscap paper were required to record all the names." A few days later Seward himself presented almost 40,000 names on a petition supporting Crittenden. The previous week he had presented a petition with 25,000 names from New York. All supported Crittenden's measure.[89] As a result, Seward continued to push compromise everywhere; but again, Lincoln had little feel for what was going on in Washington so was no closer to approving one.

Meanwhile, Seward encouraged his friend and collaborator in the House, Charles Francis Adams, to make a conciliatory speech. On the thirty-first, Adams did just that and it was a big hit with upper South Unionists. Robert Hatton thought the "admirable speech" would "do great good" and brightened the prospects for "an adjustment." Other Southern Unionists hailed Adams's "spirit of conciliation." George D. Prentice, powerful editor of the *Louisville Journal*, called Adams's speech "the most finished and masterly as well as the most significant expression of the spirit of conciliation that has yet been made on the Republican side."[90] As January came to a close, Seward's efforts were having a telling effect.

At this time, Seward increasingly focused his attention on a two-pronged approach: first, he sought to bring a compromise plan to fruition (a revised Border State Plan or the New Mexico Plan); second, he sought new ways to convince Abraham Lincoln a compromise was necessary. An example of the latter can be found in the effort Seward (and Weed) made to convince some leading men of New York to write Lincoln urging him to accept compromise. These business leaders agreed and wrote Lincoln a formal letter. First, they counseled that the small radical wing of the Republican Party would never accept compromise, even a small one; next, they argued the benefits of compromise would "far outweigh the losses" because Southern moderates could then reject secession and keep the menace from spreading. They supported the Border State Plan, firmly believing it would "hold the upper South in the Union" and thereby avert war. But in spite of their strong plea, Lincoln did not move toward compromise.[91]

Another example of Seward's new approach was his letter to Abraham Lincoln on January 27. It was a long and important one where he cited the numerous contacts he had developed with upper South Unionists and noted they were men in real leadership positions. He went on to appeal to Lincoln for a conciliatory policy in a more confrontational way: "The appeals from the Union men in the Border States for something of concession or compromise are very painful, since they say that without it their States must all go with the tide." He then positioned his case for compromise: "in any case you are to meet a hostile armed confederacy when you commence — you must reduce it by force or conciliation" feeling Lincoln would surely resist using force. Next he posited the reaction in the North to force (here he was presenting the views of New York's financial barons, among others): "The resort to force would very soon be denounced by the North. The North will not consent to a long civil war." And finally, he laid out his own position for the president-elect: "But that every thought that we think ought to be conciliatory, forbearing, and paternal, and so open the way for the rising of a Union party in the seceding States which will bring them back into the Union."[92] Seward's more aggressive stand was driven partly by the expanding compromise momentum. McClintock concludes, "By late January, a majority of Northerners favored some form of compromise."[93]

As January came to a close, Abraham Lincoln was on a journey to say goodbye to his family in rural Illinois, out of touch with the unfolding scene in the nation's capital. Henry Seward, at his best in the political intrigue of Washington, had taken charge of events and was confidently pushing ahead with plans for solving the national crisis, which now firmly included a compromise on the territorial extension of slavery. While his Southern strategy increased the risk of a direct confrontation with the president-elect, headstrong Henry thought he had the situation fully under control. February would produce astonishing results for Seward's conciliatory policy as the Union light would shine brighter and brighter.

4

FEBRUARY—UNION LIGHT, SHINE BRIGHT

[T]he challenge to the Democrats came from new political entities, the emerging Union parties, whose most distinguishing characteristic was a base of support in which slaveowners were incidental and irrelevant.— Daniel W. Crofts

February, the shortest month of the year, would prove a long one for the Washington establishment. For Henry Seward, February began on a high note. His laborious efforts with Virginia Unionists had paid off handsomely with the Virginia legislature's call for a peace conference, and some twenty-one states responded with delegations when the conference convened. "At Washington, John Tyler told the Peace Convention that 'the eyes of the whole country are turned to this assembly, in expectation and hope.' He called for a triumph of patriotism over party and for rescuing the nation."[1] New York reacted quite favorably to the call, "Governor Morgan, a strong ally of Weed and Seward, noted that 'the great mass of people in this State, and of the entire North,' desired a peaceful resolution to the crisis and advised acceptance of Virginia's invitation."[2] Henry Seward, sensing victory, began to push his Union Party concept with real vigor as he met with arriving delegates.

Weed was constantly sending Seward distinguished men from New York to use in his efforts to promote a conciliatory policy. A typical example is this short note Weed sent to Seward in early February: "My friend E. A. Miller, of New York, will hand you this. You met him once at my house. He is a most intelligent and excellent man, willing to go farther than you can for Peace, but sound at heart. I commend him to your regard."[3] Seward welcomed powerful New Yorkers who supported his compromise efforts. In early February Seward received a confused response to his letter of January 27 from Abraham Lincoln. On the one hand, Lincoln categorically refused to support compromise on the territorial extension issue. "I say now, however, as I have all the while said, that on the territorial question — that is, the question of extending slavery under the national auspices—I am inflexible. I am for no compromise which assists or permits the extension of the institution on soil owned by the nation." On the other hand as previously noted, he stated in would (or might) support Seward's New Mexico Plan. "Nor do I care much about New Mexico, if further extension were hedged against."[4] Seward now sensed he had a very complex situation evolving with the president-elect.

On February 4 the election in Virginia was held to choose delegates to a state convention to consider secession, and Virginia's Unionists won an astounding victory, beating the secessionists 69 to 31 percent in the most populous (and important) state of the South. This victory by Virginians opposed to secession had major implications beyond just the numbers, for it illustrated that a fundamental realignment of Virginia's political parties was in progress. The moderates, both antisecession Democrats and former Whigs, were joining forces to form a new political entity to promote unionism and oppose secession. Hard-core radical Southern Democrats, those who favored secession at any cost, were the opposing party. And this new entity — quickly dubbed the Union Party — was attracting a sizable majority of the state's voters, 69 percent in this election alone. Intriguingly, most were not slave owners and most were of the rising middle class.[5] Henry Seward realized what was going on; white middle-of-the-road Southerners with their distaste for rich plantation owners were not about to risk all for the sake of slavery.

To repeat for emphasis, the vast majority of Southerners did not own slaves and "they were not about to fight the wealthy slave owners war." Seward and Weed, now realizing this new development had true appeal — where economic differences, geographic differences, and *slave owning differences* were merging to create a political sea change — sought ways to exploit it. If they could drive the majority of Southerners away from the secessionists and toward moderate Northerners, it could be their way out of the dilemma with radical Republicans. A new political majority composed of Southern and Northern moderates could even bring the president-elect around to see the light. Henry Seward, ever the visionary, felt once moderates were in control of the government, a peaceful way to end slavery could be devised, using the successful approaches practiced by European governments that he had studied on his recent trip there. Seward knew many European leaders he could turn to for advice, and he knew how to craft proposals that would appeal to a majority of Americans. Visionaries are forward thinkers, Seward could well have developed a plan to eliminate slavery over time.

Seward was elated with the election results in Virginia that coincided with the convening of the Peace Conference. His confidence soared as the results he had hoped for were, indeed, coming to fruition. Henry Adams, from his insiders view, recorded: "I've seen no big men lately to speak of, except Seward, who dined here yesterday.... He is in communication with pretty much everybody; says he receives as many letters from Virginia as he ever did from New York. Scott and he rule the country and Scott's share in the rule is but small."[6] Henry Seward was on a roll, but so were the secessionists. Also on this day—February 4, 1861—a convention of the seceded states began meeting in Montgomery, Alabama.

About this time, Seward, realizing the president-elect's intransigence on territorial expansion was emerging as *the* problem, took still another tack with Lincoln. Since their sharp exchange of letters on compromise had not been satisfactory, Seward now urged Lincoln to come to Washington as soon as possible to participate in the deliberations first-hand. He hoped if Lincoln could see for himself the heartfelt appeals of Southern Unionists for compromise on the territorial extension, he just might acquiesce. But Lincoln declined to come to Washington until the end of the month. Seward also had to deal with the radical Republicans in Congress, for they now reacted to the compromise momentum by obstructing plans for compromise at every turn. Seward had only a handful of Republican colleagues in the Senate who favored conciliation—Jacob Collamer of Vermont, James F. Simmons of Rhode Island, James Dixon of Connecticut, and Simon Cameron of Pennsylvania were among them.

On the fifth, Lincoln called on Horace Greeley who was in Chicago on a lecture tour (partly to pay his respects to Greeley for his work at the Republican nominating convention) and conferred with him for several hours. Seward was highly irritated with the report of this meeting. Greeley had become a true thorn for he was not only the leader of the anti–Seward forces in New York, but he also aligned himself with the Chase and Blair factions of the Republican Party, all were opposed to any compromise with the South. Seward came to view them as enemies of peace; if left to their own, they would push the nation into war for their own political gain. He came to despise them as much as he did the radical secessionists and the radical abolitionists. On this day President Buchanan informed the South Carolina commissioners (several men who had come to Washington to "negotiate" the return of federal property to their state), that Fort Sumter would not be surrendered.

On February 9 Jefferson Davis and Alexander Stephens were elected president and vice president of the newly formed Confederate States of America. Both were viewed as very able statesmen. Davis was elected "not because he was a rabid fire-eater like Rhett or Yancey, but because he was a moderate and comparatively reasonable, or thought to be so."[7] Stephens, in fact, could lay claim to having been a Georgia Unionist and had argued against immediate secession, although he quickly joined the secessionists after Georgia's vote. February 11 was a day of truly remarkable coincidence for the nation. From Springfield, Abraham Lincoln and his rather large party departed for Washington. The trip would take twelve days and include stops in many Northern cities. From his Brierfield Plantation in Mississippi, Jefferson Davis departed for Montgomery. His trip would take just five days but included stops in many towns of the lower South as well. Both were heading for their inaugurations.

By early February Seward had come full circle from his thinking in early December and now felt saving the Union was of ultimate importance. If a compromise on slavery extension had to be made, so be it. He saw an extraordinarily complex political web with many Republicans in Congress as intransigent as Lincoln, either because of their radical political views or because they did not fully comprehend what was going on or driven by personal reasons (as the case with Greeley). In a poignant note to Weed on the fifth, Seward filed this report: "Last night a caucus of uncompromising members of Congress was held, under the engineering of P. to denounce me and exclude me from the Cabinet, 55 members of the House (one half of them Republicans) were expected. Some 20 attended."[8] These "uncompromising members" chose to ignore public opinion and the compromise momentum it represented.

The political situation facing Henry Seward in February was drifting toward resolution. The Republican Party, "an unstable minority coalition of true anti-slavery radicals and of opportunist groups which were essentially moderate," began to lose support, especially in key lower North states. Pressured by Southern Unionists, by the conservative majority in the North, and by the nation's financial and business leaders to accept compromise, many rank and file Republicans signed petitions supporting Crittenden's compromise, which addressed the territorial expansion of slavery by re-establishing the Missouri Compromise line.[9] Seward, because of his almost endless meetings with key Washington leaders, knew that a compromise on territorial expansion would seal the deal with upper South Unionists, but he faced a near-impossible situation as secretary of state-designate because the president-elect was not cooperating. And no one, absolutely no one, had the foggiest idea of what the president-elect intended to do. What might Seward have accomplished had he been in total control?

Weed, ever mindful of the challenges facing Seward, redoubled his efforts to avert war by calling for a conference of governors, by supporting the Border State Plan, and by encouraging Virginia Unionists. He launched a more aggressive effort, personally pleading for concessions with Northern members of congress, to find peace.[10] Seward met with his Peace Conference co-conspirator, James Barbour, and began to lay plans for leaders of the new Union coalition in Virginia, using the prestige and power of its statehood, to lead the process to re-engage moderates in the seceded states.[11]

Next on the good news side of the ledger for Seward, he saw even more remarkable results when, on February 9, Tennessee voters delivered another smashing defeat to the secessionists when they voted against a proposal to call a state convention to consider secession, 53 to 47 percent. Even more remarkably, they chose Unionist delegates over secessionist by huge margins, in the event a convention would have been approved. Seward's Southern strategy now was in full stride: change the debate from slavery to union, promote a compromise plan that would be acceptable to the Border States, and isolate radicals in the lower South by reaching out to those favoring compromise.

In Washington, Southern and Northern moderates were active in the Peace Conference and began to flex their muscle in Congress as well. Seward now constantly preached "save the Union" to all who would listen. Optimism was high; even Virginia's governor John Letcher, reporting on his visit to Washington, said that "the signs all look well—much more favorable than I supposed when I went to the City." Letcher had met with Stephen Douglas and John Crittenden and became convinced a settlement was near.[12] As the Peace Conference began its work, prospects did look bright. Henry Seward was all activity—he was everywhere. Henry Adams recorded this scene of Seward on February 8: "The ancient Seward is in high spirits and chuckles himself hoarse with his stories. He says it's all right. We shall keep the border states, and in three months or thereabouts, if we hold off, the Unionists and Disunionists will have their hands on each other's throats in the cotton states. The storm is weathered."[13]

Seward was ever hopeful more Republicans would come around and see the light on compromise. Many historians, after the fact, agreed with Seward, feeling the Republicans should have seen the light and avoided a national crisis. The Republicans "raised huge clouds of controversy out of precisely those phases of slavery that lacked substance," and they fabricated the issue of territorial expansion of slavery, talking of "an imaginary negro in an impossible place." Regarding the expansion of slavery into territories yet to be acquired, Allan Nevins, one of the foremost historians of the twentieth century, concluded:

> Nor was it likely, though it was certainly possible ... that the Southern expansionists who had signally failed to gain any Cuban, Mexican, or Central American soil during the eight years of Pierce and Buchanan would be able to do so in the near future.... So far as the actual diffusion of slavery went, the Republicans could have afforded to swallow the Crittenden Compromise—for the possibilities of slavery expansion were near the end.[14]

Henry Seward, who understood Manifest Destiny better than Lincoln, saw that "slavery expansion was near the end" for it had no place to go in the Southwest territories, and certainly no place to go in the Northwest territories.

***

The convention in Montgomery, Alabama, with Georgia's former U.S. Senator Howell Cobb in the chair, had in record time adopted a Provisional Constitution of the Confederate States and elected Jefferson Davis and Alexander Stephens. These developments rattled the Washington establishment because they represented what appeared to be a new nation with a constitution and with leaders all knew were quite able. Questions were quickly raised in the press regarding what to do about the "confederate states."

But that was not all that rattled the Washington establishment in mid–February; next up was Abraham Lincoln himself. Lincoln had left Springfield on his journey to Washington on February 11 and began making speeches, the first since his election. In Indianapolis he spoke of his right to retake government property and enforce laws in the seceded states; in Columbus he stated "there is nothing going wrong"; and in Pittsburgh he declared the crisis an "artificial one," suggesting it might just go away if all would "stay calm." Significantly, he made no reference to the myriad of Union-saving compromise efforts working in Washington. To many, Lincoln's remarks seemed naïve and out of touch with what was going on, to others they seemed strong and to the point.[15]

Lincoln's speeches distressed upper South Unionists to no end; some openly declared his policy would lead to war. One of Seward's contacts in Virginia, Sherrard Clemens, summarized: "We are struggling here against every obstacle, and Mr. Lincoln, by his speech in the North, has done vast harm. If he will not be guided by Mr. Seward but puts himself in the hands of Mr. Chase and the ultra Republicans, nothing can save the cause of the Union in the South."[16] Editorials across the nation rang with derision and belittlement. What did Lincoln mean to convey by talking such nonsense the editorials asked — seven states had seceded and formed a new government — and now the new national spokesman was saying nothing was wrong? William E. Barton was unimpressed also: "He [Lincoln] can not have been wholly proud of his speeches. His attempts at humor had not been well received. His efforts at reticence had not been wholly gracious... His discussions of the grave dangers then confronting the nation ... had not been wholly reassuring."[17]

A comment from the famous Edward Everett was telling. Everett had served in both houses of Congress, been governor of Massachusetts, secretary of state, minister to Great Britain, president of Harvard, and a candidate for vice president in the 1860 election. No one in America was more highly respected. "These speeches thus far have been of the most ordinary kind, destitute of everything, not merely of felicity and grace, but of common pertinence. He is evidently a person of very inferior cast of character, wholly unequal to the crisis."[18] Unfortunately, in Lincoln's early days as president-elect and as president, many of the nation's leaders did not respect him, Henry Seward among them. Seward was distressed, almost beyond belief, with Lincoln's speeches. He now felt the horns of his dilemma sharpen dramatically, for his soft approaches to compromise were being met with Lincoln's confrontational messages, often delivered in a flippant, off-hand manner. Interestingly, Seward chose not to confront Lincoln directly, but sent Weed to meet his train in Rochester and attempt to counsel restraint. He held off for a face-to-face encounter — this was his strength — as the president-elect was due to arrive in Washington in just a few days.

On February 13 the Electoral College met in Washington, voted, and Abraham Lincoln was officially declared president-elect. Great relief greeted this news as rumors had circulated for weeks that forces were at work to prevent the vote count. Seward, in fact, had hired about a hundred local strongmen to secure the Capitol — yet another example of Seward in charge. In addition to Seward's contingent, "Gen. Scott had his troops all under arms, out of sight, but ready, with guns loaded, horses harnessed and matches lighted so that they could take the field at a moments notice. But there was no enemy."[19] Meanwhile, the Peace Conference was busily drafting its compromise plan, Seward in constant touch with its leaders.

By mid–February, Seward and Weed had increased their focus on the emerging Union Party as upper South Unionists began to take charge in Kentucky, Tennessee, North Carolina, Virginia, Missouri, and Maryland. Moderates in the North were also taking charge as abolitionists increasingly came under attack and radical Republicans were being supplanted. If a party of moderates quickly developed (as the Constitutional Union Party did during the just-completed presidential campaign), certainly it held great promise for Seward and Weed. This fact was not lost on other political thinkers. James Barbour, the highly regarded Virginia Unionist and another key Seward correspondent, wrote a long letter to Seward urging him to arrange a compromise promptly. He offered this sage advice:

> You may lose a portion of your own party North. But you place yourself and
> the new administration at the head of a national conservative party which
> will domineer over all other party organizations North and South yet many
> years to come. You above all men have it in your power to bring the really
> conservative elements North and South into an organization the most useful
> and the most peaceful yet seen in this country.[20]

Seward and Weed had built the Whig Party in New York State (some say the nation), they knew how to do these things— and "you above all men have it in your power" was not lost on Henry Seward. These Southern moderates were not interested in the stuff of "higher law" or "irrepressible conflict." Henry Seward was the man they turned to when the going got tough because they viewed him as a true national leader.

The pro–Seward press was also trumpeting this new party. An editorial on February 12 in the *New York Times* stated: "We have evidence now of a

Union Party in the Southern states. The government has friends, the Constitution has supporters there with whom to treat. Conciliation and compromise become now acts of friendly arrangement, instead of surrender to open and defiant enemies."[21] For Henry Seward though, the intriguing question was, could he use this emerging Union Party as a way out of his dilemma? If he could demonstrate to Lincoln the overwhelming numbers the moderates represented, and the relatively small numbers the radicals represented, perhaps Lincoln would see his reasoning.

As February moved along, the tension for Henry Seward grew day by day, especially so since Lincoln began making his speeches. In fact, Weed was worried his dear friend might be worn down by the constant pressure he was under, the constant badgering by radicals, and now the grave concerns expressed about Lincoln's speeches. Seward had shown signs of wear and tear as the winter progressed. Knowing the time was fast approaching for his friend to confront the president-elect, Weed, in a moving and heartfelt letter written on the fourteenth, offered Seward the following advice:

> In the cars, most of the night, I was thinking of the ordeal you are to pass. It is to be great trial of wisdom and temper; in wisdom you will not fail; but of our tempers, at sixty, we are not so sure. Of my own I am sure, that it is far less amiable then it was twenty five years ago. I do not now, as then, bear with perverse, unreasonable and absurd People. Nor is it indispensable that I should, for I am indifferent to their ill-will. But it is not so with you. In the position you are about to assume all the qualities that won men and made you popular are required. To be a successful you must be a popular Secretary. And this popularity depends largely upon manner and temper. You had both once, and they made you strong. How much more you need them now when hemmed in and hedged in by envy, jealousy, and hatred?[22]

In addition to his activities promoting compromise, Seward was also keeping the pressure on Lincoln regarding cabinet appointments—especially that of North Carolina's John Gilmer. Gilmer had informed Lincoln earlier in the month that he would accept a cabinet post if Lincoln would agree to a compromise on territorial expansion, something to appease upper South Unionists and stem the tide of secession. Weed knew first-hand of Gilmer's "conditional" acceptance and now began to sense Gilmer was losing interest as Lincoln had not made a statement on compromise and was making hostile remarks in his recent speeches. Gilmer was a "must-have" cabinet appointee for Seward as he was a key part of his Southern strategy for holding the upper South — by appointing Southerners to the cabinet so demonstrate to the South that the Lincoln administration intended to be national in its representation, and conciliatory in policy.

But much more was at stake because the cabinet offer to Gilmer was one of the cornerstones for conciliatory Republicans in their quest to dominate the party. Behind the scene, Seward and Weed were in a no-holds-barred struggle with the radicals for control of the Republican Party. Seward and Weed wanted a cabinet composed primarily of former Whigs, and primarily moderates, people who would support Seward's Southern strategy and be compatible with each other. The opposition was led primarily by former Democrats, Ohio Governor Salmon Chase, the Francis P. Blair family, and the faction of New Yorkers (Republicans and Democrats) now led by Horace Greeley. They sought to curtail Seward's influence in the new administration, not only on patronage appointments and the awarding of government contracts, but on his policy of compromise with the South as well.[23]

Adding to the fray, Lincoln had let Weed (and thereby Seward) know that if Gilmer did not accept an appointment to the cabinet, he would most likely turn to Montgomery Blair as his second Southern appointee. Blair, although more of a moderate than Chase or Greeley, was a staunch no-compromise Republican. Thus, losing Gilmer would be a multiple blow to Seward and Weed, it would put an anti–Seward, anticompromise man in the cabinet and signal a victory for the hard-liners to those in the know. As conciliatory Republicans searched for the elusive formula acceptable both to Southern Unionists and the Republican rank and file, Seward and Weed knew they had to dominate the cabinet. Greeley "emblazoned the masthead of the *Tribune* with the slogan: 'No Compromise! No Concessions to Traitors!' and launched an editorial vendetta against his former crony, Weed."[24] Greeley assailed Seward with the same virulence. The stakes were very high for Henry Seward and, as it turned out, for the nation as well.

Seward had previously recommended Charles Francis Adams for secretary of the treasury, Southerners Robert E. Scott, James Barbour, Randall Hunt, and Meredith P. Gentry, and still others as possible cabinet choices. Lincoln was having real trouble with his cabinet — Chase versus no Chase, Judd versus no Judd — and especially the potential appointment of Simon Cameron (who had lots of friends, but also lots of enemies). The Chase-Blair-Greeley faction of the party, along with Norman Judd, opposed Cameron, as did the contingent of Pennsylvanians headed by Governor-elect Curtain. Seward, through Weed, now expressed his deep concern to Lincoln about the potential Welles, Blair, and Chase appointments. "Lincoln was learning. Hard experience had caused him to shift from his early view that the southern appointments would be difficult ones, and to adopt the realistic view that nearly every man taken from the section which had elected him would cause trouble enough to tax his sanity."[25] For weeks, much of Lincoln's quality time in Springfield was consumed with the cabinet selection process.

On February 16 Jefferson Davis arrived in Montgomery. Unlike Lincoln, he had traveled alone. On the eighteenth, before a large and enthusiastic crowd of whites and blacks, he was inaugurated Provisional President of the

Confederate States of America. "Our present political position has been achieved in a manner unprecedented in the history of nations. It illustrates the American idea that governments rest on the consent of the governed, and that it is the right of the people to alter or abolish them at will whenever they become destructive of the ends for which they were established." Somehow Jefferson Davis seemed to have forgotten what "the right of the people" meant — many of the people of the lower South had not voted for the establishment of the Confederate States of America, nor had he himself been elected by popular vote.

On this very same day Abraham Lincoln made a speech to the New York Legislature, "It is true that while I hold myself without mock modesty, the humblest of all individuals that have been elevated to the Presidency, I have a more difficult task to perform than any one of them."[26] Politicians are politicians. While Lincoln had been greeted enthusiastically by crowds along his route since his departure from Springfield, not so in New York City, the financial center of the nation. Long a Democratic stronghold, New York gave him a cool reception. According to the *Herald,* "the masses of the people did not turn out. There was a faint cheer as Mr. Lincoln entered his carriage at the railway station, but none of those spontaneous movements for which our people are noted." Wife Mary Todd was snubbed by New York society as well. *Leslie's Weekly* reported, "We are requested to state that Mrs. August Belmont did not call on Mrs. Lincoln during her stay at the Astor House."[27]

Lincoln's mostly successful trip to Washington then took a strange twist. On February 21, while Lincoln was in Pennsylvania, Allan Pinkerton, a detective of some reputation working for the railroad carrying Lincoln, reported on a plot to kill the president-elect the next day as he transferred trains in Baltimore, an upper South city with strong secessionist leanings. Lincoln met with his closest advisors, Norman Judd and David Davis, and others accompanying him, and after much debate decided to alter his schedule and secretly go through Baltimore in the middle of the night. Wife Mary, totally opposed, erupted in a violent rage; some reports suggest she had to be restrained. So after his speech to the Pennsylvania legislature on the evening of the twenty-second, Lincoln quietly left his hotel (dressed in a tam and loosely fitting overcoat) and boarded a special one-car train accompanied only by his bodyguard, Ward Lamon, who carried two pistols, two derringers, and two large knives. They arrived in Philadelphia, got in the last car of the regularly scheduled train for Baltimore, and once there safely transferred to the train for Washington, arriving in the nation's capital about 6 A.M. on Saturday, February 23. When the press heard about this later that day, the story exploded. A *New York Times* reporter learned of the details, including what he called a "disguise" and newspaper cartoonists portrayed the president-elect "sneaking" into the capital in all sorts of unfavorable dress.

Clearly Seward had been upset with Lincoln's speeches. "[I]t need not be left to speculation what Seward, the self-appointed 'premier,' thought of the remarks that Lincoln had made since his departure from Springfield." Lincoln's published remarks shocked Seward as they were not conciliatory in tone and they indicated Lincoln might be on a different course.[28] Many leaders of the North had not been impressed with the president-elect and they had let Seward know about their feelings. Lincoln had spoken repeatedly at towns and cities along his route, and "his speeches, under the circumstances, were evasive, trite, and often flippant. It was at this time Samuel Bowles said, Lincoln is a 'simple Susan.'"[29] And many of these leaders, both North and South, were urging Seward, who had kept the country from disintegrating over the secession winter, to take charge of the "untested and untried" president-elect.

Seward was not a confrontational type by nature; however, he knew the time had come to confront Lincoln. He genuinely felt he knew the situation with Southerners better than anyone, and he genuinely felt his Southern strategy was the way to go. And to Seward (and many others), it truly appeared Lincoln did not understand what was going on.

> The gravest deficiency exhibited by Lincoln on this trip, however, was not his *gaucherie* in such matters as wearing black gloves with evening dress, but his continued failure to appreciate the secession movement. Earlier, he had revealed his underestimate only to private individuals, but now, when his elevation to the Presidency was imminent, he gave public evidence, in speech after speech, that he regarded the crisis as self-liquidating.[30]

Seward, as a result of scores of interactions with upper South Unionists, knew the crisis was not "self-liquidating." Seward's close friend and collaborator, Charles Francis Adams, was also dismayed with Lincoln's performance, recording in his diary that "in this lottery, we may have drawn a blank."[31]

Lincoln's inauspicious arrival in the nation's capital in the early morning hours of February 23 was just noted. A few comments are in order relative to Seward's role in the affair. Henry Seward clearly was the most informed insider in Washington. His networks were unparalleled. When he spoke to the Senate on January 12, nearly one hundred Baltimoreans had come to hear him — he had friends in Baltimore, lots of them. Seward, like the detective Allan Pinkerton, had heard rumors about a potential plot in Baltimore to assassinate the president-elect. General Scott and his war department informers had heard the same rumors. Seward and Scott compared sources and agreed to dispatch Seward's son, Fred, to take notes from them to Lincoln in Philadelphia. Years later Fred Seward recorded the moment:

> Mr. Lincoln himself, conversing with his friend Leonard Swett, intimated that, while he had been impressed by the Pinkerton warning, yet he had about made up his mind not to be influenced by it, unsupported as it was by any other evidence. When, later in the evening, I arrived with the letters

from my father, General Scott and Colonel Stone, resulting from a different investigation, it became manifest to him that at least the matter had too much importance to be disregarded.[32]

Seward's role in the affair appears to have been decisive for when Lincoln received his note, from the leader of the Republican Party in Washington, he had to take the threat more seriously. But the Baltimore plot was never substantiated and the effort to sneak the president-elect into the nation's capital diminished Lincoln badly at a most critical moment, when the nation longed for a strong and well-respected leader.

For Seward and Weed much was at play during this critical time. On the nineteenth, Weed had sent Seward a cryptic note: "I did not see Mr Lincoln till this morning... Judge Davis and Mr Lemmon stayed with me. They insist that I must be in Washington next week, when Cabinet and Inaugural questions are being settled... I do not care to put on Paper things which should not be left to any chance of exposure."[33] Most cabinet posts had not been decided upon at this point and the Chase-Blair-Greeley faction was fiercely vying to control Lincoln's incoming administration. Washington was bubbling over with political intrigue. Weed had won over Judge Davis, perhaps Lincoln's closet advisor, to Seward's position. He notified Seward on the twentieth that "Judge Davis, a devoted friend of Mr Lincoln, is wise, discreet and efficient. Confide in him as you do in me."[34]

Weed had met with Lincoln in New York City with the sole purpose of pushing for Seward men in the cabinet, but the meeting had *not* been successful. Weed sent Seward a graphic letter dated the twenty-first, which is produced here in its entirety because it illustrates so clearly the incredible interactions Seward and Weed had as events unfolded.

> I had an hour with Mr L. yesterday. The conversation was unified to a single point [the cabinet], in relation to which I have no reason to suffice that he listened with profit. Nor shall I unasked, renew the subject. His Inaugural is prepared but I have no intimation of its character. I should like to tell you what was said, and what views are entertained, but of course cannot on paper. My solicitude in response to the Country is not diminished. The designs of enemies concerning me have not failed to produce an effect [Lincoln had been badgered by anti–Seward men to be wary of Weed]. Talk freely with Judge Davis. He is right, true hearted and earnest; but I fear is not heeded. I had also an hour with Mr Hamlin this morning. Nothing, in the right direction, is to be expected from him, though he assented to much that I said [Weed and Seward were never impressed with Hamlin].... P.S. Not the slightest unfavorable impression has been made in the P's mind against you. I am sure that his trust in you is full and strong. He has not as I supposed, committed to Judge Logan. You have a delicate task before you.[35]

Most accounts have Seward greeting Lincoln at the Willard Hotel on Saturday morning where he was taken by Congressman E.B. Washburne, who had met him at Washington's train station. Lincoln's first day in Washington as president-elect was a full one. After a breakfast with Seward, they proceeded to the White House to meet President Buchanan. Seward took charge immediately, making the introductions as he assumed the role of Lincoln's manager. Lincoln met the White House staff and Seward then took him to meet General Scott (who was not home). Next, they rode around Washington for some time on sort of an orientation trip. Seward dropped him at the Willard in the afternoon and went to the train station to pick up Mary and the children. Lincoln met with the Illinois delegation headed by Stephen Douglas, with Francis P. Blair Sr. and son Montgomery, and with several other officials and a host of private citizens. Seward got Mary and the children to the Willard and the family had a pleasant reunion in their suites. Lincoln went to Seward's house for dinner (Hannibal Hamlin was there also) and then returned to the Willard to meet delegates from the Peace Conference, a meeting Seward had suggested. Lincoln held an impromptu reception for members of Congress present in the hotel and at 10:00 P.M. he received members of Buchanan's cabinet, talked with a host of private citizens, and retired to bed very late, a truly exhausted man.[36]

On Sunday morning, February 24, Seward picked up Lincoln at the Willard and took him to St. John's Church. Fred Seward recorded years after the war, "On his way home from St John's Church ... Mr. Lincoln had said to my father: 'Governor Seward, there is one part of my work that I shall have to leave largely to you. I shall have to depend upon you for taking care of these matters of foreign affairs, of which I know so little, and with which I reckon you are familiar."[37] Indeed, during Seward's months-long tour of Europe in 1859, he had interacted with many leaders. Seward was prepared "for taking care of these matters of foreign affairs" and much more, he undoubtedly thought Lincoln's comment "of which I know so little" applied across the board. But Henry Seward was in for a rude awakening.

The above scene was repeated daily for the next few days with Seward constantly at or near Lincoln's side. Dignitaries from all over the capital called at the Willard, including Vice President Breckinridge and General Scott. On Monday, February 25, Seward took Lincoln to Capitol Hill for introductions to members of Congress and the Supreme Court. Of course, Lincoln did hold receptions and meet with delegations without Seward present. And in some of these meetings Seward was maligned. Of particular importance were the groups pushing for the appointment of Salmon P. Chase to a cabinet post. Chase, a strong radical Republican, would in Seward's view oppose his Southern strategy in its entirety. The appointment had to be blocked at all costs. By late February only Seward and Edward Bates had accepted cabinet posts, the remaining five spots were still to be determined. So the stakes were high for Seward as these face-to-face meetings with the president-elect com-

St. John's Church, Washington, D. C., where Seward took Abraham Lincoln on his first Sunday in the nation's capital, February 24, 1861 (Seward House, Auburn, New York).

menced. If he was to control the government, he had to dominate the cabinet, Chase, above all, simply could not be in it.[38]

A real problem for Seward at this time was trying "to connect" with the president-elect. He did not know Lincoln; almost no one in Washington did. Seward had had only one extended conversation with him and that had been some thirteen years earlier at a campaign stop in Boston. Lincoln had such a small staff (only John Nicolay and his assistant, John Hay) that Seward, uncharacteristically, had trouble penetrating the inner circle. Seward's intelligence about Lincoln's leanings on appointments or on what he would do on compromise was therefore very weak. So Seward did what many savvy politicians would do, he would make a proposal to Lincoln and then have friends call on him to reinforce the idea. He kept the pressure on by having New York delegations and various others meet with Lincoln to promote a pro–Seward cabinet and to promote compromise as well.

In analyzing the scene at this time, Kenneth Stampp suggests that "a more modest man then Seward might have taken [Lincoln's speeches and his reluctance to support compromise] as convincing evidence that [he] did not intend to be dominated by a 'premier,' that he expected to follow a course of his own choosing." But Seward was the nation's leading Republican and was responsible, more than anyone else, for Lincoln's election, so why would he not think that the "self-effacing and untried Lincoln could do anything but submit to his will"? Weed had met with David Davis and Leonard Swett the previous August, had exchanged letters with them after the election, and an "accommodation" had been reached, or so he thought. So in characteristic Seward style, "he proceeded with complete confidence that his would be the controlling voice in the government, that he could make commitments which Lincoln would never dare disavow."[39] And to be sure, Seward was making commitments.

As a result, these last few days of February were exceedingly tense ones for Henry Seward. Many emotions were at play. Until Lincoln's arrival, Seward had had command of the Washington scene. Now Lincoln became the centerpiece. Seward, accustomed to being at the center, strove mightily to control events and to control Lincoln. Again, the stakes were exceedingly high for him and for the nation. Then suddenly, for Seward things seemed to sour as "the impression grew that Lincoln would make no concessions to southern Unionists." In a stunning reversal of fortune, "all at once, Seward's Union-saving schemes began to crumble. His supposed influence in the new administration appeared barren."[40] Seward could read the political winds better than most, he knew this course had to be reversed, and quickly.

Seward had repeatedly given assurances a compromise would be forthcoming to a host of Southern Unionists and to a host of Northern moderates. Now he had to deliver. The burning question in his mind became, Would

Lincoln follow his lead? During these last days in February, Seward was working near 'round-the-clock. He employed Weed to keep the interviews coming on cabinet appointments (which Weed did) and he arranged meeting after meeting of outstanding men from across the nation, who favored compromise, to see the president-elect. He constantly urged all men of stature to remonstrate with Lincoln early and often. The horns of his dilemma were now very real, he felt the pain.

One such meeting of prominent men was a conference between Lincoln and the Peace Conference delegation headed by former Kentucky governor Charles S. Morehead, and including two distinguished Virginians, former minister to France William C. Rives and Judge George W. Summers, leader of the Unionists in the Virginia State Convention, as well as Mexican War hero Col. A. W. Doniphan of Missouri and James Guthrie of Kentucky, former secretary of the treasury. Lincoln had used an Aesop's fable to try to deflect the impassioned plea for compromise from these upper South Unionists. Morehead was so exasperated he blurted, "I appeal to you, apart from these jests, to lend us your aid and countenance in averting a calamity." From Henry Seward's view, the meeting had a more telling moment when Rives, the oldest and most well respected of the group, asserted that if coercion (force) was used against the seceded states, Virginia would secede. "At this, according to Morehead's account, Lincoln leaped from his chair, advanced one step toward where Rives was standing, and cried, 'Mr. Rives, Mr. Rives, if Virginia will stay in, I will withdraw the troops from Fort Sumter.'"[41] Whether the events happened precisely as recorded by Sandburg will never be known, but Rives undoubtedly told Seward of the encounter.

Seward, now in a full court press, pushed compromise at every turn during these perilous last days of February. Another significant visitor was Stephen Douglas. As noted, Seward had been interacting with Douglas and Crittenden to construct a compromise proposal. Douglas, like Seward, now saw the growing majority of moderates favoring conciliation. He urged compromise and he counseled Lincoln in this rare one-on-one session to follow Seward's advice and conciliate the South. But more important for Lincoln, Douglas "pledged that he and his Democratic followers would not try to gain political advantage from the crisis. 'Our Union must be preserved,' he told Lincoln solemnly. 'Partisan feeling must yield to patriotism.'"[42] Douglas, stung by the secession of seven Democratic states in the lower South, went on to urge Lincoln to call a national convention and to issue the call in his inaugural address. This meeting presented the president-elect with an extremely opportune moment to solve the crisis, the leader of the Northern Democratic opposition was indicating his willingness to work with him in a bipartisan effort to save the Union from civil war. As Lincoln tried desperately to assess the situation, Seward's frustration mounted hourly.

Still another effort to promote national reconciliation was Seward's effort to persuade Lincoln to revise his inaugural address. Lincoln had given Seward a copy for his comments as soon as he arrived in Washington and the very next day, February 24, Seward sent a strongly worded letter to the president-elect. "A tone of desperate earnestness marked the letter Seward sent to the president-elect. He warned bluntly that the original draft would, if delivered, drive Maryland and Virginia out of the Union. Insisting that he had developed a better understanding of the situation in the South than any other Republican, Seward urged Lincoln to reconsider."[43] Seward, never prone to confrontation, illustrated in the letter the near-epic frustration he felt at this moment. He could see his extraordinary efforts to save the nation wilting away. He now took a calculated risk to get the president-elect's attention by writing a blistering condemnation of his inaugural address.

Seward was disheartened that he had not received a more positive response from Lincoln on his Southern strategy; but on Tuesday afternoon, February 26, Seward received a crushing body blow. Lincoln had gone to the Senate where he polled the Republican senators on their choice for secretary of the treasury, Simon Cameron or Salmon Chase. A majority of the senators favored Chase, and Lincoln decided to offer him the post. Seward immediately heard the news and was exceedingly distraught. John Gilmer had opposed the radical Chase from the outset and on hearing the news formally withdrew his name from consideration for a cabinet post. Upper South Unionists were greatly alarmed as the appointment "seemed a calculated insult to the conciliatory lobby." Henry Adams considered it "the death blow to the policy of Mr. Seward."[44] Although Chase would not accept until after the inauguration (because no one told him he had been nominated), it was a stunning setback for Henry Seward, for moderate Republicans, and for upper South Unionists.

The last few days of February also saw the Peace Conference complete its work and adopt a set of proposals similar to the Border State Plan. They were submitted to Congress for ratification. Partisan debate took over the Senate and despite urgent pleas by Crittenden, Douglas, and others, Republicans continued to obstruct passage by raising rules of order objections. The House was more favorably disposed but only barely. At this critical juncture, the moment of truth had come for Henry Seward. Lincoln had given him no indication he was willing to accept a compromise on territorial extension and without the president-elect's support, Seward had no chance to persuade any sizable number of congressional Republicans to accept one either. And without compromise on territorial extension of slavery, Seward knew the upper South could not be kept in the Union and war was a strong possibility.

On the last day of February, decision time had come for Henry Seward, he was faced with supporting the Peace Conference proposals and risking a direct confrontation with the president-elect (and with congressional Republicans) or backing down. He backed down. Most Republicans, including Abraham Lincoln, supported the calling of a national convention to solve the sectional crisis, as reported in the press for weeks, not the Border State Plan that included a compromise on territorial expansion. They preferred to put off the decision on compromise to a later date. But upper South Unionists needed a compromise on territorial expansion, and they needed it now. These Union-loving Americans needed to demonstrate to moderate Southerners (their constituents) the incoming Republican administration would work with them. It was critically important for them to allay the fears that had been spawned by the radical press, in the North and in the South, that Republicans were out to destroy the South.

Seward, knowing a vote against the Peace Conference proposals could destroy his standing with moderate Southerners, with great consternation voted for the Republican-backed national convention proposal. Seward had little choice. In his face-to-face meetings with Lincoln, they had failed to reach agreement on compromise. This left Seward totally exposed. He desperately needed more time to build a consensus, to expose Lincoln to more moderates, and to encourage the emerging Union Party. But it was not to be as the Congress was set to adjourn, so he did what he did. Seward's vote against the Peace Conference proposals stunned and greatly disappointed his Southern allies. "Southern moderates, hard-pressed to answer Southern Rights criticism that the Peace Conference was a sellout, found their position made even more precarious by Seward's action."[45]

In spite of the wrenching decision Seward was forced to make in the Senate on the last day of the month, he and Weed continued to pull out all stops to influence Lincoln. On this Thursday, the New Yorkers dominated Lincoln's schedule.

> A variety of New York delegations appeared in Parlor No. 6, and in the evening there was a gala dinner at the National Hotel, in honor of Lincoln and Hamlin, given by the New York capitalists, E. G. Spaulding. Guests included nearly all the prospective cabinet. Though the Seward faction predominated, a few of the opposition were included, as if either to make peace or to demonstrate to them the Seward group's potency.[46]

Seward, first and foremost, was a politician, and he knew the game was not over until it was over. He continued to press on, realizing a showdown with the president-elect was now imminent.

In the last few hours of this incredible day, Seward's interactions with the president-elect became sharper almost minute by minute. He was truly disgusted with Lincoln's cabinet choices, and they had not resolved their impasse over the territorial extension of slavery. Abraham Lincoln did not believe moderate Southerners would align with the radical secessionists. He thought unionism would prevail with or without a compromise, and he felt a compromise would weaken, if not destroy, the party that had elected him. Henry Seward, because of his months-long interactions with Southern Unionists, knew a compromise on territorial extension was necessary and he was quite willing to manage its effect on the Republican Party. In fact, he was willing to jettison the radical wing of the party if it meant saving the nation from war.

So as February came to a close, political cross currents and political maneuverings abounded in the nation's capital. Washington had become a scene of real confusion. The Republican Party, the party about to control the White House, remained bitterly divided. Abraham Lincoln, as president-elect, was in a position to tip it either way, toward compromise or toward confrontation. But up to this moment in time, Lincoln had blocked all significant compromise proposals and prevented Seward from implementing his Southern strategy to accommodate upper South Unionists, and thereby hold the eight upper South states firm to the Union. Henry Seward, now forced to adjust to the facts on the ground, prepared a bold, decisive course of action to regain control.

***

February witnessed a stunning show of support for the Union. Antislaveholder sentiment in the upper South, fermenting for years, now burst forth with astounding numbers of moderate Southerners rejecting calls for immediate secession. On February 28 North Carolinians rejected a proposal to call a state convention to consider secession by a narrow margin (about 650 votes), but elected a huge majority of Unionist delegates in the event a convention was called. This provided Seward a much-needed victory. The Peace Conference proposals were being defeated in Congress, but that news had not reached North Carolina because the events in Washington were unfolding at the same time as the election. Other than the carrot of compromise, what else could account for these results in North Carolina, which were representative of the upper South? Part of the explanation can be found in the traditional political differences driven by geography, with the less-wealthy central and western sections of Virginia, Maryland, and North Carolina (the eastern sections in the case of Tennessee and Kentucky) lined up against the wealthier eastern (or western) sections. The secession movement exacerbated these old animosities in a fundamental way: the secessionists were posited as the rich, aristocratic slavocracy with the antisecessionists as the "middle American" non-slaveholder. A "class difference" attitude emerged in the new Union Party movement. Seward and Weed had connected with the rising middle class and drew most of this group into the Whig Party decades earlier, eventually propelling the Whigs to national prominence.

For years, the slaveholding aristocracy of the South had worried about nonslaveholders, who represented a substantial majority of Southerners; specifically, would they rally to support slaveholders if the time came to fight for slavery? The coalition that formed this new Union Party delivered the answer: "hell no." William Holden, influential Raleigh newspaper editor and a Democrat, broke with his party over secession and became a leading North Carolina Unionist. As the secession crisis unfolded, "Holden defined the struggle in North Carolina as a contest between 'the people' and the 'oligarchs.'" He branded secessionists as "enemies of the people" calling many rich boys who had "never earned a dime for their own support."[47] These were powerful words from a highly regarded and influential Southern editor and they exposed a fundamental flaw in Southern unity, the possibility of class warfare.

Likewise, in Tennessee this antiaristocratic, and antislaveholder, theme resonated with its two most famous unconditional Unionist. Democrat Andrew Johnson charged the aristocrats with duplicity stating the protection of slavery was a "pretext and not the real design" of the secessionists; rather, their "true intention" was "to form an independent government in the South 'as far removed from the people as they can get it.'" He concluded "there is not merely a conspiracy on foot against the existing government; but the liberty of the great mass of people.'" Secessionists, he belligerently claimed, were oligarchs who did not give a hoot about democracy. Knoxville's equally famous unconditional Unionist, the newspaper editor William G. Brownlow (former Whig and a lifelong political opponent of Andrew Johnson) joined with Johnson in the fight to keep Tennessee in the Union. Brownlow trumpeted in his editorials "there were no parties left," only "Union men and Disunionists." In his view, Unionists were "the real people," who "irrespective of parties" stood against "the Slavery Aristocracy," a group of "overbearing tyrants" who wanted "poor white men" so they would have the manpower "to fight their battles." Indeed, this "rich man's war — poor man's fight" notion was a significant factor in the new Union Party advance in early 1861.[48] Seward and Weed grasped this fundamental political change and understood the implications for the new pro–Union coalition. Most of these men were former Whigs. They now saw their opening.

***

The month of February had begun for Henry Seward on a great high. He was the leading spokesman in Washington for the Republican Party *and* the new administration, his work with upper South Unionists had paid off handsomely — with Virginia, Maryland, Tennessee, Kentucky, Missouri, and North Carolina all strongly rejecting secession. And the surge of compromise spirit in the North was largely his doing. He was truly "king of the Hill" in the nation's capital until Lincoln's arrival. But with the arrival of the president-elect, Seward's position began to change.

In true contrast, the month ended with Henry Seward hoisted on the horns of his dilemma. Events had forced him to vote against the Peace Conference proposals in the Senate, proposals similar to the ones he had been promoting all winter long. In spite of the incredible political successes Seward had engineered, Lincoln rejected his cabinet recommendations and prepared to appoint Gideon Welles, Montgomery Blair, and the dreaded Salmon Chase. And unbelievably from Seward's point of view, Abraham Lincoln began to forge his own policies and plans, chief among them his rejection of overtures from the various delegations and individuals seeking compromise, thus thwarting his Southern strategy. Lincoln began to develop the style of a political loner, by keeping his own counsel on the crucial issues, making it difficult for Seward (or anyone else for that matter) to anticipate his moves.

And keeping his own counsel included remaining stubbornly "shut-mouthed" about the secession crisis. Throughout the secession winter, Abraham Lincoln had made no public statement to assuage the South or to inform the North, in spite of desperate cries for him to say something about disunion. Stampp notes Lincoln's earlier speeches gave "few clues to his thoughts" on secession, "the main issue before the American people after the election." Secession consumed the public mind, and "that was why his continued silence was so exasperating."[49] What he did do, however, was to oppose, privately and confidentially, all efforts to reach compromise on the extension of slavery; and then, on his trip to Washington make a series of harsh statements mocking the compromisers. Had he come to Washington to participate in the debates first-hand, as Seward had urged, the outcome could have been very different. Recalling the eloquence of the Gettysburg Address, we can only ponder what a statement about national unity and the ties that bind might have accomplished to quiet public uproar and move the nation toward reconciliation.

Seward had been well aware of the potential Lincoln problem on territorial extension, first through Weed and then from his direct correspondence with the president-elect. But throughout, Seward felt certain Lincoln would follow his lead once he interacted with him face-to-face. Seward was extremely confident of his persuasive powers—as he should have been — and Weed had assured him of the "arrangement" with Lincoln's advisors. There is little question that from his point of view, Seward felt he had earned the right to be premier: not only had he gotten Lincoln elected, but his adroit handling of the national crisis during the secession winter had kept most of the nation together. In addition, Weed's constant and steadfast assistance to the president-elect (who needed all the experienced help he could get) since the nomination cannot be overlooked.

It must be remembered Seward and Weed were classic nineteenth-century politicians—they thought they had made a deal with Lincoln's team whereby Seward would lead the new administration—and they assumed the deal would be honored. In late November/early December Leonard Swett and Thurlow Weed had exchanged fascinating letters, as a follow-up to the secret August meeting where they had agreed Seward would be secretary of state in the event Lincoln was elected. Swett wrote Weed on November 26 from Bloomington, Illinois:

> The great contest is ended, and we have achieved more than an ordinary victory... We all feel that New York, and the friends of Gov Seward, have acted nobly. They have not only done their whole duty to the Republican Party, but have been generous + magnanimous. Judge Davis, who favored me with a perusal of your letter to him, the other day, + myself both regret we have not been able to have an interview with you. We hope at some convenient time we may yet do so. In the meantime, we should be exceedingly glad to know your wishes and views and to serve you, if at any time it should be in our favor.... Of course nobody is authorized to speak for Mr Lincoln, but he is a just man.

In the left-hand margin Swett wrote, "let us hear from you often."

Weed replied to Swett on December 2:

> "Your welcome Letter was received yesterday ... We have achieved a great victory ... but we are to encounter a "sea of difficulties." ...I am anticipating troubles not generally appreciated by Friends.... I cherish a pleasant recollection of the circumstances which made me acquainted with Judge Davis and yourself. I should be happy to see you both and if, in your judgments, a consultation would be useful, I can meet you, quietly, at any time and place you may indicate.... If Mr Lincoln has leisure to glance over the enclosed Editorial, please hand it to him.[50]

So the process of negotiating Seward's role in the new administration had commenced immediately after the election.

David Donald, after reviewing Seward's record, concludes:

> Seward ... was confident he could persuade the President-elect to agree that the fever of secession should be allowed to run its course in the Deep South while Unionism should be fostered in the upper South by avoiding all provocations ... he counted on his enormous intelligence and undeniable charm to win over the President-elect and was constantly with him at breakfasts, meetings, receptions and dinners. Delighted with Seward's ebullience and lack of pomposity and sharing his fondness for jokes, Lincoln appeared docilely to follow the lead of his premier.[51]

But in his early days in Washington, Lincoln was in "surveying mode" and Seward was learning the man was not about to "docilely follow the lead of his premier."

Indeed, Henry Seward had used every influence he knew to pressure Lincoln on cabinet choices and on compromise. He had arranged delegation after delegation to meet with Lincoln. Stephen Douglas had come, Unionist leaders from the Virginia State Convention had come, Kellogg had been sent to Springfield to plead for compromise, Weed had been busily at work on Norman Judd, Leonard Swett, David Davis, and others close to Lincoln, and a virtual host of distinguished national leaders from all walks of life had written Lincoln or had come to argue Seward's cause. He had even engaged the pro–Seward press to apply what he thought would be the finishing touch on Lincoln, to settle the matter of Seward's power in the new administration once and for all.

> A letter to the *New York Evening Post*, which was obviously inspired [if not written] by Seward and which was published just after Lincoln reached Washington, showed Seward's deep sense of frustration because of abolitionist opposition and because he had not had Lincoln's support. The writer of this letter declared that Seward's enemies were trying to drive him out of the Cabinet. They were also seeking to defeat any form of compromise with the South, and in so doing claimed Lincoln as an ally. A *New York Times* editorial applauded this letter, denounced Greeley and the abolitionists in general, and expressed confidence in Lincoln.[52]

Henry Seward had left no stone unturned in his quest for cabinet dominance and in his quest for a compromise with the South. But now, he seemed to be headed for failure.

In spite of his bitter disappointment over cabinet choices, Henry Seward was not about to give up the fight. He had had a remarkable three months during the secession winter. He had worked tirelessly and with consummate political skill to keep the nation from totally disintegrating — and he had almost pulled off a compromise that would have saved the nation from war. Now he faced an uncertain future despite his astonishing political successes. Henry Adams recorded it this way:

> Those who saw and followed Mr. Seward during all the anxieties and cares of this long struggle ... would not be likely to forget his cheerfulness, his steadiness, his clear perception, his inexhaustible resourcefulness, his unfailing tact, his influence in guiding the actions of others, his power of bringing diverse connections into a vast combination, his promptness in abandoning unattainable objectives, and his pertinacity in seeking as much as praticable. With all this "armory of weapons," he fought, during these three months of chaos, a fight which might go down in history as one of the wonders of statesmanship.[53]

The concluding comment belongs to the best of the Lincoln biographers, David Donald. As the secession winter unfolded, Donald captures the crux of it all: "All eyes now turned to Springfield, where an inexperienced leader with a limited personal acquaintance among members of his own party groped his way, on the basis of inadequate information, to formulate a policy for his new administration."[54]

What Henry Seward could have accomplished had he been president-elect will be explored in the Epilogue. We now turn to March 1861—a month of true madness.

5

MARCH MADNESS

> Moderates both North and South outnumbered the antagonistic
> minorities in each section who fed on each other, gradually eroding
> the center. An undoubted majority of Americans preferred that the
> center hold and expected it to do so. Widespread surprise and aston-
> ishment thus greeted its sudden collapse in mid–April 1861.— Daniel
> W. Crofts

Friday, March 1, was a day of unimaginable tension for Henry Seward. He now faced the real prospect of losing his political status in the administration, in Washington, and indeed, the nation. By reluctantly supporting the proposal to call a national convention rather than the proposals sponsored by the Peace Conference, he "apparently concluded the Republican endorsement for a convention looked better than nothing at all." Concerned with "the effects of an unsuccessful effort to get Republicans to accept more," he did what he could do. But upper South Unionists and Northern moderates were stunned, and Seward's public stance to abandon the Peace Conference doomed his support among many as they felt betrayed.[1] Seward knew the time had come to challenge the president-elect, and he knew the risks would be very high. But he was not about to accept ignominious political defeat. In Charleston Harbor the Confederacy assumed control of military affairs and President Davis named Gen. P. G. T. Beauregard, recently disposed Commandant at West Point, to command all forces surrounding Fort Sumter.

Seward arranged a conference with Gen. Scott, who was now supporting his conciliatory policy, to coordinate an approach to Lincoln. Seward then summoned Weed to Washington. They conferred and laid plans to reverse their fortunes. First on the agenda was the now unequivocal requirement to have Simon Cameron, the moderate Republican who was once again a Seward ally, receive a cabinet appointment. Seward had arranged for Lincoln to receive "invited guests" only on this Friday, and Cameron was one of the first to appear. Cameron had three separate meetings with Lincoln and finally accepted the secretary of war post late in the evening.

Next, Seward had a confidential and private interview with the president-elect. At great risk to his political status, and indeed his standing within the new administration, he boldly challenged Lincoln. "Frustrated and despondent," he told Lincoln he could not work with Salmon Chase and "must insist on excluding Mr. Chase if he remained." Even more bluntly, he told Lincoln his inaugural address must be modified so as to have a more conciliatory tone.[2] He reiterated his position on a compromise for the upper South and made a last-minute appeal for Henry Winter Davis (a Seward man) over Montgomery Blair for postmaster general. As the acknowledged leader of the party, as the man responsible for Mr. Lincoln's elevation more than any other, and as the man who had kept the country from disintegrating, Seward felt he deserved better than what he had been given. He then issued his demands for participating in the new administration — change the inaugural address, no hard-liners in the cabinet, a compromise acceptable to Southern Unionists. Lincoln, taken aback, did not respond immediately.

On Saturday March 2, Lincoln was in near-seclusion and only special guests were received at the Willard. Weed, working behind the scene, coordinating moves with Seward, arranged for Lincoln to meet with a delegation of New York merchants. Headed by Simeon Draper, the delegation descended on Lincoln to support Seward's plea to exclude Chase from the cabinet. Lincoln told them if the cabinet slate broke, it would break at the top (implying Seward would be removed); the delegation left in great dismay. Next, Seward arranged for two delegations from Virginia to be received. Each pleaded with Lincoln not to appoint Chase (or Blair) and to accept a compromise along the lines of the Border State Plan. Seward and Weed had moved into high gear again, the moment for demonstrating their political clout had come, but Lincoln appeared not to bend.

Remaining overly confident even at this exceedingly uncertain moment, Seward took an extraordinary step — he made contact with Jefferson Davis "through an intermediary" and stated boldly "that the Lincoln government would be dependably conservative." Then Seward "received reports Davis was pleased. The President of the Confederate States of America was for Seward too."[3] Senator William Gwin, a Tennessee attorney and physician who had moved to California and been elected senator from that state, was an old friend and colleague of Seward's, and acted as the intermediary. This episode is a yet another example of the breadth and depth of Henry Seward's contacts. Few in the North could have even received a reply from Davis, much less a positive one. As will be discussed in the Epilogue, had Seward been president-elect, this kind of political maneuver, if even needed, would have had much broader implications.

From mid–December onward, Seward received letter after letter urging him to action. One such letter stated, "The Nation looks to you, under providence, for its salvation. It is feared that Mr. L. is not equal to the emergency of the times." Another from a North Carolina Unionist opined, "All eyes are turned to Mr. Seward & not to Abraham Lincoln for a peaceful settlement.... Mr. Lincoln is looked upon as a 3rd rate man, whilst you are called the Hector or the Atlas of not only the Cabinet but ... of the whole North." Seward's prestige and acknowledged political acumen even crossed party lines. Edwards Pierrepont, a prominent Democrat from New York City, wrote to William Evarts, leader of the Republican Party in the state, "There is no man of sense in the Democratic Party who does not think that Seward at the head of the Cabinet will give your party more strength, both north and south, *than any other man in the nation*. There is but one opinion upon this matter."[4] These were strong words from a Democrat, but they seemed to reflect the sense of many of the nation's leaders in early March.

Given this unprecedented level of support from so many quarters, his abiding confidence in his own abilities, and the level of influence he thought he would have with the president-elect (again Weed felt he had a firm commitment from the Lincoln team that Seward would be the controlling voice in the new administration), Seward was perplexed and dismayed that Lincoln had not responded immediately to his demands. He now decided it was time to deliver his first "broadside." Late in the afternoon of March 2, Henry Seward stunned Lincoln by withdrawing from the cabinet. He "dashed off a curt note: 'Circumstances which have occurred since I expressed ... my willingness to accept the office of Secretary of State seem to me to render it my duty to ask leave to withdraw that consent.'"[5] It was a dramatic moment for Abraham Lincoln, and for Henry Seward as well.

Was Seward bluffing? Was he merely testing the inexperienced president-elect? Could the nation's leading Republican walk away from the cabinet just hours before Lincoln was to take the oath of office? Crofts' view: "He [Seward] calculated that Lincoln would hesitate to start his presidency amid such an open and visible rupture of the party. Of course, Seward was bluffing: any hope for the policies he favored depended more than ever on the effectiveness of his own counsel within the administration."[6] Carefully orchestrated, Weed had Seward's friends in New York quickly spread the news of Seward's withdrawal. Some of Seward's closest friends thought he should carry through with it promptly. Upon receiving Seward's note, Lincoln was reported to have uttered his famous line, at least as recorded by John Nicolay, "I can't afford to let Seward take the first trick."[7]

On Sunday morning, March 3, Seward called at the Willard, where an enormous crowd had gathered in hopes of seeing him and Lincoln as they left for church. But on this Sunday "11 o'clock came and passed and no 'Uncle Abe.'" Seward "was seen going in, but as time passed it became probable that the visit of Mr. S. had another object, and the crowd melted away." Lincoln remained in the hotel all day, Seward for most of that time. This was not a day for church.[8] The first truly momentous decision of the Lincoln presidency was at hand.

Seward now used his well-known persuasive powers to the fullest. He demanded a compromise acceptable to Southern Unionists and, most important on this Sunday morning, he demanded a conciliatory inaugural address (along the lines he had recommended in his letter of the twenty-fourth). The address had become the crisis of the moment for Seward as its scheduled delivery was just hours away. Seward bent to the task with a sense of true urgency for he was sure the original address, if given, would do great harm. Lincoln was to hold a dinner party for prospective members of his cabinet in the evening. Dinner parties were common during inauguration week but not so for Abraham and Mary, as Washington society did not put out the welcome mat for the mid-westerners.

Also on this tension-filled Sunday, Seward received a letter from Gen. Winfield Scott stating he believed it "impractical" to relieve Fort Sumter. Daniel Crofts notes, "Judged either by its timing or its contents, Scott's was an extraordinary document." Seward had withdrawn from the cabinet but Scott still sent *him* the letter "obviously written in response to Seward's direct solicitation." Scott suggested several possible courses of action and in the process used five words that subsequently made the letter famous: "Erring sisters, depart in Peace!"[9] For Scott, general-in-chief of the U.S. Army, to write Seward instead of the president-elect with such advice was just extraordinary. Seward's stature and presence within the Washington establishment was second to none; indeed, General Scott evidently viewed him as "the premier."

In spite of his incredible workload and the high tension of the moment, Seward plowed ahead with true gusto. Will, his youngest son, wrote home regularly and on March 3 in a letter addressed to his sister, Jenny, he observed: "Father is overrun with callers of all kinds and there is at least half dozen every minute of the time waiting for a private consultation, every mail brings from seventy five to a hundred letters ... but he does not seem particularly annoyed and is in better spirits than I have seen him for a long time."[10] Henry Seward had the temperament, political experience, and vision to save the nation from war.

Monday was Inauguration Day. And it soon became clear Seward had carried the day on the inaugural address as "Lincoln decided to make substantial last-minute revisions" to it. It is said Lincoln "rose before dawn ... to alter the document" and in the end "accepted Seward's advice to delete both a reaffirmation of Republican orthodoxy on the territorial issue and a threat to recapture federal property in the seceded states." Lincoln heeded almost all of his suggestions and the speech became much more conciliatory in tone.

The vow to seek "a peaceful solution of the national troubles, and the restoration of fraternal sympathies and affections" used Seward's exact phraseology. Lincoln's eloquent conclusion, "We are not enemies, but friends. We must not be enemies," was inspired by Seward also.[11] Seward's gamble appeared to have paid off, for Abraham Lincoln moved toward conciliation and peace.

Despite great fears about disruption, the inauguration went off smoothly. Lincoln's address was praised for the most part only by Republican newspapers. Democratic papers in the North and most papers in the South did not give it high marks. William Herndon, Lincoln's longtime law partner from Springfield who was at the inauguration, recorded, "There was some applause, not very much nor very enthusiastic."[12] Much more important to the peace of the nation than public reaction to the address, however, Lincoln had sent Seward a carefully worded note before the inaugural address asking him to reconsider his withdrawal. "It is the subject of the most painful solicitude with me; and I feel constrained to beg that you will countermand the withdrawal. The public interest, I think, demands that you should and my personal feelings are deeply enlisted in the same direction. Please consider and answer by 9 o'clock A.M. to-morrow."[13]

After the ceremony, Seward and Lincoln had a long, one-on-one confidential meeting at the White House. Although no record of the meeting exists, Seward knew he had won on the inaugural address and now "closed the deal" on his conciliatory Southern policy. He conferred with Weed during the evening and on Tuesday morning withdrew his resignation, acknowledging Lincoln's "opinions and wishes" that he do so and pointedly noting "our conversation of last evening." Seward had carried the day and now had new political life as the private meeting with Lincoln undoubtedly produced a commitment to follow a conciliatory Southern policy. But Seward did not win on the cabinet selections and continued to doubt whether Lincoln's plan for "a compound Cabinet" would work. He wrote Frances, "I believe I can endure as much as any one; and may be that I can endure enough to make the experiment successful."[14]

Although some claim it was Abraham Lincoln who had "taken the first trick," what mattered was who gained the most politically. And politically, both Henry Seward and Abraham Lincoln gained some ground as Lincoln took the reins of government. Lincoln gained his cabinet choices as Chase, Welles, and Blair all received (and accepted) appointments. Seward gained not only on the more conciliatory inaugural address, but on one issue as big as the cabinet — the agreement to pursue a conciliatory policy toward the South.[15]

While there are no records of the many secret conferences Seward had with Lincoln during these first few days of March — the White House was in such a state of chaos no one thought it important to record such discussions —

they were highly signifi-
cant because Lincoln
moved quite strongly in
the direction of Seward's
Southern policy after the
inauguration. In 1861,
there were four primary
federal government func-
tions or activities in the
states: enforcement of
federal laws; delivery of
the mails; collection of
duties on imports; and,
maintaining federal prop-
erty. David Potter sum-
marized:

> It is an astonishing
> fact, and one which
> has been strangely
> ignored by history,
> that Lincoln
> planned, at the time
> of his inauguration,
> or soon after, to sus-
> pend every one of
> these four types of
> activity....This, then,
> was the much
> vaunted "firm" pol-
> icy of Lincoln. He
> would assert the Fed-
> eral authority vigor-
> ously — but he would

Seward's wife, Frances, in the garden at her Washington home in 1862. She never adjusted to Washington, preferring instead to be at her home in Auburn.
She "suffered" frequent, and often undiagnosed, illnesses (Seward House, Auburn, New York).

not exercise it. He would enforce the laws — where an enforcement mecha-
nism existed. He would deliver the mails — unless repelled. He would collect
the duties — offshore. He would hold the forts — at least the ones which
Buchanan had held, and which seemed capable of holding themselves.[16]

Seward's threatened resignation and its subsequent withdrawal produced an
astonishing turn around on the substance of Lincoln's firm policies toward
the seceded states. As the Lincoln presidency began, Seward kept the road to
peace open by avoiding an immediate confrontation with the Southern Confederacy.

Tuesday, March 5, was a bad day for Abraham Lincoln. When he arrived
at his desk in the White House on his first official day at work as president,

a report from the just departed secretary of war, Joseph Holt, including a dispatch from Maj. Robert Anderson, awaited him (some evidence exists he received the report the previous night but this was the first time he fully digested the contents). Anderson's report stated his provisions on hand would last about six weeks, it would take 20,000 troops to defend the fort, and unless resupplied he would be forced to surrender. Henry Seward (through General Scott) already knew the contents. Lincoln was stunned by Anderson's report. Donald's poignant comment: "Lincoln was not prepared for this emergency. As yet there was no executive branch of the government. The Senate had yet to confirm even his private secretary, John G. Nicolay. None of his cabinet officers had been approved."[17]

Abraham Lincoln had an enormous capacity for growth and in time would master the complexities of running the country, but at this critical moment he was "not prepared." To repeat Donald's graphic comment, "as he [Lincoln] freely admitted later, when he became President 'he was entirely ignorant not only of the duties, but of the manner of doing business' in the executive office." Because he had so little experience in management or in using staff, "he tried to do everything himself." And other than a few Washington insiders like Henry Seward, "there was no one to teach him rules and procedures, and he made egregious mistakes." He thought he could give direct orders to military officers. He thought he could reorganize the government by executive order. He thought he could make managerial changes without the consent of the cabinet departments. "The difficulty with Mr. Lincoln is that he has no conception of his situation," Sen. Charles Sumner concluded. "And having no system in his composition he has undertaken to manage the whole thing as if he knew all about it."[18] Horace Greeley would call at the White House on this first day of business to press Lincoln to remain firm and offer no compromise to the South. Henry Seward, ever the political counter puncher, would stay late that night to confer with the president, in part to offset Greeley.

Matters could not have been much worse at the White House as it was a "mob scene" every single day, starting from day one, because no one seemed to understand the need to screen visitors. Often hundreds of people would be standing in the hallways or in the anterooms waiting for their time. And often truly important visitors could not get through the crush to deliver urgent messages or to have critical meetings with the president. Office-seekers took up most of Lincoln's time as the White House was open to all from morning to late at night. "Sometimes the petitioners were so numerous that it was impossible to climb the stairs." William Pitt Fessenden, senator from Maine, observed they looked like an "ill-bred, ravenous crowd," while Lincoln thought that he was considered "fair game for everybody of that hungry lot."[19]

The new president was warned repeatedly by his cabinet officers, friends, and by leaders of Congress to control access to the White House, but he was unmoved. "With a sad smile he explained to Henry Wilson, the Massachusetts senator, that these people 'don't want much and don't get but little, and I must see them.'"[20] Lincoln's naïve response, although the grist for wonderful stories about how he was so good to the common man, was telling. "The pressure was so great, Nicolay wrote, that 'we have scarcely had time to eat sleep or even breathe,"— much less have quality time to deal with the suddenly growing crisis.[21] Confusion and disorder, while always present to some degree at the beginning of any administration, were beyond the pale at this White House. While the nation was disintegrating, the White House was in chaos. Freehling speaks so eloquently about chance occurrences and the differences they made as the nation drifted toward war, Could a more experienced executive taking charge have made a difference?[22]

But then again, there was Henry Seward. While not occupying "the seat" at the White House, the premier certainly had ideas about what needed to be done. And he began to take charge of the scene. From his point of view, the chaos at the White House played into his hands just fine. Seward was more than content to let the president spend his time dispensing minor political offices and shaking hands with a horde of visitors while he assumed the work of running the government and saving the nation. He took control immediately, first by assuming command of the president's schedule — all cabinet meetings and appointments of key visitors would be scheduled through him. Second, he dominated the president's scant free time, always seeming to know when a few moments were available. Both efforts brought howls of protest from the other cabinet officers, but Seward moved ahead nevertheless.

On March 6 the first cabinet meeting was held. It was an introductory affair with little substance discussed. The new president, having met members only once or twice, had to become acquainted with his new team. Earlier in the day, Lincoln had to explain to an indignant Salmon Chase, who had learned of his nomination to the cabinet from Senate colleagues, that someone in the White House had failed to notify him of his appointment. Lincoln humbly asked Chase to serve for "it would be embarrassing if he did not serve." Lincoln chose not to mention Anderson's letter describing the situation at Fort Sumter or General Scott's advice that Fort Sumter be abandoned as the Army could do nothing to relieve it. Seward was receiving daily communications from Southern Unionists urging that Sumter be abandoned (and Fort Pickens in Florida, too).

The elections of February in Virginia, Tennessee, and North Carolina had stopped secessionism in the upper South. In fact, secessionism had lost ground in every slave state that had remained in the Union — and most leading contemporaries of Seward and Lincoln agreed secession would not succeed in the lower South unless buttressed by the more populous and wealthy states of the upper South. Seward continued to arrange for upper South Unionists to see the president. Two such meetings, with leading men from Tennessee and Virginia, on March 6 are noteworthy. The Tennesseans asked Lincoln "how his inaugural was to be understood," and Lincoln assured them "that it meant peace." He promised them to do "all in his power to avoid a collision." Joseph Segar, one of the Virginians consulting with Lincoln, returned to the Virginia State Convention in Richmond with "every assurance that the policy of the Administration is peace and conciliation."[23] Now Seward sought to consolidate his victory on conciliation at every point by having the president make statements to leading Southern Unionists (and many others as well) of the administration's peaceful intentions.

On March 6 Will Seward wrote another letter home to Jenny. Although the words of an adoring son, Will captured the feelings of many of his father's close friends:

> Today he assumes the duties of the office of Secretary of State and with it more responsibility & care than seldom ever falls to the lot of one man, by one half of the country denounced as a man dangerous to their institutions and by a large portion of the other half equally denounced on account of his conservatism, should the country be saved from civil war and dissolution it can only be by his guidance of the present administration and his courage to pursue a course for which friends and neighbors will desert him, this he will do, although he should sacrifice everything except honor but what to me seems very hard is that he will be obliged to bear all mistakes of the administration and will receive little or no credit for all the fortunate actions made under his direction.[24]

The very next day Weed sent Seward a letter echoing much of Will's sentiment:

> There is general regret among our Friends that you are in the cabinet. But I adhere to the opinion that you conquered wrong, tho' it may be that continued wrong will drive you out. Injustice with their ... appointments would furnish evidence of ulterior designs [Weed is referring to Chase-Blair-Greeley faction]. If Mr Lincoln knew how entirely the hopes of the Whole Country are resting on yourself he would open his eyes. I want much to know policy is to be pursued towards Fort Sumpter [sic]. Can you say a word by letter?

Weed was quite worried about Fort Sumter, recognizing abandonment was the *sine qua non* for Seward's Southern policy. The ever-astute political operative, Weed also recognized it would need to be explained carefully to the North to ensure public support. On the afternoon of March 4, he had written Seward:

> Many things press upon me, so many that my hair is turning very white... Let me hear from you at Albany by return mail, as to what is to be done with

Fort Sumpter [*sic*] and when? I can understand much from a few words. I have an important vitally important suggestion about the consulate at Paris. Keep it open if possible till I see you.[25]

Fort Sumter presented Seward with the opportunity to convince leaders of the new Unionist movement in the upper South that the administration was for peace. As these leaders began to consolidate power, they warned him repeatedly that the only thing they feared was a military confrontation between Washington and Montgomery. Virginia Unionists strongly supported Seward's Southern policy; conversely, Virginia secessionists just as strongly opposed it. Unionists applauded Seward for his policy based on "diplomacy rather than bayonets and bullets." Reports of federal withdrawal from Sumter sent secessionists into hopeless despair, "a perfect agony of apprehension," as they knew their cause had "no shadow of a chance to push secession any further" and more important "every Southern man who favored it will be tomahawked." Seward's collaborations with upper South Unionists had left secessionists with only one option, they "were praying for an armed clash involving federal forces." Otherwise, their cause in the upper South was dead.[26] And as virtually everyone in the conciliatory lobby knew, any attempt to resupply Sumter would cause "an armed clash." Seward moved ahead as if he had convinced the President on this course of action.

But Seward, the ultimate Washington insider, still sought to broaden support for abandonment of Sumter by enlisting fellow conciliators—Democrats, Constitutional Unionists, whomever. Seward contacted Crittenden, Douglas, Adams, and some others. He got much needed support from Douglas. "On March 6 and 7, Stephen A. Douglas took the floor of the Senate to defend Lincoln's Inaugural Address as a 'peace offering.'" Seward had briefed him on the harsh first draft. Douglas stated the president favored peaceful reunion and, in a move that stunned Republican hardliners, stated the administration would "even abandon Fort Sumter rather than risk provoking an incident there." Crofts documents that "circumstantial evidence suggests that Douglas, in making predictions about Sumter, echoed information he had received from Seward."[27] Seward most likely had persuaded Douglas to deliver the message of the administration's peaceful policies. And who better to deliver the message than the leader of the Democratic opposition, a masterful political stroke that was typical of Henry Seward.

On March 7 and 8 John Gilmer wrote a series of letters to Seward outlining better than any other Southern Unionist the situation in the South. The secessionists "only hope," Gilmer noted, was that "some sort of collision will be brought about between federal and state forces." He wrote Seward four letters in which he noted repeatedly "the seceders in the border states and throughout the South ardently desire some collision of arms." Gilmer, and virtually every other Southern Unionist in the know, implored Seward to abandon Sumter as quickly as possible: "There must be no fighting, or the conservative Union men in the border slave states ... will be swept away in a torrent of madness."[28] Also on the seventh, federal military forces continued to abandon forts in Texas, giving the impression the government in Washington was not going to fight to retain federal property in the seceded states. Upper South Unionists viewed these reports as evidence of Seward's conciliatory policy taking hold.

Regarding the Gilmer letters, it is important to emphasize the recipient was Henry Seward. While other leaders of conciliation also received letters (Douglas and Crittenden especially), Southern Unionists focused the bulk of their attention on Seward, as they thought he would be the leader of the new administration. They reached out to him with letters, with editorials in newspapers they controlled, and with personal visits in truly astounding numbers. Many have labeled Seward as too radical or too extreme for Southerners because of his "higher law" and "irrepressible conflict" speeches, but the record during the secession winter does not support the claim. Most upper South Unionists viewed Seward as the one to save the nation from disintegrating. They viewed him as the leader of the conciliatory Republicans (which was correct) and as the premier (which in Seward's mind, at least, was correct), and they turned to him time and time again as the crisis unfolded. No one else in the Republican Party was even close to his level of interaction with Southerners.

On March 8 Henry Seward was ill (or feinting illness) and remained in his house most of the day. On March 9 the second cabinet meeting was held. At this one, Lincoln formally told the cabinet of the situation at Sumter (he had earlier mentioned it to some members) and it was discussed at great length. Most agreed with Seward (and General Scott) that no military force was available to relieve it; Sumter would have to be abandoned. Lincoln seemed to lean in that direction but made no commitment. Montgomery Blair was the only cabinet officer unequivocally opposed to abandoning Sumter, and he said so forcefully. Blair told his father of the cabinet meeting discussion (which was at least unethical) and the senior Blair (a fierce no-compromise Republican) stormed into the president's office stating evacuation of the fort would be "virtually a surrender of the union," calling it treason. The senior Blair apologized on March 10, stating he had said "things that were impertinent." But his message to Lincoln was quite clear.[29] The bellicose attitude of the radical Republicans, epitomized by the Blairs, indicated they were quite prepared to risk a confrontation with Montgomery, although no one had a clue what that would mean.

Of course, Seward knew of the Blair meeting at once, but at first was not overly concerned. He knew the Blairs' viewpoint represented only a portion of the Republican Party, and only a small portion of the voting public. Taking

The entrance to Seward's Washington home looking out the front door. The entrance gate to the White House can be seen in the left center background (Seward House, Auburn, N.Y.).

no chances, though, he constantly reinforced his Southern policy with Lincoln by sending him messages supporting peace from upper South Unionists and from Northern moderates; virtually all favored abandonment of Fort Sumter. Seward was now convinced, if his Southern policy could be implemented promptly, upper South Unionists would unite cordially with their counterparts in the North (Gilmer and others had so advised). And these Southern moderates hoped they could begin working with Unionists—the Cooperationists— in the lower South to fine a way to restore the Union. Some even predicted a counterrevolution against the radical secessionist minority could be arranged, even including the possibility of armed conflict, to bring back the seceded states.[30]

**

Seward had convinced himself, partly as a result of his extensive interactions with upper South Unionists, that secession was a minority movement in the lower South and that with "proper encouragement" it could be contained there and eventually reversed. Moreover, he felt Weed was the right man to exploit disloyalty in the Confederacy, working closely with key upper South Unionists such as Gilmer. One early historian of the conflict concluded that at the beginning of the secession crisis there was considerable opposition to secession in most southern states, "in general, those that opposed leaving the Union in 1861 were old-line Whigs [Seward and Weed's colleagues], who were either outspoken unionists or unionists at heart, the up-country element, the foreign element, and many others who hoped for an ultimate peaceful settlement of the questions causing trouble."[31] Plantation owners, indeed, were a decided minority in each and every Southern state and even they were not united. The secession of the lower Southern states had occurred in great haste, and many felt, like Seward, a turnaround could be engineered, if an acceptable compromise was in hand.

Though a majority of Southerners who favored the Union did so assuming a compromise was forthcoming, a truly stunning piece of evidence of pro–Union strength can be found in the number of Southerners who eventually fought for the Union, compromise or no compromise. After Lincoln's Proclamation of Insurrection was issued, a state paper that many Southerners viewed as a declaration of war on the South, an amazing number of Southerners still supported the Union. "Officers in the federal army included over 160 Southerners who commanded federal brigades and fought with distinction, some one-quarter of federal generals were born in the South, and Southern-born officers held many, many colonelcies and other ranks. Estimates conclude that as many as 200,000 Southern-born soldiers fought for the Union, and only about twice that number composed the entire Confederate army in the field at any given time."[32] Often an overlooked fact is that even after the war began, huge numbers of Southerners rejected secession unconditionally and chose to fight for the Union, and this included more than a few men from the lower South, northern Alabama one of the most conspicuous examples.

**

On March 9, amid the crush of visitors at the White House, Lincoln wrote a hurried note to General Scott asking answers to a series of questions about Sumter. Also on this Saturday, upper South Unionists delivered yet another blow to the secessionists when Missouri chose to reject secession. Antisecession momentum continued to build and "for several weeks in March ... Unionists became cautiously optimistic that the administration would preserve the peace." If an armed confrontation could be avoided, "they thought the crisis could be surmounted, the Union restored, and their political dominance in the upper South solidly secured." As a result, "the new Union Party began to display vigorous signs of strength and potential permanency. A firm determination to ignore 'old party divisions' characterized the new mood."[33]

Many conciliators felt the upcoming Virginia elections, scheduled for late May, would prove the pivotal event in eliminating secessionism once and for all in the upper South. Virginia Unionists expected a landslide victory (if peace was maintained) with the Union Party then established as the dominant political force in the state. Tennessee and North Carolina had similar elections scheduled for August with similar outcomes anticipated. And Kentucky, Missouri, Maryland, and Delaware would surely follow the states to their south. Henry Seward was a politician, first and foremost, and saw great potential for the nation (and himself) in this new political movement. Seward "was starting out afresh for a Union party, the well-informed Washington correspondent James E. Harvey noted privately." He felt secession could be dealt a mortal blow because this new Union Party of political moderates would be highly motivated to bridge differences between North and South. "Informed observers understood Seward's thinking. The Confederate commissioners in Washington reported its basic features to their superiors in Montgomery. Seward, they judged, stood ready to 'merge' the Republican party into a 'Union party,' so as to hold the upper South and to stir a Unionist backfire in the seceded states."[34]

Regaining political dominance obviously was a huge motivator for all Unionists in the upper South, especially former Whigs who had been sidelined by the collapse of the Whig Party during the 1850s. Now they saw their political fortunes rebound dramatically. Former Whig leaders in Virginia, for instance George W. Summers, Alexander H. H. Stuart, John Minor Botts, and John B. Baldwin, were more than anxious to resume their political careers. The huge majorities they commanded after the election in February delighted them beyond belief. These were politically astute men, they were practical politicians, they relished power and clearly saw the stakes and, like Henry Seward, they clearly saw the winning combination. Avoid a confrontation with the new confederacy, and the moderates of the South would regain political dominance.

On March 11 General Scott replied to Lincoln's note about Sumter stating the fort could not be defended without a fleet of Navy vessels and a commitment of armed forces of some 25,000 men. "Scott's military advice dovetailed with Seward's political calculations. Nor was the convergence mere coincidence. The two were 'working like hand in glove' at this juncture."[35] That same day Seward sent a note to Weed asking if the legislature of the state could not call for a national convention, which he said "would be agreeable to the Administration in all its parts."[36] But all was not rosy for Seward's Southern policy. On March 12 he received a pointed note from Weed:

> The surrendering of Fort Sumpter [sic] is to be bitter thing for the people. Such sharp disgrace will overwhelm us. Can it not be averted? I am sure that I could have arranged for its being Provisioned with the Secession Commission. This, I infer, will have occurred to the Administration, and is certainly better than a Retreat, the necessity for which it will be hard to convince our People of. Do save us from such humiliation.[37]

Weed sensed public opinion in the North was toughening and, indeed, it was as news of abandonment of Sumter was reported in the press. Seward, of course, felt public opinion could be managed and in fact public opinion did change dramatically a few days later as news of the military imperative of abandonment became known.

In a more ominous development for Henry Seward, on March 13, Lincoln met with a former Navy officer, Gustavus Vasa Fox (Montgomery Blair's brother-in-law) at Blair's suggestion. Fox, a thirty-nine-year-old Navy veteran, had some experience with Southern ports as a result of his naval career and had been meeting with Gen. Scott for some time promoting a plan to resupply Sumter by sea. He proceeded to present his plan to Lincoln that included landing supplies in small boats with larger gunboats offshore in support. Lincoln listened intently. Also on this day, Seward received a response from Weed on his earlier request for calling a convention. Weed again brought up Sumter commenting on the initial reaction of many legislators: "I will see whether the legislature can be moved towards a Convention. The Fort Sumter mortification is too sharp to ask it just now."[38]

Seward, through a series of intermediaries (first Senator Gwin and finally, Justice Campbell of the Supreme Court), began interacting with "commissioners" sent to Washington by Jefferson Davis. The commissioners wanted their "government" recognized by the secretary of state — they even threatened to attack Fort Sumter if refused. Whether they were bluffing or not was impossible for Seward to determine at the time, but he desperately wanted to avoid any confrontation at the very moment it seemed his Southern policy would be successful. He discussed the situation with Lincoln and both agreed the commissioners could not be seen, formally or informally, and recognition of their government was out of the question. Seward drafted a resolution essentially stating the Confederate States of America was unconstitutional. He did not deliver the resolution, which would have ended the negotiations and could have led to an immediate attack on Sumter, but he continued his clandestine relationship with the commissioners.

As Seward felt certain his Southern policy would be carried out, he sent word to the Confederate commissioners the administration would abandon Sumter and opt for peace. "The Secretary [Seward] and the commissioners alike sought delay, though for exactly opposite reasons." The commissioners sought more time so their government could become more established and Seward sought more time so his Southern policy could solidify support in the upper South.[39] On March 14 the cabinet met twice to review the situation at Sumter.

March 15 saw the most important cabinet meeting to date. The president, after presenting the Fox plan to resupply Sumter, asked each cabinet member to give him an opinion, in writing, "Assuming it to be possible to now provision Fort-Sumpter [*sic*], under all the circumstances, is it wise to attempt it?"[40] On March 16 Lincoln received the written responses from his cabinet. John Nicolay recorded: "As requested, the members of the Cabinet returned somewhat elaborate replies, setting forth their reasons and conclusions. Two of them, Chase and Blair, *agreeing with the President's own inclinations* [emphasis mine], responded in the affirmative; the five others, Seward, Cameron, Welles, Smith and Bates, advised against the measure."[41] Lincoln made no decision as Seward, the senior man in the cabinet, led the opposition, stating it would provoke war. "With his advisors divided, Lincoln was unable to reach a decision.... Like any other administrator facing impossible choices, he postponed action by calling for more information."[42] Writing years after the event and with his decided spin, it is interesting to note Nicolay used the words "the President's own inclinations" meaning Lincoln leaned toward resupplying the fort. If Nicolay is correct, then Lincoln's commitment to Seward's Southern policy had weakened (if it had ever been that strong) by mid–March and he was leaning toward the resupply mission.

Next, in his effort to get "more information" Lincoln made two unusual moves. First, he asked Secretary of War Cameron and General Scott to send someone to Charleston, under the guise of arranging for the evacuation, to get a first-hand view of the fort and the Confederate batteries opposed to it. Lincoln had taken a real liking to Fox, so knowing of Lincoln's preference, they chose Fox for the mission. Whether Fox was qualified or not to make an assessment on the highly complex plan to land supplies by sea at the fort (some suggest he was not), he was so overly committed to his plan it is hard to imagine he could have made any kind of balanced assessment. Fox desperately wanted to attempt a resupply mission come what may, and he wanted to command it. But almost all of Lincoln's military advisors thought it could not succeed. So, could Lincoln have expected a "balanced" report from such a partisan source? If Lincoln did favor resupply and risk war (as Nicolay's words suggest), he certainly could use the anticipated report from Fox (which would undoubtedly conclude an expedition could be successful) as justification to move forward.

Second, in an even more unusual move, Lincoln sent Stephen Hurlbut, an Illinois lawyer who was born in Charleston, and Ward Lamon, his body-guard, to Charleston to "sample public opinion." Hurlbut and Lamon would come back with a report more useless than Fox's. According to their report, there was "no attachment to the Union" in South Carolina. Of course, South Carolina, the acknowledged hotbed of secession, was the wrong place to sam-ple public opinion in the South. With the explosive scene that March in Charleston Harbor (troops marching to and fro), it was also precisely the wrong time to sample opinion there. The two were also charged with deliv-ering messages to South Carolina authorities. Hurlbut, as a young lawyer, had moved to Illinois and came to know Lincoln there. Lamon was a big, clumsy man known for his drinking habits and in no reasonable way could be con-sidered a political emissary. Nevertheless, Lamon strutted around Charleston as if he were an "official of the administration" and went so far as to prom-ise Governor Pickens and General Beauregard that Sumter would be evacu-ated. Incredibly, "he even proceeded to discuss the type of vessel which should be used and the details of evacuation" with the South Carolinians.[43] Lincoln, who knew so few senior players on the stage in Washington (or the country for that matter), was compelled to turn to relative novices for important advice.

Meanwhile Seward was playing the political game with Sumter as only he could. Feeling he had won the debate over Sumter (and constantly think-ing his viewpoint would prevail) Seward informed the New York press Sumter would be evacuated in a few days; he sent the same message to his fellow con-ciliators in the North and upper South Unionists as well. As a result, the cab-inet decision (or so he thought) about Sumter became well known. Seward's efforts produced a groundswell of public support for abandoning the fort. "Neal Dow, the Republican leader from Maine, wrote that evacuation of the fort would be 'approved by the entire body of Republicans in this State' because it was 'undoubtedly a Military *necessity*.'" Even his bitter nemesis in New York, Horace Greeley, did not favor risking war. "Greeley's powerful *New York Tribune* spoke of allowing the Southern states to go in peace and opposed the use of any force."[44] Weed saw public opinion change rapidly too. Only the most radical no-compromise Republicans adhered to resupplying the fort, including the Blairs, Salmon Chase, Zach Chandler, Ben Wade, Thad-deus Stevens, and a few others. But even some radical Republicans saw the military necessity and grudgingly supported abandonment, Charles Sumner a notably example. Although Northern moderates were not unanimous, a substantial majority favored abandoning Sumter in mid–March. And in the upper South, a vast majority favored immediate evacuation. Of course, radical Southern secessionists and radical Northern Republicans favored a confrontation, to support their respective agendas.

Seward, as noted, had taken it upon himself to notify the Confederate commissioners that Sumter would be evacuated, but on whose authority? Nicolay, after the war, supported Seward and thought that he was simply stating his opinion that orders would be shortly issued to evacuate Sumter. Seward "undoubtedly believed every word of this at the moment" as he had declared his views to Lincoln in writing and the cabinet had followed him, voting five to two in favor of abandonment. General Scott had drafted an order to abandon Sumter, dated March 11, and the order was on the president's desk. As it turned out, though, Lincoln had not made a final decision, but he kept it to himself, and no one knew him well enough to understand. Seward, believing Lincoln had made a commitment to follow his Southern policy and abandon Sumter; indeed, believing he was "the premier," acted accordingly.[45]

March 18 found Horace Greeley again at the White House to promote the radical Republican agenda with the president. But Seward, ever the overconfident politician, felt Greeley and the radicals were successfully countered, especially on Sumter, by the cabinet vote, General Scott's recommendation, and his early March commitment from Lincoln. Seward now moved to flex his political muscle on diplomatic appointments. In 1861 some ambassadorships were among the highest-paid jobs in the nation and, coupled with the prestige factor, they were highly sought. The top "plum" of diplomatic posts was ambassador to Great Britain, the Court of St. James. Lincoln favored William L. Dayton of New Jersey while Seward pushed for his old friend, Charles Francis Adams, whom he had previously recommended for secretary of the treasury. Seward won this struggle, too; when Adams expressed his appreciation to the president, Lincoln replied rather brusquely: "Very kind of you to say so, Mr. Adams, but you are not my choice. You are Seward's man."[46] Dayton would become ambassador to France and was successful largely because Seward's friend from New York, the urbane John Bigelow (who spoke perfect French), was dispatched to be the number two man in Paris. Anson Burlingame from Massachusetts, another Seward man, would serve exceptionally well as ambassador to China.

Seward would not win all the diplomatic appointment battles, of course, but he was a dominant factor in virtually every significant decision. And with regard to Adams, "one of the most capable and skillful diplomats ever to serve the United States," he had made a superb choice.[47] But Adams never quite got over the crude reception he had received at the hands of the president and he never really warmed up to Lincoln. Sandburg summarized Adams's view, one shared by many in the nation's leadership in March:

That a man of the brains and experience of Seward was Prime Minister, Adams considered a piece of luck for the country, while on the other hand he held the opinion that from the birth of the United States Government no other "experiment so rash had ever been made as that of elevating to the head of affairs a man with so little previous preparation for the task" as Mr. Lincoln had.[48]

In mid–March, Lincoln wrote an order to establish a military bureau, Attorney General Bates had to tell him he did not have authority to do so. Seward continued to play the role of premier. While Lincoln and the rest of his cabinet continued to debate the Sumter situation, Seward moved ahead. He sent two men to Richmond to inform George W. Summers the fort would be evacuated very soon, knowing that Virginia's Unionists would react very favorably. He shared his hope that a hands-off policy would lead eventually to peaceful restoration of the Union with moderates throughout the land leading the way, including those in the lower South.[49] Whether Seward was acting with Lincoln's authorization is still not certain, but on March 19 he arranged for New York congressman John Cochrane to see Lincoln. Cochrane had just returned from Richmond and delivered to Lincoln the message that Seward's promise to evacuate Sumter within a few days had had a most decided effect on the Virginia State Convention with Summers and his Unionist allies delighted beyond belief. "By March 19, if not before, Lincoln thus received full information about Seward's contacts with the Virginians and about his pledges regarding Sumter."[50] But on this same day, pushed by the Blairs and now supported by Salmon Chase, Fox had another conference with Lincoln where he reviewed again the possibility of a successful resupply mission to Sumter.

In spite of no-compromise Republican intransigence, Seward's Southern policy was having an effect in both North and South as a compromise was now anticipated. The premier was moving the nation toward peace, or so he thought. Meanwhile, Abraham Lincoln, harassed and exhausted, continued to be overwhelmed by office-seekers and other visitors at the White House. Sometimes he would shake hands with the crowds for hours. He found out on March 20 his sons had the measles. He looked very tired.

Radical Republicans continued to pressure Lincoln on the Sumter resupply mission; for them it was a *political* necessity, military imperative be damned. Lieutenant Fox had set off for Charleston and his report would be forthcoming in a few days. The Republicans passed a new higher tariff despite strong opposition by New York City commercial interests who worried about lower South ports taking away their business because of the old lower tariffs in effect there. Weed sent Seward a note about pending appointments, but struck at the tariff: "The Tariff Law is to give infinite trouble, every way and every where."[51] Financial interests began to worry about how the government would remain solvent without sufficient tariff revenues (as unbelievable as it sounds today, in 1861 the main source of federal government revenue came from tariffs on imported goods). "In late March, as in January, the Treasury Department again had to float substantial loans. Its principal creditors, the powerful and influential large merchants of New York City, had strenuously opposed passage of the new tariff and now urged its repeal."[52] Public opinion in the North, always fickle during this time, wavered between conciliation and confrontation with the South.

March 21 found Fox in Charleston, where he visited Fort Sumter and talked with Major Anderson (he also talked with the South Carolinians). March 22 and 23 were not good days for Henry Seward. Confusion reigned in the nation's capital and throughout the land. Lincoln had made no public statement on anything and had not signed the order directing the evacuation of Sumter. Rising concern over revenue collections and the impact of the new tariff began to take hold as the financial elites saw the possibility that secession might indeed produce a negative economic impact. The *New York Times* for a moment changed support for Seward's conciliatory policy and in an editorial urged that the ports in the seceded states be closed, destroying commerce and bringing economic ruin. Seward faced this new dilemma with resolve. He parried these concerns by stressing that finding ways to increase federal revenues could be managed much easier than war — here was the mark of a true statesman.

Radical Republicans kept badgering Lincoln about Sumter, stating over and over the fort could not be abandoned, and "a caucus of Republican congressmen warned the President that failure to reinforce Sumter would bring disaster to the party." Lyman Trumbull, Lincoln's "voice" in the Senate, introduced a resolution stating "it is the duty of the President to use all means in his power to hold and protect the public property of the United States."[53] Seward, with his upper South and Northern allies, still believed the seceded states could be enticed to rejoin the Union peacefully; however, a growing body of Northern opinion now favored letting them "go in peace." The *National Intelligencer* called peaceful separation "wisdom and sound policy" while the *New York Times* reported "growing sentiment throughout the North *in favor of letting the Gulf States go.*"[54]

While there was real division of opinion about what to do about the seceded states, the majority of the Northern press, echoing the majority opinion of Northerners, rejected war in the spring of 1861. James Gordon Bennett's *New York Herald* had the largest daily circulation of any newspaper in the nation, rivaled only by Horace Greeley's *New York Tribune,* which had the largest weekly circulation of any paper in the country. And Henry Jarvis Raymond's *New York Times* was rapidly growing in influence because of its erudite editor. All three came out against war in March.

> Though officially nonpartisan, the *Herald* tended to take a Democratic slant
> ... the *Herald* took an outspoken pro-compromise position, consistently
> berating the Republican party and the Lincoln administration for refusing to
> offer essential concessions. The *Herald* warned incessantly that the upper
> South would soon follow the cotton states out of the Union unless the Crit-
> tenden Compromise were rapidly adopted.[55]

The *Tribune* did not favor offering the South a compromise but opined that the government was supposedly based "not on force but on reason; not on bayonets and battalions, but on good will and general consent ... To war on the Seceders is to give to their yet vapory institutions the strong cement of blood ... But let them severely alone." Raymond in the *Times* put it more eloquently:

> The true policy of the government is unquestionably that of *masterly inactiv-
> ity* ... The object to be aimed at is, the conversion of the Southern people
> from their Secessionism. The appeal of the Government must be to the
> minds of the people ... Force, as a means of restoring the Union, or of per-
> manently preserving it, is out of the question.[56]

Henry Seward, responding to the press, to the public, to Southern Unionists and Northern moderates, took the stance that war had to be avoided at all cost, as his actions throughout the month so clearly demonstrate.

Abraham Lincoln continued to be buffeted from all sides. He was not sleeping well and reports suggested that he looked "worn." On March 23, finally, he restricted visitors to the White House and held another long cabinet meeting as he sought the best course. Major Anderson, who had had considerable discussion with G. V. Fox during his recent visit, sent a strongly worded report to the War Department (through his normal chain of command) stating he did *not* agree with Fox's view regarding the feasibility of resupplying Sumter by sea. Anderson was the man on the ground and knew the South Carolinians would not let boats of any size unload supplies at the fort (after all, he was there when President Buchanan's resupply ship, *Star of the West*, was fired upon in January). Sunday, March 24, would be a day of true consternation for the president.

For Seward it was a day of consternation as well for he knew the time had come for him to produce on his pledge for the abandonment of Sumter, and he felt quite strongly it was time for the president to sign General Scott's order. His friends in Virginia were especially anxious. George Summers had written him asking "what delays the removal of Major Anderson?" reiterating the positive effect it would have on Virginians and the disastrous effect if it were not done.[57] Through his clandestine contacts, Seward continued to hold off the Confederate commissioners by offering the evacuation of Sumter in lieu of recognition. The "Sumter discussion" had been going on for almost three weeks in the cabinet and the nation now expected it to be done. Seward knew the time had come for action.

Monday began the final, fateful week of March. Fox returned from Charleston with an optimistic report on the resupply of Sumter, it even went so far as to suggest that it could be accomplished with a minimum of ships and men. Again, Fox's credentials seem marginal for delivering such a report — he had been a lieutenant in the Navy (a mid-level rank), he had been out of the service for five years, and although he had some experience sailing to Southern ports while in the Navy, it can hardly be argued this qualified him to be an expert in tactical naval maneuvers. Yet Lincoln, in spite of Major Anderson's strong reservations, and the nearly unanimous opposition of his senior military advisors, chose to rely on Fox's judgment for the most momentous decision of his new presidency. Could a more experienced head of state have made a difference?

On March 26 the cabinet met again for several hours to discuss Sumter. For Abraham Lincoln, decision time was fast approaching. For Henry Seward, the decision had been made — or so he thought — and he was focusing his efforts on getting the order to evacuate the fort signed. On the twenty-seventh, Seward received a cryptic note from Weed (note the wide range of issues addressed): "I am glad to see Appointments making in Southern States. The Tariff Law is to give infinite trouble, every way and every where. I understand that Lt. Gen. Campbell of Bath is an applicant for a consolate. He is unworthy. Chandler is in a rage about something.[58] Weed gave no hint he knew the Sumter decision was still undecided, he conducted business as usual with Seward, commenting on the tariff, a consulate appointment, in essence a rather routine exchange.

On March 27 Lincoln received the report from Hurlbut and Lamon, who had found virtually no support in Charleston for the U.S. government. Of course, this could not have been a surprise to anyone who had been in Washington during the secession winter. Lamon had conferred with both Governor Pickens of South Carolina and General Beauregard, commander of Confederate forces in Charleston Harbor, while Hurlbut was "sampling public opinion." Potter observes:

> Lamon's dogmatic promises of evacuation, coupled with the general expectation in Washington, led to a widespread and unqualified belief that the question was settled.... It is clearly evident that a general understanding existed that Major Anderson was to be withdrawn. It is also evident that Lincoln shared in this understanding.[59]

Nicolay, though, would not have agreed "Lincoln shared in this understanding," but Henry Seward was certainly of this opinion as his assurances to virtually everyone so indicated.

Yet, somehow, the situation was not settled. March 28 would prove the pivotal day. The Senate adjourned after approving a host of Lincoln's nominations for government and diplomatic posts. General Scott had sent Lincoln a note, likely drafted or edited by Seward, suggesting the time had come to abandon Sumter *and Fort Pickens*, and that the order on Sumter should be signed forthwith. Scott asserted that both forts should be abandoned to "soothe and give confidence to the eight remaining slave-holding States, and render their cordial adherence to this Union perpetual."[60] Scott now crossed the line from making a military judgment to making a political judgment.

Many conclude this political judgment was a blow to Abraham Lincoln. The general, as previously mentioned, had informed the president the military effort required to resupply Sumter (25,000 men, a fleet of ships) was too substantial for the military to accomplish on short notice. Seward had championed this theme, the military necessity, as the practical justification for abandoning Sumter and this had helped carry the day on the vote at the cabinet meeting on March 15. But again, Nicolay, after the war, firmly stated that Lincoln had not been leaning toward evacuation, "The idea of the evacuation and abandonment of the fort was so repugnant that Mr. Lincoln could scarcely bring himself to entertain it."[61] Many of Lincoln's contemporaries considered him a most mysterious man. Often he kept his own counsel. He had few intimate associates in Washington. So it is impossible to know just how he felt about abandoning the forts during March or how his thinking was evolving, Nicolay was perhaps the man closest to him at this moment. And if Nicolay felt "abandonment of the fort was so repugnant" to the president, then perhaps Lincoln was looking for some such opening, as Scott's political judgment afforded, in order to reveal his true feelings. We do know General Scott had given the president an order instructing evacuation of Sumter more than two weeks earlier and it had not been signed — and Henry Seward, the premier, needed it to be signed forthwith.

Regarding Fort Pickens in Florida, Lincoln had ordered the reinforcement of the fort on two separate occasions since he took office, but his orders had not been carried out, some argue for good reasons, others argue subterfuge. Some suggested if Lincoln could retain Pickens, he could use it as a "face saver" with the North, in the event he proceeded with the abandonment of Sumter. But again, abandoning *both forts* was the message Seward had been receiving, loud and clear, from his daily interactions with upper South Unionists for weeks. No doubt, he now sought to press the Pickens issue with Lincoln, feeling the Sumter issue had been resolved. Seward, the master of political tactics, had his demand for signing the order on Sumter and for abandoning Pickens, delivered by an intermediary, this time the commander in chief of the U.S. Army.

Most have criticized Scott for making a political judgment rather than sticking to his expertise, military affairs. David Donald called it "shocking advice." But in Scott's defense, he most likely *was* delivering Seward's message, not his own. A summary of key events that had occurred up to this moment:

- On March 15 the cabinet voted against resupplying Fort Sumter;
- The vote was known throughout the country and most citizens assumed Sumter would be evacuated;
- Seward had notified the Confederate commissioners that Sumter would be abandoned;
- Over two weeks had passed since Scott drafted his order for Major Anderson to surrender Sumter and it had not been signed by the President;
- Ward Lamon, whether authorized or not, had promised Governor Pickens of South Carolina that the fort would be evacuated;
- Major Anderson, in command of Sumter, had made it very clear he not only thought a resupply mission would fail, but he needed a decision on what to do promptly.

General Scott, who had the highest regard for Seward (and probably thought of him as the premier), and knowing the state of the nation's military forces better than anyone, undoubtedly agreed with Seward's assessment: the time had come to surrender both forts. Neither thought the president was acting "presidential" at this point in time, so a gentle nudge was in order, thus the note. Scott had had conversations with Ward Hill Lamon after his return from Charleston and was led to believe Lincoln was ready to sign the order to evacuate Sumter. Seward, having thought the Sumter question settled, probably persuaded Scott (or wrote it in himself) to include Fort Pickens in his note so the whole thing could be wrapped up at once. But Scott's note turned out to be a very big mistake. The move backfired. The scene unfolded as follows.

The Lincolns had scheduled their first state dinner for the cabinet and a few noted guests, including General Scott, for the evening of the twenty-eighth. Before dinner, Lincoln had called the general to the White House, and Scott thinking this private meeting the perfect time to deliver his note, did so. Lincoln, truly worn out with his nerves near the breaking point, exploded in rage at reading the message, lashing out at the old general and shouting that he would find someone else to lead the military if Scott would not follow orders. Scott, truly shaken by Lincoln's violent reaction, asked to be excused from the dinner party and left.[62] After the dinner Lincoln asked his cabinet officers to stay for a special session.

> Then, in a voice choked with emotion, he told them of Scott's recommendations. Blair erupted that the general was not offering military advice but "playing politician." Except Seward, whose views Scott was echoing, the

others tended to agree. Lincoln gave notice that he would hold a formal council the next day. That night he slept not at all, aware that the time had come for decision.[63]

On the morning of March 29, Lincoln appeared to have made his decision to resupply Sumter, but at the cabinet meeting held later that day he still asked each member to vote on the mission. Seward took the lead in responding. With the hostile reception of Scott's proposal to abandon Fort Pickens from the night before, Seward now had to improvise quickly in order to save face and maintain his standing with the president. Seward proposed abandoning Fort Sumter and at the same time sending a naval expedition to the Gulf Coast to reinforce Fort Pickens, thereby maintaining "the possessions

Seward's home in Washington, D. C., where Lincoln was such a frequent visitor other Cabinet members became irritated (Seward House, Auburn, New York).

and authority of the United States." He stated this "new and vigorous move" would preserve "his policy of peace and procrastination."[64] He did not carry the day.

Sensing Lincoln was now toughening up, Blair and Chase strongly backed resupplying Sumter (Chase now unequivocal) and Gideon Welles joined them in support. Seward, still adamantly opposed, could only gather the support of Caleb Smith. Bates ended up taking a noncommittal position, and Simon Cameron was absent. The cabinet now stood at three in favor of resupplying Sumter with two opposed and two undecided. But Lincoln had made up his mind, in spite of or despite his inharmonious cabinet. He ordered the resupply effort to move forward: "I desire that an expedition, to move by sea, be got ready to sail as early as the 6th of April next" was the exact language of the order.[65] Seward, totally stunned, left the meeting in complete dismay.

Somehow the radical Republicans had won. Either they persuaded Lincoln to change his mind or Lincoln had been inclined to resupply Sumter all along as Nicolay suggested. G. V. Fox had made an impression on Lincoln to be sure, as had congressional Republicans. Horace Greeley had played a decisive role, using editorials in his widely read *Tribune* to blast Seward and his conciliatory policy at every chance. And of course, the senior Blair had been instrumental for he had lobbied Lincoln incessantly from the day the president took office. In fact, Lincoln, exhausted and ill from the strain, nevertheless took time to tell Francis Blair Sr. "the good news" later in the day.

The role of Horace Greeley cannot be underestimated. He was the bitterest of Seward's enemies, and he was an extremely bright and perceptive editor. He saw in the new Union Party the work of Seward and Weed, and he correctly surmised it would be a party with Seward at the helm, this he could not tolerate. He continually blasted Seward in his March editorials. "The Tribune had steadfastly opposed compromise since the crisis began." Greeley was unimpressed with Southern Unionism and opined, "The behavior of the 'Union party, so called' ... simply gave countenance to 'the current Southern assumption that Republicanism menaces the rights and safety of the South' ... Greeley therefore condemned as 'foolishness' Seward's efforts 'to shape public policy to suit border slave states.'" Greeley flatly stated Seward's policy would "ruin the Republican party." He urged Lincoln to toughen up and "prepare to meet force with force."[66] Although Greeley had supported peaceful separation earlier, in the closing days of March he took a more pronounced stance of hostility toward the South, and toward Henry Seward as well.

Throughout the secession winter, Seward had been accused (correctly) by some in Congress and some in the North of abandoning a key Republican Party principle (the territorial extension of slavery) in his effort to reach out to Southern Unionists. Greeley, because of his diabolical hatred of Seward, simply could not swallow Seward's policies toward the South or his efforts to promote a Union Party, for that would surely result in Seward's political gain. Greeley would oppose almost anything Seward favored, irrespective of whether it was good for the country or the right thing to do. It should be noted the course of American history sadly is replete with cases where personal animosities among key national figures caused serious deterioration to otherwise manageable circumstances—Hamilton and Burr heading the list. And in some cases these personal disputes resulted in catastrophic outcomes for the country. Personalities, chance occurrences, the timing of key events—all played a role in the march toward war. Had Greeley not parted with Seward and Weed in 1855 (for whatever reasons), he would have been much more likely to support Seward at the nominating convention, and just as important, to have supported him throughout the secession winter as well.

Abraham Lincoln was in a political quandary at the end of March. Dealing from his position of political inexperience, he had tried to balance all sides in the struggle over a conciliatory Southern policy, the same approach he had used with his balanced cabinet appointments. But on this issue, whether to offer a compromise acceptable to Southern Unionists or take a hard-line position and risk war, he had found no way to reach a balance. In a state of near total exhaustion from overwork and stress, not a time to make the most momentous decision of a lifetime, he chose the course that would risk war.

> The strain under which Lincoln labored in arriving at this decision was immense. All the troubles and anxieties of his life, he told Browning, did not equal those he felt in these tense days. The pressure was so great that Mary Lincoln reported that he "keeled over" and had to be put to bed with one of his rare migraine headaches.[67]

The morning of March 30 found Seward still in a state of shock, but he chose not to accept defeat. Seward did not keel over from the strain but pressed on, still confident he could persuade Lincoln to reverse his course on Sumter. He was convinced a substantial majority of Northerners favored actions that would avoid war (and newspaper reports of the period generally support his view). With his "abandon both forts proposal" shot to pieces, Seward quickly offered the president a plan for a relief effort to Pickens. Seward would adopt this as his compromise position on the forts, feeling if he could reverse the decision on Sumter he could sell some sort of rationale to Southern Unionists regarding Pickens. He conferred with Weed as to the next step, aware that his political standing in the nation was, once again, at stake. He bent to the task of devising a new strategy with unmatched earnestness. After his collapse from the migraine headache, Abraham Lincoln, finally recognizing he could no longer see everyone who came to the White House, ordered his appointment hours limited to 10 A.M. to 3 P.M.

Henry Seward, never at a loss for ideas, moved ahead with the reinforcement of Fort Pickens plan and redoubled his efforts to change the president's mind on Sumter. He conferred with Winfield Scott and they decided to manage the Fort Pickens affair and let Welles, Blair, and Fox manage the Sumter expedition, if it were to come to fruition. They (Seward and Scott) felt a careful effort at Pickens, if accomplished in a subtle, non threatening way, just might be palatable to moderate Southerners. By leaving the more hazardous Sumter effort to Fox, whom Lincoln would appoint "commander," they laid plans to "out fox" Fox. Seward had recommended Capt. Montgomery Meigs, an engineer in the Army who was managing the construction of the Capitol, to lead the Pickens expedition. Seward had taken Meigs to see Lincoln immediately after the cabinet meeting on the twenty-ninth.

On the morning of the thirty-first, Meigs again met with Lincoln, this time with Col. Erasmus D. Keyes, General Scott's military secretary. After a cursory review of the plan, Lincoln ordered the Pickens expedition to proceed along with the Sumter mission. With the Pickens effort now under way, Seward launched a series of desperate moves to reverse Lincoln's decision to resupply Fort Sumter.

***

For Henry Seward, and for the nation as well, March truly had been a month of madness. Like February, March began for Seward on a high note. His bold confrontational maneuver, some say bluff, to withdraw from the cabinet had worked: Lincoln made last-minute changes in his inaugural address along the lines Seward recommended, making it much more conciliatory in tone, ending, "we are not enemies, but friends." More important, Lincoln had agreed to follow Seward's conciliatory policy toward the South. Largely as a result of his efforts, the compromise spirit had surged in the North and in the upper South as well. Seward reached the zenith of power on the "ides of March" when the cabinet voted five to two in favor of abandoning Fort Sumter, which had become the centerpiece of his Southern policy.

The last half of the month saw public opinion in the nation sway to and fro, for and against compromise, but with a clear majority in the North still opposed to any action that would risk war. Upper South Unionists consistently urged abandonment of Forts Sumter and Pickens, and anxiously awaited the upcoming elections in the next months. Radical Republicans, who represented such a small minority of the nation's voters, were so vociferous in their opposition to abandoning Sumter they appeared more numerous. Lincoln's stunning decision, announced at the cabinet meeting on March 29, to reinforce Fort Sumter threw Seward into a tailspin. But ever the resourceful and over-confident politician, he parried the blow and immediately sought to reverse Lincoln's decision. As March came to an end, little did Henry Seward know *the point of no return* was a mere two weeks away.

6

THE POINT OF NO RETURN

The war was greeted in its first few weeks almost as a festival. Everybody seemed relieved. People went out and celebrated, both in the
North and in the South. There were parades, bands playing, flags
flying; people seemed almost happy. Large numbers of troops were
enlisted...the grim awakening would come later.— Bruce Catton

Easter Monday, April 1, 1861, was not a good morning for Abraham Lincoln, Henry Seward, or the nation. The two principals in the new administration were again at odds, and the risk of war for the nation had suddenly
increased dramatically. Henry Seward, after conferring with Thurlow Weed,
had his son Fred deliver his famous (or infamous) memorandum to the president, "Some thoughts for the President's consideration." No document of
its kind from a presidential counselor, either before or since, has been produced — ever. For the most part, Lincoln historians have given Seward's
"thoughts" low marks; some even suggest they were a travesty. And if examined from the point of view of defending Lincoln, they are correct.

But if the thoughts are examined from the view of defending Seward, a
different picture emerges, especially at this particular moment in time. During his first weeks in office Abraham Lincoln was characterized as indecisive,
adrift, even confused. He was spending inordinate time greeting visitors and
dispensing minor political offices. On the other hand, Seward had a program
to save the nation from war "based on isolating the states that had seceded
by cultivating the border states that had not." From Seward's point of view,
this Southern strategy was the way to solve the national crisis. Seward felt he
was "the premier" and he felt he had earned the right to be the dominant voice
in the new administration. No one had worked harder than he to get Lincoln
elected, no one had worked harder than he to keep the Union from disintegrating further over the secession winter, and no team had provided such an
unprecedented level of support to Abraham Lincoln as Seward and Weed. And
indeed, Seward was incensed with Lincoln about Sumter, feeling the president
had reneged on his commitment to follow his conciliatory Southern policy.

As a politician who knew the "rules of the game," he felt he was owed more clout. "It was while he was in this state of mind that Seward composed a notorious paper."[1]

The stature of the author — the nation's most well-known and popular Northern politician, the leader of the country's moderate (and majority) element, and the man widely viewed as the leader of the Republican Party — cannot be overlooked. Indeed, on this April 1, many of Henry Seward's contemporaries thought of him as the *de facto* leader of the country, many thought of him as the premier. And Seward, always overly confident and headstrong, had not been impressed with Abraham Lincoln during his first weeks in office; nor had many others. Van Deusen notes, "[A]s Seward's hopes of peace and reconciliation faded, he became impatient with Lincoln, and in this he was not alone." The lack of any statement about the rebellion from the White House had caused much grumbling in the North.[2] Seward had spent months cultivating upper South Unionists, the men he knew were so critical to saving the nation from war; and now, in his mind at least, the president was about to throw it all away with his decision on Sumter.

In addition, it is important to realize just *who* Governor Seward thought he was writing to on April 1, 1861. It was not the Abraham Lincoln who would grow into a great president, it was a terribly inexperienced and untested man who happened to be seated in the White House. No one in the country, except perhaps a few of his cronies in Illinois, considered Abraham Lincoln a great man on April 1. He was viewed by his harshest critics as a mere lawyer from Springfield who was, to use Lincoln's own words, an "accidental instrument." Henry Seward — the former governor, leading senator, "Mr. Republican" — no doubt felt he should be in the White House and that Lincoln should not. A comment by the nation's political "prince" captures the view of many at this critical juncture. Charles Francis Adams, after conferences with Seward and other prominent men at the capital, recorded in his diary: "The impression which I have received is that the course of the President is drifting the country into war, by its want of decision. Everywhere at this place is discouragement, not loud in words but in hopelessness of a favorable issue. For my part I see nothing but incompetency in the head. The man is not equal to the hour." Seward, himself, described Lincoln as having "no system, no relative ideas, no conception of his situation — much absorption in the details of office dispensation, but little application to great ideas."[3] Thus, from the defending Seward view, the "thoughts" were from the leader of the country writing to someone who needed to be led.

***

Henry Seward found himself in yet another political quagmire on April 1. Given the circumstances, Seward, with Weed's concurrence, felt he needed to deliver a second "broadside" as threatening resignation again was no longer an option. So he chose his thoughts as the vehicle. The key points in Seward's thoughts and comment follow.

> We are at the end of a month's administration and yet without a policy either domestic or foreign. This, however, is not culpable, and it has been unavoidable. The presence of the Senate, with the need to meet applications for patronage, have prevented attention to other and more grave matters. But further delay to adopt and prosecute our policies for both domestic and foreign affairs would not only bring scandal on the Administration, but danger upon the country.

Whether the administration did or did not have a domestic policy (historians for the most part support Lincoln's view that his inaugural address stated his policy), contemporary reports suggest many leading men in the nation agreed with Seward, James Gordon Bennett a leading example. Since Lincoln had made no public statement about the South, the forts, or the crisis in general, the press (which did represent the public's views in many ways) repeatedly chastised Lincoln for not making a statement that would soothe the country or just clarify his administration's position. This was true of the Democratic newspapers in the North for sure, but it was true of the moderate Republican newspapers (such as the *New York Times*) as well. And it was entirely true of virtually all of the moderate Southern newspapers, those representing upper South Unionists. As to foreign policy, no contemporary reports suggest Lincoln had developed a foreign policy as he was particularly unknowledgeable about foreign affairs (as he himself had mentioned to Seward upon his arrival in Washington in late February).

> Seward urged Lincoln to "change the question before the public from one upon slavery, or about slavery for a question upon Union or Disunion. In other words, from what would be regarded as a Party question to one of Patriotism or Union. The occupation or evacuation of Fort Sumter, although not in fact a slavery, or a party question, is so regarded."

Seward emphatically urged Lincoln to change his decision and give up Sumter, which many viewed as a party issue, thereby demonstrating to the nation the administration was above party politics and showcase the administration's "national representativeness"—and its peaceful intentions. Seward more than most politicians knew the score: most non–Republicans (over 60 percent of the electorate) and a sizable number of Republicans (perhaps as many as 50 percent) favored abandonment of Sumter. Thus, a substantial majority of Americans favored abandonment. Seward's political logic saw the opportunity to demonstrate in one stroke bipartisanship and the conciliatory nature of the new administration by withdrawing from Sumter. At the same time, he recommended defending all other Gulf ports and recalling the Navy from foreign posts to prepare for a blockade. Seward had reluctantly agreed to the reinforcement of Fort Pickens to maintain his standing in the cabinet and because he reasoned many upper South Unionists might accept it. Seward thought he could "sell" the reinforcement of Pickens to moderates. Indeed, in his view, the difference was that Sumter had come to be looked upon as a showdown between the extreme elements in the country. The radical Republicans were constantly calling for a show of force at Charleston, the cradle of secession. Radical secessionists demanded federal withdrawal, nothing else. Pickens did not have that level of association.[4]

> Seward next addressed foreign affairs: " I would demand explanations from Spain and France, categorically, at once. I would seek explanations from Great Britain and Russia, and send agents into Canada, Mexico and Central America, to rouse a vigorous continental spirit of independence on this continent against European intervention, and if satisfactory explanations are not received from Spain and France, I would convene Congress and declare war against them."

On March 30 Seward had received word Spain had "annexed" Santo Domingo (after a revolution there) and with cooperation from France was about to annex Haiti as well, thereby reestablishing a European presence in

Palais Legislatif in Paris. Seward visited here in 1859 to meet with French political leaders; he was welcomed enthusiastically (Seward House, Auburn, New York).

the Western Hemisphere. In addition, France had threatened intervention in Mexico, where a revolution was threatened. Seward hoped (albeit without evidence) an effort to counter meddling by European powers in the Hemisphere might strengthen the Union cause in the upper South.

In addition, there had been rumors throughout the fall (and even some "documented" reports) of British agents trying to spread terror through the South by arming slaves. "Governor Conway [of Arkansas] did not believe that Northerners were the real villains in the piece. His was the original discovery that British agents were responsible, and he darkly declared that if all the facts relating to them could be made public and documented, the patriotic people of the United States would be astonished."[5] Whether challenging foreign governments would strengthen the Union cause or not surely is questionable, but in Seward's mind it could provide an explanation for the Pickens expedition if nothing else.

Seward's proposal can be understood only by recognizing that his paramount concern was "the American domestic crisis" and that "his foreign proposals followed logically from his domestic proposals." His great hope was to maintain peace "both at home and abroad. The evidence is quite conclusive that he wanted a foreign *crisis* rather than a foreign *war*. Seward's objective remained consistent. He still hoped to secure peaceful reunion by relying on southern Unionism."[6]

> Finally, Seward sought to regain the role of premier, which he thought he had secured in his early March rapprochement with Lincoln. He ended his thoughts, "But whatever policy we adopt, there must be an energetic prosecution of it. For this purpose it must be somebody's business to pursue and direct it, incessantly. Either the President must do it himself, and be all the while active in it; or devolve it on some member of his Cabinet."[7]

Seward implied he was ready to be the premier and his message "teemed with practical ideas, many of which were later implemented." The forts on the Gulf Coast were eventually reinforced and naval vessels were recalled from abroad to set up a blockade. France and Spain were put on notice that their actions in the Western Hemisphere were unacceptable. Representatives from the government were sent to Canada and Mexico to coordinate hemispheric activities.[8]

Seward, no doubt, felt Abraham Lincoln had made a very bad decision regarding Sumter and war was now probable. Furthermore, he had not developed any confidence in the president by April 1 (nor had anyone else for that matter). And it was Lincoln who had collapsed under the strain, not he. So as the nation's leading Republican, he surely felt he was justified in sending his thoughts to *this* chief executive at *this* moment in time. Again, in his mind, he was the premier — he felt he had earned the right to call the shots — and it was time for him to gain control of a deteriorating situation from a man who was acting neither presidential nor knowledgeable about national or international affairs.

***

Lincoln, of course, did not like Seward's thoughts. He wrote a reply, which was evidently never delivered, that responded to the first and last points, essentially stating that the administration had policies that were outlined in his inaugural address and he, as president, would see that they were carried out. There is no way to discover what Lincoln actually told Seward. David Donald concludes:

> Lincoln left no record of how he felt about this extraordinary document ... recognizing how sharp his reply was, he probably did not send it. He kept the only known copy in his files and most likely discussed the memorandum with Seward, managing to combat its arguments without hurting the Secretary's feelings.[9]

Unlike Lincoln, who tended to make decisions alone, Seward's style was to seek consensus. He reviewed his thoughts with both Thurlow Weed and Henry Jarvis Raymond seeking their support, he almost always tried to enlist others to second his "doings." Weed was in Washington during the last few days of March so Seward interacted with him regularly. Raymond, summoned to Washington for a midnight meeting at Seward's home to discuss the thoughts, wrote a blistering editorial in his *New York Times* on April 3 supporting Seward, and attacking a "do-nothing government." He went on to urge embracement of the hands-off policy so to disarm "the fears of War which now unite, by outward pressure, the Southern people," and make it possible "to organize a Union Party in every Southern State." The next day Weed, in his *Albany Evening Journal*, warned Lincoln not to use force to challenge the secessionists and pleaded for "reconciliation."[10] Lincoln was extremely sensitive to negative press: "Mary Lincoln recalled newspaper assaults gave her husband 'great pain.'" In fact he would seek revenge on Raymond for this editorial putting out the word that the editor of "that" paper would never receive a position in his administration.[11]

At the same time he was coordinating support for his thoughts, Seward was working with his New York friends to delay (or scuttle) the Sumter expedition. Gustavus Fox had been sent to New York Harbor to see the famous ship owner and financier William H. Aspinwall to lease one of his ships for the expedition. He also had to procure provisions (through Navy channels) and to arrange for a government loan to pay for the expedition (as the government was broke). Aspinwall balked at the idea of resupplying Sumter and so informed Lincoln. "Fox was sure that Aspinwall's hesitancy about the project and Marshall's opposition to it were 'all political' in motivation. 'Capt. Marshall has been to Washington for two weeks and wishes to know if Mr.

Seward goes for it.' Seward's influence again!"[12] Montgomery Blair, on receiving this news from Fox, immediately went to the White House to protest Seward's supposed meddling. Lincoln told Blair to push ahead with all speed and to order Fox back to Washington for consultations. Once again, it is important to note William Aspinwall and Capt. Marshall were most interested in Henry Seward's opinion, caring little for the Lincoln-approved proposal.

Meanwhile, confusion reigned at the White House. A message from Major Anderson had just arrived where he stated his supplies would only last another week and he pointedly asked when the order to evacuate the fort would arrive. A few days earlier Lamon had told Anderson that the president would shortly direct the abandonment of the fort, Anderson believed him, and he was now extremely anxious to comply. The president, suffering acute anxiety of his own, waited impatiently to hear news of the successful reinforcement of Fort Pickens. General Scott (and Henry Seward) knew Pickens could be successfully reinforced because of its location (relief ships could reach it by sea and be out of range of shore batteries), but somehow failed to convince the president. Because the cabinet was so new and incapable of working together (Chase hated Seward, Seward disrespected Welles, Blair disliked everybody) and the White House was not yet functioning well, miscommunication, misinformation, even deceptions abounded.[13]

Seward, though, kept moving forward (forward at least in his mind) by sending a telegram to George Summers at the Virginia State Convention, urging him to come to Washington immediately. Of course, in the telegram he could not tell Summers that the president had reversed course and now intended to resupply Sumter. The subject was not only too sensitive to put in writing, but in 1861 there was no way to send a secure (confidential) message via telegraph. But Seward desperately needed Summers in Washington to help him persuade Lincoln to change his mind on Sumter.

As if Seward had not enough to occupy his time, April 1 also found him at the White House with Capt. M. C. Meigs and Lt. David D. Porter of the Navy to present their secret plan to reinforce Fort Pickens. Seward had convinced Lincoln that many questionably loyal employees were still at their jobs in the Navy Department, so the Pickens plan would need to be kept secret — even from Gideon Welles, secretary of the Navy and Simon Cameron, secretary of war. Lincoln not only approved the secret plan (including keeping it from Welles and Cameron), but signed the orders on the spot. He had come to rely on Seward: often when Fred Seward brought him papers for signature, he would quip, "Your father says this is all right, does he? Well, I guess he knows. Where do I put my name?"[14] The secret orders included making the warship *Powhatan* part of the Pickens expedition, the same ship Gideon Welles had designated "flagship" of the Sumter expedition.

By April 3 Seward and Lincoln were both desperate to confer with the Virginians. Seward asked his able assistant, Robert S. Chew, to recommend someone who could be entrusted to take a secret message to George Summers in Richmond. Chew recommended Allan B. Magruder (a Washington lawyer and native Virginian who was closely aligned with upper South Unionists), and brought him to see Seward. After interviewing Magruder and determining his acceptability for the job, Seward took Magruder to see the president. Lincoln asked Magruder to go to Richmond and bring Summers immediately to Washington to consult about a matter "of the highest importance." Lincoln told Magruder: "Tell Mr. Summers, I want to see him at once, for there is no time to be lost; what is to be done must be done quickly.... If Mr. Summers cannot come himself, let him send some friend of his, some Union man in whom he has confidence."[15]

The cabinet met most of the morning of April 3 to continue the hand-wringing discussions about Sumter, and Lincoln continued to promote his aggressive policy. Seward had one ace left; that is, have the Virginians vote against secession (thus keeping Virginia in the Union) in exchange for the abandonment of Sumter. Both Seward and Lincoln had discussed this "state for a fort" proposal and, indeed, Lincoln had discussed it with two delegations of Southern Unionists in February. If the Virginians would defeat a secession ordinance, Seward felt Lincoln might still reverse his course on Sumter — "the fort" — for he would then have secured "the state." Time was running out to save the nation from civil war.

Magruder left on the next train for Richmond and arrived late in the evening of April 3. He met at once with Summers, who said he could not go to Washington because he had to manage the effort to defeat a secession ordinance that, coincidentally, had been pushed on the convention by hard-line secessionists who thought they had enough support to pass it. Summers hurriedly consulted with members of the Unionist leadership of the convention and, still not knowing what was up, they prevailed upon Col. John B. Baldwin, a distinguished lawyer, former state legislator, and hard-core Unionist, to represent them before the president. Summers had great confidence in Baldwin, knowing they were of the same cloth. So Magruder, with Baldwin in hand, left Richmond late in the evening and they were both in Seward's office on the morning of April 4. Seward stressed the urgency of the meeting to Baldwin and immediately took him to see the president. This would be the meeting at which Lincoln was again to propose a fort for a state or, as he said, "a state for a fort is no bad business."

The secret meeting between President Lincoln and Colonel Baldwin took place at 11 A.M. on April 4 in a bedroom at the White House. No staff member was present to record the discussion and nothing in writing was conveyed to Baldwin — no offer, no proposal, no letter, nothing — so it is impossible to reconstruct with any certainty what truly happened. However, nothing came of the meeting, and Baldwin left greatly disappointed, even somewhat confused about why he had been summoned. After the war, a great controversy arose about this affair; that is to say, whether Lincoln actually made a formal offer to Baldwin, the "state for a fort." It will never be known, but we do know Lincoln met that very afternoon with Gustavus Fox to approve the final plan to resupply Sumter. So whether or not the president had any intention of offering a fort for a state, he certainly moved down a path to do otherwise.

Lincoln's new path now decidedly risked war — but was the nation prepared to go to war? Lincoln had asked General Scott for daily reports regarding military preparedness and manpower and Scott began sending them in early April.

> This memorandum [Scott's daily report] was supplemented two days later (April 5) by a detailed report from the Adjutant-General to the President, which showed the full strength of the army of the United States and its distribution to be as follows: Department of the East, 3894; Department of the West, 3584; Department of Texas, 2258, Department of New Mexico, 2624, Department of Utah, 685; Department of the Pacific, 3382; miscellaneous, 686; grand total, officers and men, 17,113.[16]

Clearly, the United States government was not prepared to start a war in April 1861.

For Seward's part, he continued to arrange for Virginia Unionists to meet with the president in his last-ditch efforts to avert war. Weed ends a cryptic message to Seward on April 5: "There is a war stir and cry here today. If there is to be an earnest movement let 'Fred' say 'Yes' in a Telegraph to Blatchford to-morrow morning."[17] Some in the North were beginning to swing again toward taking a tough stand with the seceded states, partly because of exasperation at the "do nothing government," but the majority of Northerners likely still favored some form of compromise to avoid war at this point.

The first of Seward's last-ditch meetings occurred on Friday evening, April 5, with a delegation of Virginia Unionists led by Joseph Segar and John Minor Botts. Lincoln now knew of the vote at the Virginia State Convention, where secession had been defeated decisively. The Virginians presented a plan to Lincoln and the cabinet "by which the federal government would promise not to use military force in the South and the Confederate government would promise to seek no treaties with foreign powers. A national convention would then attempt to devise terms for reunion." But Lincoln refused to agree not to use military force in the South. This position so upset Segar, he predicted the nation was on the verge of war when he returned to the Virginia State Convention the next day.[18] The cabinet had had a very tense meeting that morning to review Sumter. Lincoln was described as "ill at ease, and not self possessed."[19] Seward, his anxiety heightened to the extreme, continued to push on.

The second last-ditch meeting took place on Sunday evening, April 7, when Botts, an unconditional Unionist and former congressman, had a one-on-one meeting with Lincoln. He urged withdrawal from Sumter as a "necessary condition" to keep Virginia from seceding. It was in this private meeting that Botts claimed Lincoln told him he had offered the fort-for-a-state proposal to Baldwin. After the war (and after Lincoln's tragic death), Botts and Baldwin were summoned before a congressional committee, the Joint Committee on Reconstruction (the committee of the Congress controlled by radical Republicans). The committee was trying to determine if Lincoln had offered such a proposal, and if so, why the Virginians had not accepted it — they wanted to punish Virginia Unionists who had joined the Confederacy for not accepting the proposal. Both Botts (who had not joined the Confederacy) and Baldwin (who had) testified under oath as to whether Lincoln offered the fort-for-a-state proposal. Botts claimed he did; Baldwin claimed he did not. The controversy has remained unresolved to this very day.[20]

After the war Baldwin would remark that his meeting with Lincoln was "the most significant event in his life"; indeed, most Americans would say the same about a one-on-one interview with the president of the United States. Also after the war, Allan B. Magruder, who had brought Baldwin to Washington, recorded his conversation with him immediately after the Lincoln interview, and his notes support Baldwin's view that no fort-for-a-state offer had been made. Seward surely thought an offer should have been made, and in his interview with Baldwin immediately after the meeting he found Baldwin confused.[21]

Why Abraham Lincoln, widely regarded as one of the most accomplished writers ever to assume the presidency, did not put a proposal in writing for the Virginians to consider, or at least have Seward, another accomplished writer, do it, is subject to conjecture. Nothing in writing was ever given to any Unionist of such an offer, either to Baldwin or Botts or Summers or whomever, nor was any follow-up message from any official of the administration ever made to anyone at the Virginia State Convention about the matter. Intriguingly however, the president did put his thoughts in writing a few days later, when he next met with Virginia Unionists.

It must be noted, again, the Virginians did deliver "the state" part of the equation as they voted against a secession ordinance by the lopsided margin of 89 to 45. They committed themselves to the Union based on the strength of Henry Seward's assurances that the forts would be evacuated. Seward received confirmation of the vote the morning of April 5, and he knew (and so must have Lincoln) the Virginians were planning to recess their State Convention as soon as preparations for the upcoming statewide elections were complete. But Lincoln, who evidently had decided to resupply Sumter, could not respond with "the fort" part of the equation. Richard Current observes,

> [I]n after years most Lincoln biographers and most Northern historians accepted and elaborated upon his [Lincoln's] own retrospective version of his [Sumter] policy.... On reexamination, however, Lincoln's version of the Virginia matter appears to be questionable ... to say nothing of the interpretations which Lincoln-defending historians have put upon his own defense.[22]

Henry Seward, despite his extraordinary statesmanship and his incredible efforts to find a solution to the national crisis, was about to lose the game as the "state for a fort is no bad business" solution drifted away. Surely Seward was as perplexed as anyone in the nation. Current deserves the last word: "For all the endless argument, nobody really knows what Lincoln intended or expected when he made up his mind to let that fateful expedition go."[23]

⁎

A digression from the daily narration of events to review again South Unionists and Henry Seward at this critical moment. Upper South Unionists were firmly in control of the border states, as noted above, Virginia had voted two to one against secession, Maryland was following Virginia's lead in lockstep, North Carolinians had voted against even calling a convention to consider secession, Tennessee had swung almost entirely against the secessionists, and Kentucky (in spite of having a prosecession governor) was closely aligned with Tennessee. Almost all leading contemporaries of Seward agreed, without these five upper South States, the Confederacy had little chance of success. Seward, as noted, had made it his driving principle to save the border and save the nation.

Over the secession winter upper South Unionists (many former Whigs like himself) responded to Seward in droves, not only because they viewed him as the ablest Northern statesmen, but because they truly believed he would call the shots in the new administration. And Seward himself was confident he would do so. When he, early and often, promoted the peaceful intentions of the incoming president, most people believed him without question — and most people in the North supported him. Some historians argue that a peaceful solution was merely wishful thinking on Seward's part, but these political moderates did not think so.

And contemporary evidence supports the moderate's view. "Local and state elections in late March and early April gave more ammunition to Republicans who warned of the threat to the party. Around the North anti–Republicans either won or gained considerable support...they trumpeted their success as a sign 'that a formidable reaction has commenced in the North' against Republican belligerence."[24] Southern Unionists' interactions with Northern moderates in Congress confirmed the rising support for compromise, and their interactions with the Washington social set constantly confirmed Seward's status as the leader of the new administration. It is vitally important to remember that very few of these Southern Unionists knew Abraham Lincoln — they had never seen him, they had never heard him speak, they had never interacted with him in any way. And it is vitally important to remember also, in this era, face-to-face meetings were *the* primary way to resolve issues.

All winter long, Henry Seward had promoted a studied, steady, and calm approach to resolving the national crisis, and throughout the tumultuous month of March he seemed to be in charge. As April began, Southern Unionists did not see, could not see, Lincoln's sudden change in attitude toward the South. They firmly believed "that peacekeeping and reunion would be a protracted process" so they began to plan for the Border State Conference, where representatives from all upper South states would convene in Kentucky to devise a Union-saving compromise. The Virginia State Convention was due to adjourn by mid–April and reconvene in the fall. The Border State Conference was scheduled after the Virginia state elections in May because Unionists expected to capture control of the state legislature. They were busily consolidating their enormous gains in the convention delegate election and were extremely confident they would "bury" the secessionists in the upcoming state election.[25] George Summers, it was widely rumored, would be appointed U.S. senator by the new legislature, and having a moderate Southerner in the Senate from the key state of Virginia would be a great boon for upper South Unionists, and for Henry Seward as well.

Throughout the upper South, secession had been decisively defeated and Unionists were eagerly anticipating strengthening their new Union Party in upcoming elections scheduled over the coming summer. Then the process to build the party into a regional and national force could begin as the process to end secession was completed. The only thing that could defeat them was a military confrontation between Washington and Montgomery. Almost all leading men in the border, whether Unionists or secessionists, saw this fact clearly. So it was with this in mind that so many Unionists from Virginia and the upper South responded to Seward's call and made the extraordinary effort to come to Washington to plead with Abraham Lincoln for continuation of a conciliatory policy. As rumors of military preparation surfaced all sought to counsel Lincoln on the wisdom of a peaceful policy toward the South. No greater effort has ever been made in the history of this nation to persuade a chief executive on a particular political policy.

***

After meeting with John Baldwin, Lincoln met with Gustavus Fox on the evening of April 4 and approved the final plans to resupply Fort Sumter. He drafted a letter, for Secretary of War Simon Cameron's signature, to Major Anderson saying that the fort would be resupplied, asking him to hold out until the relief fleet arrived if he was able to do so. Seward met with Baldwin after his meeting with Lincoln and sought mightily to persuade Baldwin of the administration's peaceful intentions, before Baldwin left on his return trip to Richmond. But Seward knew he was running out of time, and "this sudden turn of events pointed directly toward war." Unbelievably, "it jeopardized the period of delay for which [Seward] had played so skillfully, and it threatened to nullify all his efforts."[26] What else could he do to keep the peace?

Seward had received the welcome news that the Virginia State Convention defeated an ordinance of secession on the morning of April 5. He now made a series of desperate, final efforts to avert war. As previously mentioned, Seward and Winfield Scott had taken charge of the Pickens expedition (which became an "Army affair"), and left the Sumter expedition to Gideon Welles and Montgomery Blair (which became a "Navy affair"). Seward, so familiar with inter service rivalry, now sought to have the Pickens (Army) effort succeed at all costs, even at the expense of the Sumter (Navy) effort. It was a "frantic rear-guard action" where Seward "in every way possible" sought "to shift Federal action from Fort Sumter to Fort Pickens." Seward had shown little interest in Fort Pickens before the evacuation of Sumter had been overturned, but now he strove with all his skill to "divert the action to the Florida fort."[27]

Seward, General Scott, and a few others knew Sumter had little military value.[28] Resupply of Sumter was, as Seward suggested in his April 1 memorandum, a political issue primarily and one pushed on Lincoln by the outspoken, hard-line Republicans who viewed Charleston as the heart of secessionism, felt the South Carolinians needed to be punished, and needed it done to confirm their "clout" within the new administration. Public opinion changed so often it is impossible to know whether most Republicans favored resupplying Sumter in early April, but thousands had signed petitions to Congress supporting compromise. Democrats in the North, however, remained opposed for the most part.

> After listening, as a banker's dinner guest in New York, to the conversation of three of them — the prominent lawyer Samuel J. Tilden, the former (and future) governor Horatio Seymour, and the historian-publicist George Bancroft — the ubiquitous English newsman Russell concluded that "the Government could not employ force to prevent secession." These men could not bring themselves to allow their old opponents, the Republicans now in power, to dispose of the armed forces of the Union against their brother Democrats in the Southern States.[29]

Seward, ever the confident politician, felt public opinion could be managed and that the majority in the North did not favor risking war, so he and Scott concentrated real effort on trying to substitute Pickens for Sumter.

The story now gets quite convoluted. As noted above, Seward had had Lincoln sign secret orders for the Pickens expedition that included making the *Powhatan,* the largest and most imposing warship in the Navy's fleet, part of the Pickens expedition. The secretary of the Navy and the secretary of war were not informed of the Pickens expedition because Seward had convinced Lincoln of the need for complete secrecy. Lincoln did not realize the *Powhatan* was included in the Pickens order. Seward may have calculated if he could truly cripple the Sumter expedition by removing its key ship, perhaps the experienced Navy men around Welles would convince him to postpone it. In any event, late on the evening of April 5, Seward was forced to see Welles because of conflicting telegrams received from the men preparing the convoys in New York Harbor. They had become totally confused as to what to do given that two expeditions seemed to be under way — and neither group understood what the other was doing. Seward now had to inform Welles the *Powhatan* would not support the Sumter expedition. Welles, who had just ordered the *Powhatan* to support the Sumter expedition, was incredulous and demanded to know why. Seward then told Welles about the Pickens expedition, and Welles exploded in a fit of rage (and rightly so). Seward could not calm him, and Welles insisted they go to the White House to discuss the matter with the president, which they did. Commodore Silas Stringham accompanied them, and they arrived just before midnight. Lincoln, who was about to go to bed, was shaken by the "mad scene." He sided with Welles and ordered the *Powhatan* reassigned to the Pickens expedition, despite Seward's strenuous objections.

But ordering something done and having it carried out were often miles apart in nineteenth-century Washington (twenty-first century too). Seward, with great reluctance, sent a dispatch early on April 6 to Lt. David D. Porter (soon to be made admiral), who commanded the *Powhatan,* stating the president wished the ship to return to New York Harbor to be made part of the Sumter expedition — he signed it "Seward." Porter (who had just sailed the *Powhatan* out of the harbor) then reviewed his original orders, signed by Lincoln, which made him part of the Pickens expedition; he concluded that an order signed by the secretary of state could not supersede one signed by the president. He continued on to Fort Pickens and wired back to Seward: "I received my orders from the President and shall proceed and execute them."[30]

How far Seward went beyond prudent behavior "to checkmate" the Sumter expedition is conjecture. Glyndon Van Deusen, the ablest of Seward's biographers, felt he pushed the envelope pretty far, but was not imprudent. Another example of Seward's behavior at this chaotic time was his interactions with James E. Harvey, Washington correspondent for the *Philadelphia North American and United States Gazette* and *New York Tribune*. Harvey, while not an admirer of Seward, had been drawn to Seward because of his Southern policy, which he fervently supported. In fact, "Harvey was lobbying openly for Seward's time-buying palliative ... and giving sympathetic coverage to a Seward-inspired plan to appoint non–Republican southern Unionists to Lincoln's Cabinet." Now Seward (along with Secretary of War Simon Cameron), as part of their desperate effort to sidetrack the Sumter expedition, began sending information to Harvey about the mission to resupply Sumter. Harvey, in turn, began sending it to Charleston. The most controversial of his telegrams was one on the morning of April 6: "Positively determined not to withdraw Anderson. Supplies go immediately, supported by a naval force under Stringham, if their landing be resisted."[31]

For Seward to have given Harvey confidential information about the Sumter expedition was certainly indiscreet; some would argue worse. And again Van Deusen gave Seward the benefit of the doubt.[32] But Gideon Welles certainly did not give Seward the benefit of the doubt. In fact, he bitterly accused Seward of trying to prevent the resupply of Sumter — and said Seward was well aware the *Powhatan* was to be the flagship of the Sumter expedition. The Navy Department did have its share of Southern sympathizers, so at least part of Seward's secrecy was justified; had he informed Welles of the Pickens expedition, it could have been leaked to the Confederates by Southern sympathizers still at work in the department. But Seward's views on Sumter were crystal clear and no one in the cabinet misunderstood his unequivocal opposition.

In another desperate move on April 6 that dovetails with the leaked information to Harvey, Seward met with Lincoln to discuss making the Sumter expedition public. Several cabinet members had suggested this at the March 29 meeting, including Welles. The thrust of the proposal was to avoid having the Administration appear to be the belligerent in the event fighting broke out. Seward had given his word to the Confederate commissioners that no resupply effort to Sumter would be attempted without prior notification and he wanted to avoid provoking the Confederates at all costs. He even may have hoped public disclosure would produce a negative reaction in the North where public opinion seemed to be moving in favor of letting the lower South go in peace. Lincoln, who had been leaning in favor of making a public statement, then approved notifying Governor Pickens. Seward immediately dispatched Robert S. Chew to deliver the message. Chew left Washington for Charleston on this Saturday, April 6, as G. V. Fox in New York worked feverishly to get the Sumter expedition under way. Ominously, on the afternoon of April 6, Lincoln met with the governors of Indiana, Ohio, Maine, and Pennsylvania, instructing them to prepare their state militias for possible action.

Sunday, April 7, found Navy lieutenant John L. Worden dispatched to Fort Pickens with explicit orders for the Navy commander there to land the troops on his ships at Pickens. After consulting with Seward in the morning, John Minor Botts had his one-on-one meeting with the president after dinner. He pleaded for abandonment of Sumter, but Lincoln said it was too late. Seward was walking a tightrope with the Confederate commissioners as they were seeking an explanation about reports of war preparations going on in New York Harbor. Attempting to reassure them of the administration's peaceful policies, he sent this soon-to-be-famous cryptic message through his emissary Justice Campbell: "Faith as to Sumter fully kept; wait and see."[33]

Monday, April 8, began the second week of April 1861—it would prove the most fateful week in the nation's storied existence. Robert Chew arrived in Charleston and read Lincoln's message to the governor saying that Sumter would be resupplied but not reinforced. Governor Pickens notified General Beauregard, who immediately placed all Confederate forces on full alert. In Washington, the Confederate commissioners, unsatisfied with Seward's promises and now in receipt of confirmed reports of war preparation in New York Harbor, demanded a reply to their request for recognition of the Confederate States of America. Seward's reply, drafted weeks earlier, was sent immediately—unsigned. It flatly rejected their demand. So Seward's "negotiations" with the Confederates finally broke down. Had Seward been deceitful or manipulative? David Potter concluded; "But, at a heavy cost to his personal credit, Seward had prevented for four full weeks the precipitation of a diplomatic crisis which might have had immediate military repercussions."[34] Henry Seward, almost single-handedly, had kept the nation from war.

In New York Harbor, the revenue cutter *Harriet Lane*, loaded with supplies, departed for Fort Sumter. At the Virginia State Convention in Richmond, alarmed by the reports of military preparations in the North, a group of conditional Unionists, led by former congressman William B. Preston, succeeded in passing a motion to send yet another delegation to Lincoln to urge him not to abandon his conciliatory policy toward the South and risk war by resupplying Fort Sumter. The delegation consisted of Preston, George W. Randolph (a secessionist), and Alexander H. H. "Sandy" Stuart (a staunch Unionist and brother-in-law to John Baldwin). At Washington another ominous development was taking place on this day. General Scott called for militia to defend Washington itself as rumors had surfaced that Maryland and Virginia secessionists might attempt to seize the capital. Lincoln, after holding a secret meeting with Pennsylvania governor Andrew G. Curtin about calling up his state militia, sent him a wire: "I think the necessity of being ready increases. Look to it."[35]

On Tuesday morning April 9, the rented steamer *Baltic*, with "commander" Gustavus Fox onboard, set sail from New York Harbor for

Charleston. Lincoln spent most of the day in interviews with political office-seekers and approved a host of minor political appointments. On Wednesday April 10, the warship *Pawnee* left Hampton Roads for Fort Sumter. A terrific storm raged off Cape Hatteras. Significantly, on this day General Beauregard in Charleston Harbor received a telegram from Confederate secretary of war Leroy Walker, instructing him in the event of an attempt to resupply Sumter to demand the evacuation of the fort at once. If the garrison refused, Beauregard was instructed to "proceed, in such manner as you may determine, to reduce it."[36] Heavy rains had drenched Richmond and central Virginia (the same storm that was now off Hatteras), washing out rail service to Washington and delaying the Preston delegation's departure from Richmond. Telegraphic and newspaper reports continued to circulate in Richmond (and throughout the nation) describing war preparations in New York Harbor.

But upper South Unionists remained firm in their conviction that the administration would honor Seward's commitment to pursue a conciliatory policy and refused, at first, "to believe that Lincoln had reneged on the promises of peace and a withdrawal from Sumter."[37] Many in the North who favored conciliation were concerned as well fearing "a clash at Sumter might unite the South and divide the North." It was critically important for Lincoln, in their view, to justify his position relative to resupplying the fort. Lincoln issued orders barring newsmen from all government departments while at the same time permitting the leak of information about the peaceful provisioning of Sumter. In the end, Lincoln's "peaceful provisioning" was cast in the right light by leading Republican papers. Both the *New York Tribune* and the *New York Times* ran stories announcing "positively, and as if by authority" a resupply mission was on its way to Charleston. They then cast the story as Lincoln had hoped: "If rebels fire at an unarmed supply ship, and make a perfectly proper act the pretext for shredding blood of loyal citizens, on their heads be the responsibility."[38] Somehow the editors had forgotten the *Star of the West* incident in January.

On the other hand, Democratic newspapers of the North did not cast Lincoln's plan "in the right light." In fact, they leveled blistering editorials about his April policy. Bennett's *New York Herald*, the hugely influential daily, in its editorial on April 10 trumpeted: "Our only hope now against civil war of an indefinite duration seems to lie in the over-throw of the demoralizing, disorganizing, and destructive Republican sectional party, of which 'Honest Abe Lincoln' is the pliant instrument."[39] Strong words indeed, and as the resupply effort to Sumter began, Democrats of the North clearly could not be counted on to support it.

The beginning of the end for Henry Seward's long and arduous efforts to find peace would occur late morning on Thursday, April 11, in Charleston Harbor. A small boat, under white flag, left the dock and proceeded to Fort

Sumter. Three Confederate representatives were on board — Col. James Chestnut, the recently resigned senator from South Carolina; Capt. Stephen D. Lee, West Point graduate and recently resigned from the U.S. Army; and Lt. Col. A. R. Chisolm, representative of Gov. Francis W. Pickens. Jefferson Davis and his advisors had caved in to the hotheads from South Carolina and ordered Sumter attacked before the resupply mission could arrive. Former Georgia senator Robert Toombs, now secretary of state of the Confederacy and an experienced Washington insider, strenuously objected to attacking Sumter. "You will wantonly strike a hornet's nest.... Legions, now quiet, will swarm out and sting us to death. It is unnecessary; it puts us in the wrong; it is fatal."[40] Toombs, indeed, would prove prescient.

The Confederate emissaries arrived at Fort Sumter in the early afternoon and delivered a message from General Beauregard to Major Anderson that ended with "I am ordered by the Government of the Confederate States to demand the evacuation of Fort Sumter." Anderson conferred with his officers and then informed the Confederates he would not evacuate. As the Confederates were departing, however, he mentioned he would be "starved out" in a few days. When this was reported to Beauregard, he decided to wire Secretary Walker for further instructions. Walker replied that if Anderson would state an immediate date and time for evacuation and not use his guns on Charleston, then Beauregard was authorized to accept the terms and not fire on the fort. So at 11 o'clock that night, the three Confederates returned to Sumter to ask Anderson for a specific date and time for his evacuation. Anderson replied he would evacuate at noon on April 15. All knew the resupply effort from New York was on the way and due to arrive before that time so the Confederates could not accept Anderson's proposal, they required a rapid evacuation. They told Anderson his response was unsatisfactory and said that the guns in Charleston Harbor would open fire in one hour's time. They did, at 4:30 A.M. on Friday, April 12, 1861. The grandsons of those who had fought in the American Revolution began firing cannons at one another.

But April 12 would produce good news for Washington too. Lieutenant Worden had arrived in Pensacola and persuaded the Confederate commander, Gen. Braxton Bragg, to let him visit Fort Pickens. Once there, he informed the naval commander he brought special orders from the president, the commander immediately obeyed and disembarked troops from his ships. Fort Pickens was reinforced successfully because, as mentioned, the Confederates had no way to prevent reinforcements from reaching the fort by sea. Lieutenant Worden would be arrested by Confederate authorities on his return to Washington.

In Washington and other cities and towns across the nation, rumors and a few telegraphic wires reported on "action" at Fort Sumter. Leaders of upper South Unionists, such as John Gilmer, reached out to Seward, seeking an

explanation or hoping to get more satisfactory news. "I am so deeply distressed that my heart seems to melt within me," Gilmer wrote to Seward on
April 12. He went on to say, "I cannot but still believe that the course I suggested would have been wise, and the results, had it been pursued, most
beneficial.... If what I hear is true that we are to have fighting at Sumter or
Pickens, it is what the disunionists have most courted, and I seriously appre-
hend that it will instantly drive the whole South into secession."[41]

Other upper South Unionists were still optimistic however and felt the
trouble at Sumter could be handled if it was contained there; that is, no further escalation of hostilities. On Saturday afternoon, April 13, amid reports
of fighting at Sumter, Seward, who would not give up on peace, arranged for
the Preston delegation from Virginia to see the president. As the heavy rains
had delayed their departure from Richmond, they had taken a boat to Baltimore, then a train to Washington. Lincoln now took a decidedly tough stance
and told the Unionists if fighting occurred at Sumter (as was reported), he
would "repel force with force." As previously mentioned, while he chose not
to give anything in writing to John Baldwin or John Minor Botts the previous week when peace was on the line; he now chose to read this delegation
of Unionists a tough statement when war was on the line. As predicted by
Gilmer, the phrase, "repel force with force" was very bad news for Unionists
and very good news for secessionists.

As Lincoln was meeting with the Preston delegation in Washington, the
surrender of Fort Sumter was occurring in Charleston, at about 2:30 in the
afternoon. Out of ammunition and food, Anderson had few choices left.
Incredibly, no one had been killed in the thirty-four-hour bombardment,
with only a few minor injuries to the men at the fort. No one in Charleston
Harbor had been seriously injured either, although one Confederate horse
died (probably from fright). Gustavus Fox and his resupply "fleet" had arrived
off Charleston, badly battered by the terrible storm during their trip south,
and watched helplessly offshore as the bombardment took place. Debate has
continued whether Lincoln sought to induce the South to fire the first shot.
Lincoln would comment to Fox a few weeks later: "You and I both anticipated that the cause of the country would be advanced by making the attempt
to provision Fort Sumter, even if it should fail; and it is no small consolation
now to feel that our anticipation is justified by the result."[42] Seward received
the reports on Sumter with true disgust. He wrote Anson Burlingame on this
fateful day: "It will be deeply regretted if the energy of this great Government
is to have its first serious trial in a civil war instead of one against a foreign
foe."[43] With the country now poised for war, Henry Seward was inconsolable.

On Sunday, April 14, Major Anderson conducted the formal surrender
ceremony, lowering the U.S. flag at Fort Sumter to a one-hundred-gun salute.
Hundreds of Charlestonians had come in small boats (some large ones, too)

to witness the ceremony. In one of those ironic moments, as the guns were fired in salute a pile of cartridges accidentally exploded, killing two federal soldiers and wounding several others, the ceremony ended prematurely. Although telegraphic reports about Sumter had reached Washington on the thirteenth, Sunday brought official news of the surrender to both Montgomery and Washington. Jefferson Davis met with his cabinet and expressed thankfulness no blood had been shed and stated that separation was not yet final. Abraham Lincoln met with his cabinet in a long night session. After much debate, they approved his call for 75,000 troops and his call for a special session of Congress to convene on July 4.[44]

Whether intentional or not, the resupply effort had induced the firing at Fort Sumter and the nation was headed toward war. Current's argument is persuasive:

> [T]he evidence on the whole makes it hard to believe that Lincoln could have counted on a peaceful provisioning of Fort Sumter. He knew well what had happened to Buchanan's attempt to send supplies in a lone, unarmed merchant steamer, the *Star of the West*. He had little reason to expect a more friendly welcome for his own much larger expedition, which included warships.[45]

Of particular importance, Stephen Douglas conferred with the president and promised his support in maintaining the Union, thereby bringing the Democratic opposition to support the president at a truly critical moment. Lincoln's Sumter plan had worked. "The flag having been fired upon, men were eager to heed the President's call for troops, and women eager to see their sons, husbands, or sweethearts go save the country. These enthusiasts included Democrats as well as Republicans, for suddenly the issue had become one of patriotism, not partisanship."[46] Strangely, although no one could realize what was to come or that a civil war had actually begun, celebrations broke out all over the North ... and the South. As the distinguished Civil War historian Bruce Catton observed, "The grim awakening would come later."

Upper South Unionists were in a state of unparalleled anxiety, but they had not given up all hope. Many reasoned that if the federal government's provocative efforts could be held in check, they could still maintain their majority support in the upper South and a proposal to resolve the crisis could still be arranged. In Virginia many Unionists stood firm, although they realized the action at Sumter had weakened their position. William C. Rives said it was "more incumbent than ever for Virginia and the other border slave states to maintain their mediatorial position." They planned to move ahead with their May conference feeling they could lay the foundation for restoring the Union.[47] Southern Unionism was still very strong and these seasoned political leaders were not about to give up their allegiance to the Union, even after the bombardment at Sumter.

The scene would change dramatically on Monday, April 15, 1861, when President Lincoln stunned the nation, both the North and the South, by issuing his Proclamation of Insurrection. It called for 75,000 troops to put down the rebellion and called Congress into special session on July 4. The precise language of the call for troops is as follows:

> Now, therefore, I, Abraham Lincoln, President of the United States, in virtue of the power in me vested by the Constitution, and the laws, have thought fit to call forth, and hereby do call forth, the militia of the several States of the Union, to the aggregate number of seventy-five thousand, in order to suppress said combinations, and to cause the laws to be duly executed. The details, for this object, will be immediately communicated to the State authorities through the War Department.[48]

Americans were being summoned to fight Americans. Abraham Lincoln was prepared to go to war as he "could scarcely contain his anger at the Southern firebrands."[49] For Henry Seward, April 15 would prove a terribly sad and disheartening day. But what would come next?

***

Monday morning found Richmond in a state of frenzied excitement (or, some argue, confusion). The two leading prosecession newspapers, the *Richmond Enquirer* and the *Richmond Examiner,* proclaimed war had begun in headlines citing Lincoln's Proclamation. Prosecession mobs danced in the streets. Unionist leaders in the convention did not know what to believe. The *Enquirer* and *Examiner,* strongly biased toward secession, could not be trusted. At first, many leading Unionists simply did not believe the news. The reaction of "Sandy" Stuart, who had just returned the previous evening from his meeting with Lincoln in Washington, was typical:

> Stuart, who had received from Seward what he considered satisfactory reassurances about the administration's peaceful purposes, first read the proclamation at breakfast... He "did not for a moment believe that it was authentic," nor could he believe Lincoln "guilty of such duplicity." Stuart therefore telegraphed Seward to ask whether it was a "fabrication."[50]

Other Unionists reacted similarly to Stuart. Jubal Early, the staunch Unionist who would become the legendary Confederate general, "contended that it could not be authenticated until printed in a newspaper Unionists trusted.... He hoped that a 'statesman' as able as Seward could not have been 'guilty of the blunders which appear in that proclamation.'"[51] In spite of the frenzy around them, Unionist leaders in the State Convention still held such sway that the convention was adjourned shortly after noon on April 15 to await authentication of the proclamation. Throughout the upper South reaction was the same — disbelief, shock, great concern. If the proclamation proved authentic, those who had bought the Seward line would feel betrayed by what they now would consider a broken promise of the highest order.

In Washington Henry Seward felt betrayed, too. At the long cabinet meeting on the evening of April 14, Seward faced the horns of his dilemma for the last time. Lincoln would ask all for comments on his draft Proclamation of Insurrection, a declaration of war on the South. Despite promoting a conciliatory policy throughout the secession winter, which had rallied the nation and kept the country from war; despite the scores of political maneuvers he had pulled (some major, some minor); despite representing the opinion of a clear majority of Northerners; despite promoting a new Union Party in the upper South, with all its intriguing possibilities; despite threatening to resign from the cabinet and succeeding in his bluff with Lincoln; despite his famous memorandum of April 1; despite all that he had done, the nation's leading Republican now suffered total defeat. Seward had little choice but to accept the proclamation or resign — and this time a resignation could be no bluff.

Lincoln, for reasons that are still debated, had suddenly moved away from support for Seward's Southern policy and the prospect of peace it portended, and adopted the confrontational stance of the radical Republicans that invited war. Avery Craven observed:

> Whether these acts were part of a well-worked-out policy of accepting what seemed to be an irrepressible conflict, and cleverly throwing the responsibility for beginning the war onto the South for psychological advantage, or whether they were the result of blundering along with the sweep of events, we cannot say with complete assurance. We do know that, with Lincoln's assumption of control, a firmer, uncompromising temper marked the policy of the Federal government.[52]

Seward, despite his reputation as the great persuader, had failed to convince Lincoln on conciliation, and as a result, the nation was off to war with itself.

On Tuesday, April 16, when the proclamation was authenticated, many upper South Unionists had come to the end of their rope. The majority of Southerners viewed the proclamation as a declaration of war on the South that must be resisted. In Richmond, the mood of the convention was captured by William T. Sutherlin of Pittsylvania County: "I have a Union constituency which elected me by a majority of one thousand, and I believe now that there are not ten Union men in that county to-day." John Baldwin, who would vote against secession, was left to mourn the "rapid" fever that had "seized" so many heretofore Union-loving colleagues.[53] But it was "Sandy" Stuart, the unrepentant Unionist, who delivered the most prescient comment on this fateful day. He rose to speak, begged the convention not to rush into secession, warned it would bring war to Virginia, and concluded, "Secession is not only war, but it is emancipation; it is bankruptcy; it is repudiation; it is widespread ruin to our people."[54] But in spite of the incredible pleas for restraint by firm Unionists, debate began immediately. Although unconditional Unionists from the western part of the state resisted to the end, a secession ordinance was approved on April 17 by 88 to 55, a lopsided vote similar to the vote that defeated it less than two weeks before.

***

As an intriguing aside, on this very day in Richmond a group of ardent secessionists of the Southern Rights Party, by invitation only, held a secret meeting at Metropolitan Hall, about two blocks from the Capitol. There is reasonable evidence to suggest they planned a coup d'etat to overthrow the duly elected government of Virginia. They planned to arrest Gov. John Letcher, the Unionist leaders of the Virginia State Convention, and then install a government of prosecession radicals led by former governor Henry A. Wise, who was the most prominent leader in the secret meeting. The secessionist meeting had been scheduled for April 16 weeks before as publicly announced in prosecession newspapers; little did the organizers know that Lincoln would issue a "call to arms" that would be authenticated on this very same day. If Lincoln's proclamation had not been issued, and if the radical Southern Rights Party had attempted to carry out its coup and declare Virginia seceded from the Union, then what?

John Minor Botts, intimately involved in the Virginia scene, said that Lincoln's proclamation "came just in the very nick of time to save the disorganizers the task of a revolutionary movement." Botts speculated that had the proclamation not been released, Lincoln "might have received a call from the executive of this state for the aid of the general government to sustain the lawful authorities of Virginia." Indeed, it is highly likely Governor Letcher, a firm Unionist, would have requested federal troops to fight the secessionists and to protect (or restore) the state government and the Virginia State Convention. Botts was convinced that had this occurred; nothing would have "driven Virginia or other Border States into a participation with the Cotton States."[55] Ironically, Col. Robert E. Lee most likely would have been the officer in command if federal troops were sent to Richmond to rescue Governor Letcher and the leaders of the Virginia State Convention.[56]

Did Abraham Lincoln or Henry Seward know about this planned coup? There is no record that Lincoln was ever briefed on the subject, nor is there any record of the cabinet discussing the matter. But Seward certainly knew what was going on. No one in the nation was more knowledgeable about events in Virginia than he. Crofts feels this way:

> But articles about the Southern Rights meeting and its possible subversive intent did appear in a number of newspapers, both in and out of Virginia, and Seward, at least, had received warning about "the secret circular of

Governor Wise and his clique." Might Seward or Botts have raised the subject during early April conversations with Lincoln? We do not know.[57]

But we do know that here was yet another chance occurrence that had major implications for secessionism. Had Lincoln's proclamation been delayed for just a day, events in Virginia may have turned out quite differently — and the Civil War averted.

***

What about the reaction of Union-loving men in the upper South to Lincoln's Proclamation of Insurrection? Tennessee and North Carolina were both firmly controlled by Unionists. As previously noted, unlike Virginia, both states had defeated proposals to call state conventions to consider secession. In both Nashville and Raleigh, Unionist newspapers dominated and set the tone for Union papers throughout their respective states. The Union Party was growing stronger day by day as former Whigs and antisecession Democrats were combining forces to create a party with heavy majorities in both states. In Tennessee "the February 9 election results in Nashville and throughout [the state] crippled the secession movement for the next two months." In North Carolina, the vote in February for delegates to a state convention resulted in "a crushing majority for candidates of the 'Constitutional Union Ticket,' a coalition of Democratic and Whig Unionists." Unionists paraded through Raleigh on that election night in an "immense procession" and sang "The Flag of Union" all along the way. Secessionists were distraught with the victory by people they called "submissionists."[58]

April 16 changed much of this support for the Union because of Abraham Lincoln's Proclamation of Insurrection. Had there been a formal declaration of war, the effect could not have been more instantaneous and widespread. The president had, indeed, declared an insurrection, which in practical effect, though not in legal theory, was virtually declaring the existence of a state of war; and amid the storm of indignation which shook both sections preparations for war were vigorously pursued.[59]

Loyal men who had pledged their support for the Union were stunned, and when the proclamation was confirmed, many switched their allegiance to the Southern Confederacy, albeit with grave misgivings. The staunch Unionist William Holden, editor of Raleigh's most influential newspaper, the *North Carolina Standard*, opined: "The proclamation of Mr. Lincoln, calling for troops to make war on the Southern States, dissolved the Union so far as we are concerned, and summoned every true Southern man to arms."[60]

Many Southern Unionists felt the fighting at Sumter could have been explained without eroding Unionist political strength in the borderland, providing no coercive policy toward the South was instituted. Almost all Unionists pointed to Lincoln's proclamation, his call to arms against the lower South, as the decisive blow to Unionism in the region. Comments from five leading upper South Unionists illustrate this all-important point, for as Henry Seward knew too well, war could have been prevented with their support. All were highly recognized, men of true distinction, leaders in their respective states.

First, Congressman Horace Maynard from East Tennessee, one of the state's strongest supporters of the Union (he would later become a Republican):

> The President's extraordinary proclamation had unleashed a tornado of excitement that seems likely to sweep us all away. Men who had heretofore been cool, firm and Union loving had become perfectly wild... Never was published a more unfortunate state-paper. It has done more, and I think I speak considerably, to promote disunion, than any and all other causes combined.[61]

Second, Tennessee's John Bell, the Constitutional Union Party's presidential candidate and a devoted Union man saw it unfold this way:

> When John Bell heard about the proclamation, he concluded that armed force was needed "mainly for the protection of the Capitol and other points threatened, and that no invasion of the South was then meditated." So Bell "waited with eager hope and expectation" for word that soldiers would be used only for strictly limited defensive purposes. But no such explanation ever came....Bell sadly endorsed Tennessee's military preparations.[62]

Third, North Carolina's William Holden, the state's charismatic Unionist leader remarked with true bitterness:

> If Mr. Lincoln had only insisted on holding the federal property, and had called in good faith for troops to defend Washington city, the Union men of the border states could have sustained him ... but he "crossed the Rubicon" when he called for troops to subdue the Confederate States. This was a proclamation of war, and as such will be resisted.[63]

Fourth, Virginia's John Minor Botts, the unconditional Unionist who had strode so mightily to convince Lincoln to maintain his conciliatory policy on the evening of April 7, reacted to the proclamation claiming Unionism was "paralyzed by this single dash of the pen":

> Because the proclamation devastated support for the Union in the upper South and played into the hands of 'demagogues with which the land was filled,' Botts considered it 'in many respects the most unfortunate state paper that was ever issued from any executive since the establishment of the government.[64]

Fifth, North Carolina's Jonathan Worth, an outspoken Unionist and leader of the state legislature, reacted to the proclamation,

A large majority up to the time of issuing Lincoln's proclamation were firm for the Union. But then Lincoln prostrated us. He could have devised no scheme more effectual than the one he has pursued, to overthrow the friends of the Union here.[65]

Lincoln's proclamation without question destroyed a great deal of pro–Union sentiment in the upper South and drove peaceful men to take up arms. A report from the Unionist stronghold in Lexington, Virginia, home of Governor Letcher, captured it best:

[On Saturday, April 13] when news of the fall of Sumter arrived. Secessionists raised a Confederate flag in front of the courthouse, but the "more numerous Unionists"—who included many "working men"—built a higher "Union pole" with an "eagle on it," to fly the American flag. When a few secessionist cadets from the Virginia Military Institute objected, a scuffle ensued and "the Unionists handled them roughly." But on Tuesday, April 16, after news of the proclamation reached Lexington, the same men who had raised the Union pole cut it down. A month later, Rockbridge County voted 1,728 to 1 for secession.[66]

And finally, the prescient letter of North Carolina's John Gilmer, the staunch Unionist who had been offered a place in Lincoln's cabinet and the man at the center of the struggle against secession in North Carolina. Gilmer's letter to Seward of April 21 was not provocative or threatening (as many other letters sent North from Southern Unionists had been), but rather reflective and poignant. He told Seward "all hope is now extinguished" saying the administration has done "the very thing which the disunionists most desired." His hope of restoring the Union now shattered, like many of his fellow Southern Unionists, Gilmer joined the Confederacy with great trepidation.[67]

Gilmer had told Seward "there is a United North against a United South," but the facts on the ground did not support Gilmer. In the South, even after the incredible swing of popular sentiment in favor of the Confederacy after Lincoln's call for troops, still almost one-third of all Southern men who took up arms chose to fight for the Union. And in the North, soon after the proclamation was issued the early euphoria of war spirit waned and huge numbers of Northerners rejected the war effort. In a few short months, Northerners stopped volunteering for military service, a draft had to be instituted, and widespread resistance occurred culminating in the famous draft riot in New York City, which still ranks as the worst race riot in the nation's history.

No one in the administration was prepared to start a war. Messages were sent to each state to call up their militias, but then what? Not enough rifles, not enough uniforms, not enough tents or even eating utensils—sadly, it was a scene reminiscent of a tragic comedy. Weed sent Seward an urgent dispatch on April 22:

We are cut off from communications with you. This occasions intense soli-
tude. There are men and busy enough all ready, in this city to walk through
Baltimore and hold Washington. But nobody has from Washington anything
to act beyond a dispatch I received yesterday from the Secretary of War [the
call for State troops from the War Department].

The beginning of the federal war effort was characterized by supreme
bungling. Later that day Weed sent another dispatch ending "there is no
bounds to the enthusiasm of the People. But any want of energy and purpose
in the Government may cause a terrible re-action. There is just disappointment that the Government is not better prepared."[68]

But Henry Seward would not give up on peace, even after the guns fired
on Sumter and even after the issuance of the Proclamation of Insurrection.
On April 24 Seward was still working feverishly for peace as he sought to
arrange a cessation of hostilities through negotiations with the Confederate
government carried out by the German ambassador to the United States. The
condensed report:

Rudolf Schleiden [the German ambassador] had come to Seward offering
his services in arranging an armistice for three months, or until Congress
could assemble. Vice President Stephens of the Confederacy was in Richmond, and Schleiden proposed to go down there and consult with him.
Seward took Schleiden to see Lincoln, who expressed interest in the project
but would state no specific terms. Seward, who was determined that Schleiden go, procured a pass through the lines for him and that same day the
German set off on his secret mission. He had several conferences with
Stephens but could bring back no concrete proposals for an armistice.
Lincoln decided that further negotiation was useless. Seward's last effort
to avert war had failed.[69]

Abraham Lincoln had made up his mind to pursue an aggressive course
against the secessionists and there would be no turning back. After war began
and casualties mounted sharply, he may likely have had second thoughts.
David Potter's riveting conclusion:

In the months that followed, Lincoln exhibited great forbearance and charity
toward the south. That he did so may not be entirely a consequence of his
personal magnanimity. It may also have derived from a conviction that, if
the matter had been handled differently — if, indeed, he had handled the
matter differently — the conflict might have been averted.[70]

Indeed, "throughout the war Lincoln suffered emotional agony, especially in
the wake of Union defeats." After the first major Union defeat in July 1861,
in Northern Virginia, he exclaimed: "If hell is not any worst than this, it has
no terror for me."[71]

The concluding thought belongs to J. G. Randall and David Donald,
award-winning Civil War historians:

Throughout the whole situation one sees the unfortunate effect of Lincoln's April policy. Feeling that Lincoln should have given conciliation a better trial, that he should above all have avoided a crisis at Sumter, conservative Southerners were deeply outraged at what they deemed both a stroke of bad policy and a breaking of administration promises. As for his call for troops, it served in one flash to alienate that whole mass of Union sentiment, while not pro–Lincoln, was nevertheless antisecessionist and constituted Lincoln's best chance of saving the Union without war.[72]

No political leader in America that April would have agreed with this summation more than William Henry Seward.

And so *the point of no return* had been reached. The nation was off to war with itself. Abraham Lincoln had won the struggle over policy toward the South and now would lead the nation's war effort. Henry Seward's Southern policy had been abandoned and his hopes of creating a new Union Party smashed to pieces. But could William Henry Seward have saved the nation without war, and found a way to eliminate slavery peacefully, had he been president-elect and then president?

EPILOGUE: SAVING THE NATION

> But with all his faults, Seward was a remarkable, an outstanding figure in his era. He had an endless thirst for knowledge.... He enjoyed having people about him, and had the Irish facility for making himself agreeable to them, whether they were servants, clerks, politicians, or statesmen. Even his foes acknowledged his generosity.... It was well said of him that he destroyed his enemies by making them friends. — *Glyndon Van Deusen*

Could the Civil War have been averted? Was William Henry Seward the man who could have made the difference?

As demonstrated throughout this work, William Henry Seward, as secretary of state-designate, worked tirelessly to save the nation from war in spite of resistance from President-elect Lincoln and the vehement objections of radical Republicans. His near-success was due primarily to his political experience, his familiarity with the nation's leadership, and his personality. Seward had an incredible range of colleagues in Washington — Southerners from the lower South, upper South Unionists, moderate Northern Democrats, conciliatory Republicans— who respected his political abilities and who would have responded very differently to his appeals had he been president-elect. Indeed, his contacts among the nation's leadership in all walks of life were unparalleled. His political partner, Thurlow Weed, was the nation's acknowledged expert in blending business and politics to achieve political ends. Nineteenth-century America was a time when money or promises thereof played a dominant role in politics (perhaps little has changed), and no one in the nation was better at playing the "money game" than Weed.

In contrast, Abraham Lincoln was not successful in keeping the nation from war primarily because he lacked political experience (especially in the nation's capital), was unfamiliar with the nation's leadership in virtually every field of endeavor, and was prone to making major decisions alone. He had little access to political money and no one with Washington experience to help him. As the crisis moment approached (indeed, much too rapidly for the new administration), the difference in backgrounds between these two leaders was immense. One was eminently qualified to take charge of running the country on March 4, 1861; one was not. Current summarizes:

> By the standards of Seward and his friends, Seward was far better qualified for the presidency than was Lincoln. Eight years older of the two, Seward had gone to Union College, led the New York senate, been elected governor, and sat with Henry Clay and Daniel Webster and John C. Calhoun in the United States Senate while Lincoln was irregularly attending backwoods schools in Indiana, keeping store in Salem, attending sessions in the Illinois legislature, struggling to get ahead as a lawyer in Springfield, and serving a single, fruitless term in Congress.[1]

In addition to his capabilities to assume command on day one, Henry Seward was extremely popular in the North on that day. James Ford Rhodes's cryptic, yet riveting, conclusion was that "[Seward] had a great hold on the

Northern people; their faith in him was unbounded."[2] That faith was justified for Seward, as previously demonstrated, was a true visionary; he captured the imagination of Americans with his ideas for the future. While "he stood only five feet six inches tall, with a slender frame that young Henry Adams likened to that of a scarecrow," he was "a commanding figure, an outsize personality, a 'most glorious original' against whom larger men seemed smaller."[3] He opposed risking war at all costs, feeling preservation of the Union was all-important. A thought, such as Alexander Stephens's prescient remark, "revolutions are much easier started than controlled, and the men who begin them often themselves become the victims," was clearly on his mind.[4]

Of course, Henry Seward

William Henry Seward as he began his second term in the U. S. Senate, leader of the moderate anti-slavery forces (Seward House, Auburn, New York).

was not a perfect politician. To some he appeared calculating and insincere; to others radical, too much a progressive; and to still others he seemed as enigmatic as any man of his generation. But if demonstrated political skills (and money) were required to prevent disunion, if intellect and persuasive logic mattered, if face-to-face interactions counted (and they were paramount in 1860), Henry Seward had it. Abraham Lincoln would grow into greatness, but as the moment of crisis arrived, Seward was the best politician in the nation: "Seward had dash, a knowledge of political conditions, and a versatility such as none of these men possessed [his contemporaries], while his perfect tact and vigor of intellect, his enthusiasm and inspiring hope, made him the almost perfect supplement to Lincoln."[5] As president-elect, he would have controlled his own destiny and would not have had to be the "perfect supplement" to Abraham Lincoln.

To set the stage for discussion in this epilogue, a brief recap of the secession crisis — and the enormous complexity it presented to the nation's leadership — is required. William Freehling's most recent work, in what likely will become the accepted text for understanding secession, cautions his readers not to merely follow the accepted theory of why the nation went to war. North-South differences over slavery caused the sections to become estranged, for sure, but there was much more to it. In a previous work, Freehling pointed to the so-called republican theory, which holds that "Northerners cared less about abolishing black slavery than about saving white republicanism." With the Southern minority constantly demanding the Northern majority yield to compromise on a host of issues during the 1850s, many Northerners felt the time had come to defend majority rule, the basis for "American republicanism and thus America's contribution to the world."[6] Many in the North (and the South) viewed plantation owners as arrogant, paternalistic aristocrats. And the minority status of plantation owners (less than 10,000 large plantations in all the South) forced them at times to use desperate, and largely undemocratic, tactics to maintain their political power. Resentment toward them was high in the South, too.

Furthermore, as previously noted, neither the North nor the South was a monolithic entity in 1860. Many in the North supported slavery and, in fact, the majority of Southerners favored staying in the Union rather than accept a new "experimental government" in early 1861. Most Southerners did not believe the election of Abraham Lincoln was cause in and of itself to withdraw from the Union. So why war? Randall's haunting peroration: "It is not that democracy was at fault. After all, civil war has not become chronic on these shores, as it has in some nations where politics of force is the rule. One can at least say the Civil War was exceptional, that may be the best thing that can be said about it."[7]

So again, why war? Intriguingly, Freehling chronicles case after case where personalities (even eccentricities) and chance occurrences caused events to swerve in one direction or another. Could the drift to war have been partly the result of happenstance, or just bad luck? The lower South's fears about upper South Unionists and Northern moderates combining forces to create a "white republic" by ending slavery and deporting blacks (a widely discussed topic during the 1850s) adds fuel to the fire. Could the small number of radical secessionists of the South simply have been desperate revolutionaries with nowhere else to go but war? "Might-have-been history, if not romanticized and if grounded in the evidence, thus adds depth to the tales of what did happen."[8] The central question for this epilogue then, is, Could a different leader, pushing events in a different direction, have kept the nation from disintegrating?

What follows is a hypothetical scenario, using data available from the period, wherein William Henry Seward as president-elect and then president saves the nation from war, with Thurlow Weed's able assistance.

Weed had managed a magnificent campaign for his lifelong friend, Henry Seward. New York money was spread across the North and across the Borderland. Former Whigs were enlisted to work for Seward and Weed had assured the faithful they would be rewarded. In a brilliant tactical move, he had secured the vice-presidential nomination for William L. Dayton, the 1856 Republican vice-presidential nominee and one acceptable to the Know Nothing wing of the party, and it proved a popular choice; former Know Nothings rallied to Seward, although some with little enthusiasm. On Tuesday afternoon, November 6, 1860, Thurlow Weed arrived at the Seward home in Auburn, New York. He was with Henry as the telegraph brought news of election results from across the nation. Weed was confident of Republican victory. He had worked tirelessly throughout the fall campaign to bolster support for Seward in undecided states. His effort in New York State to raise money for the campaign had met with tremendous success. New Jersey, Pennsylvania, and Ohio all looked "good" as election day approached. Now the early telegraph reports confirmed Weed's optimism, with Seward running well throughout the North. Sometime after dinner, the final tallies from Pennsylvania and New York arrived. Weed, with a beaming smile, offered a toast to the next president of the United States, William Henry Seward.

As news spread through Auburn the scene unfolded spontaneously, the town erupted in celebration of their man, their hero, the president-elect. Cannons boomed, bands played, and folks marched around the town square for most of the night. Local restaurants were overrun with visitors, champagne flowed freely. Henry Seward would make a few remarks to the adoring crowd just before midnight.

Celebrations occurred in most towns and cities across the North with Seward's victory. In the South debate arose because a "Black Republican" (the

The Seward home in Auburn. Seward inherited this magnificent place from his father-in-law, Judge Elijah Miller (Seward House, Auburn, New York).

term radical secessionists used for any Republican) had been elected with only marginal support from the South. In many Southern towns there arose a genuine concern about what it meant, with some towns organizing opposition meetings. South Carolina, the most pro-secession of the Southern states where some leaders had convinced themselves that any Black Republican was unacceptable, moved toward secession. A Seward victory forced Southerners into much debate.

Wednesday, November 7, Seward and Weed conferred for most of the morning. They were extremely experienced politicians—they began the process of forming an administration immediately. Seward and Weed had run the state of New York successfully (and no more corruptly than the Democrats), and they now employed the same tactics at the national level. They "made an exceptional team" with "Seward [the] more visionary, more idealistic, better equipped to arouse the emotions of a crowd" and with "Weed [the] more practical, more realistic, more skilled in winning elections and getting things done." Seward, the visionary, "conceived party platforms and articulated broad principles" while Weed, the practical politician, "built the party organization, dispensed patronage, rewarded loyalists, punished defectors, developed poll lists, and carried voters to the polls, spreading the influence of the boss."[9]

Weed laid plans to form an "advisory group" of key New Yorkers, including leaders from business, commerce, and finance (some Democrats included), as well as select politicians from Washington. Seward assigned Weed lead responsibility to handle patronage appointments, just as he had done as governor. Weed had developed contacts in virtually every state because of his efforts in building the Whig Party into a national force during the 1840s, and he knew many newspaper editors he could turn to for advice as well. As usual, he moved quickly to reward activists in the recent campaign with patronage appointments and promises of government contracts, some with money. Mostly former Whigs, these new campaign workers formed the nucleus of a new Seward-Weed organization. Seward took on the responsibility for deciding cabinet appointments.

Seward announced he would resign his Senate seat in the coming weeks, but as radical Southern Democrats attempted to inflame reaction to his election, he returned to Washington on November 21. Weed followed a few days later. Once in Washington, they sprang into action with true vigor and a sense of real purpose. Since Seward was the president-elect, every dinner had an agenda, every appointment was calculated for effect, and every statement to the press had an objective: to calm the nation. Seward, whose "extravagant dinner parties were legendary" and "attended by Northerners and Southerners alike," now exploited his natural ability to the fullest. He was the consummate raconteur; "no one showed greater acumen in reconciling the most contentious politicians in a relaxing evening atmosphere." Seward had employed such dinners, especially during his second term in the Senate with daughter-in-law Anna serving as hostess, to befriend everyone, ranging across the political spectrum from Jefferson Davis to John J. Crittenden to Charles Sumner to Charles Francis Adams. All enjoyed being at Seward's home for he "was a superb master of ceremonies, putting all at ease with his amiable disposition" and "he would draw the company into lively conversations ranging from literature and science to theater and history."[10] Seward knew how to play politics and, it must be emphasized again, in nineteenth-century America, a time when television, radio, and instant news did not exist, face-to-face meetings were paramount.

Seward immediately sought advice and counsel from key moderate Republicans and reached out to Democrats from the North and Constitutional Unionists from the border states. Significantly, he not only engaged Southern leaders from the upper South — Unionists such as John Gilmer, Emerson Etheridge, and John B. Baldwin — but from the lower South as well. His neighbor Jefferson Davis and the enigmatic Georgia Unionist Alexander Stephens were early dinner guests. Weed now assumed the role of "chief advisor" and took it upon himself to screen visitors to the Seward house. He set up an office at the Willard Hotel and made it known he would be dispensing patronage.

Seward moved with great dispatch to understand the breadth and depth of the secession movement. He engaged William Gwin, the pro–Southern senator from California, to sound out radical secessionists; he consulted senators who favored concessions to the South — Baker, Crittenden, and Douglas — and through his long-time friend Charles Francis Adams he began meetings with key leaders of the House who favored concessions, specifically Thayer, Kilgore, and Sherman. He engaged Gen. Winfield Scott to intercede with the Buchanan administration. For President-elect Seward, November was a time to survey the Washington establishment relative to the secession crisis unfolding in South Carolina. In addition, he made some progress with his cabinet as Weed floated names under consideration in his *Albany Evening Journal* for public reaction. Seward tended to be a consensus builder and as president-elect he played this role superbly.

Radical Republicans, who were primarily interested in maintaining (and building) their own political power, began to view Seward with alarm as "the consensus builder" began to weaken their appeal in the North. Seward attacked the radicals for their uncompromising policies, stating they risked war. Greeley, in turn, attacked Seward in his *Tribune,* warning of "waffling" on the Republican platform. For Greeley, Seward was acting too much like a moderate. "[I]n fact, [Seward] was not an abolitionist" as "he had long maintained that slavery in the states where it existed was beyond the reach of the national power." Seward's vision "of a nation without slavery ... referred to long-run historical forces and the inevitable triumph of an urbanizing, industrializing society." Free labor, more efficient than slave labor, was winning out in the upper South already. Seward understood what was going on and sought time to let economic forces of the workplace do the work of diminishing the profitability of slavery.[11]

Radical secessionists — South Carolina's Robert Rhett and Alabama's William Yancey the two most well known — also reacted with alarm because Seward now stood in the way of their dream to create a "Southern Nation." They were very well aware of the movement in the upper South away from slavery and toward free labor; they were terrified their upper South "brethren" might not join their new nation. And they were always suspect of those in the upper South relative to a "commitment" to slavery anyway. They had much to be concerned about after the election for "Yankee presidential candidates [Lincoln and Douglas] had secured almost one in six southern votes," the Constitutional Unionists [Bell] who stood for peace "had collected two in five votes," and even many Southern Democrats, including their candidate John Breckinridge, did not favor disunion.[12] Nevertheless, Rhett and Yancey began to plan their revolution.

In the upper South, many factors were at play to thwart secession, central among them future economic development in the region. Many Southern moderates did not see their future tied to the slaveholders. Instead, upper South moderates saw their future tied to the border states of the lower North — Pennsylvania, Ohio, Indiana, and Illinois — where industry and trade intermingled with agriculture. John B. Baldwin and George Summers spoke frequently and passionately about the issue. "Baldwin noted wheat, tobacco, livestock, and garden crops from eastern Virginia were sold in Baltimore and other cities of the Northeast." Likewise, Summers noted that customers "on both sides of the Ohio and upper Mississippi rivers bought salt and coal" produced in western Virginia. In fact, many of these former Whigs, who represented small businessmen, shopkeepers, and manufacturing interests, "had no wish to join a southern nation dominated by free traders, who opposed any protective tariff for industry."[13] Seward and Weed understood these former Whigs and their economic interests; they had promoted just such themes when running New York State and building the Whig Party.

The radicals, North and South, were terrified Seward and Weed would rally the nation to compromise; they detested the thought of a Union controlled by political moderates. Weed began to dispense patronage appointments from his office at the Willard. The lines of office-seekers stretched for blocks and, to the radicals' great dismay, moderates in the North and in the South received each and every appointment. John Underwood, antislavery agitator from New York who had a very successful dairy farm in Northern Virginia (and married into Stonewall Jackson's family), predicted "slaveholding gentlemen will cross the Potomac in swarms and clamor at the Capitol for the privilege [and money] of serving their country in public office — Slavery or no Slavery."[14] He was right: Weed had no shortage of Southerners waiting for appointments.

Wall Street, shaken by the secession clamor, crashed on Monday, November 12. Seward responded with a soothing public statement to allay fears of a financial panic. Seward had experienced financial panics in New York (the panic of 1837 had helped him get elected to the governorship), and he knew what to do. Seward was a New Yorker first and foremost, deeply connected to Wall Street and its business leaders. His carefully worded and carefully coordinated message was calculated to have maximum impact. He promised a compromise proposal by mid–December aimed at ending talk of secession. In actuality, those favoring compromise

> were strengthened in their conciliatory feeling in the weeks immediately following the election by a lessening of zeal in the Republican rank and file....
> In Massachusetts, "Union" men in the December elections managed to defeat Republican candidates, abolitionist meetings were forcibly broken up, and the demand for repeal of the personal liberty laws [laws that protected runaway slaves] gained considerable momentum.[15]

President-elect Seward moved steadily to consolidate support for conciliation as Weed, through his network of newspaper editors, kept conciliation at the forefront of public discourse.

By mid–December Seward was in complete charge of the Republican agenda. Congressional leaders responded to calls from the president-elect; even those with sharp differences would come to the Seward house for talks. Using General Scott as the intermediary, he opened informal lines of communication with the Buchanan administration, where there were several cabinet members from the South. Seward knew first-hand most of the Supreme Court justices, even the irascible Chief Justice, Roger Brook Taney, so he had access to the Court as well. Seward's informers were everywhere and he now employed them fully to keep him apprised of changes in "political direction" and to keep the momentum for conciliation moving forward.

Seward and Weed had spent a lifetime reacting to public opinion, but more important at this moment, they knew how to influence it. They saw a substantial majority of Northerners favoring compromise in mid–December, so they moved to isolate the radicals in the North. "A Boston citizen warned Sumner [the radical Republican senator from Massachusetts] that men who passed for Republicans but had no sympathy with Republican principles were gaining great power in Massachusetts affairs."[16] Seward had won the election by responding to a wide range of issues facing voters: the strong demand for a protective tariff in New Jersey and Pennsylvania; the even stronger demand for free land in Michigan, Minnesota, Iowa, and Wisconsin; the demand to end the corruption of the Buchanan administration; and the demand to restrict the expansion of slavery. In reality, Goodwin concludes: "Had the election been fought on the single issue of slavery, it is likely that Lincoln would have lost." Seward would have lost as well.[17]

Seward quickly concluded the time had come to arrest the secession movement. As South Carolina passed its ordinance of secession on December 20, other states of the lower South seemed to be caught up in the fever. "[T]he process unfolded in an atmosphere of crisis and haste" and the state legislatures gave too much freedom to these hastily convened conventions. In some cases they did not even require their actions be put to referendum. This undemocratic process, or what upper South Unionists often called an "epidemic" or "fit of madness," needed to be halted.[18] Seward and Weed had a plan.

First, the plan called for consolidating support in the upper South. Most of these Southerners thought immediate secession was unwise and as they began to openly oppose the slavocracy, Seward and Weed supported them at every turn. Weed hastened patronage appointments to Southern moderates and made outlandish promises of other "rewards." As a result the antisecessionist party in the upper South made real gains. Seward, on the other hand,

tolerated no thoughts of aggressive action on the part of the federal government and so instructed his closest associates to inform President Buchanan.
Initially, the centerpiece of his evolving strategy was to prevent any confrontation (armed or otherwise) with the secessionists until he had consoli-
dated antisecessionist strength in the upper South.

Second, he concluded a compromise on the extension of slavery at this
moment in time was necessary to preserve the Union. He presented the
"Seward Compromise" to Congress in classic Seward style — having others
do the bidding. In a moving speech, Senator Crittenden delivered the compromise package in the Senate. Charles Francis Adams, with the prestige and
power of his name garnering wide attention, presented it to the House. The
"Seward Compromise" included a constitutional amendment prohibiting
Congress from interfering with slavery where it already existed and championed statehood for New Mexico, where slavery already existed. Thus, the
huge landmass represented by the New Mexico territory would be opened to
slavery, the balance of the Western territories closed. As president-elect,
Seward had the influence (and power) to make "the call" on compromise and
he moved the plan forward with dispatch.

The Seward Compromise immediately stymied the secession movement.
Southerners in both the lower and upper South now took stock. Upper South
Unionists received the news enthusiastically and gave it overwhelming support. In the lower South, serious debate began as radical secessionists were
put on the defensive. In the North, moderates from all parties quickly praised
the effort. President Buchanan gave it his blessing, as did Stephen Douglas.
Seward and Weed enlisted support from everywhere. The moderate Northern press and the press in the upper South hailed the proposal. New York City
financial elites rallied to its support, calling it the "right thing to do." President-elect Seward hosted dinner after dinner with congressmen to shore up
wavering members.

Seward, through Weed, increased the pressure on moderate Republicans
to accept the Seward Compromise. His efforts met with some success in both
the House and Senate as Republicans responded not only to his appeals but
also to public pressure from the North supporting compromise. Adams and
John Gilmer (both would shortly receive cabinet appointments) agreed to lead
efforts in the House. In the Senate he asked Crittenden and Simon Cameron
to lead. Upper South Unionists in the Congress, all of them, rallied to support it, and most Northern Democrats followed Douglas's lead. Even some
lower South congressmen were forced to consider it as some felt "its prompt
passage would preserve the Union."[19] A substantial majority of the nation
lined up behind the Seward Compromise; this was "the hour of Seward's
supreme greatness."[20]

Seward, with Weed coordinating the effort, made a real effort to influence public opinion. They enlisted the moderate press, the financial elites, and the intellectual community, at least those who opposed war. With Seward as president-elect, these efforts produced dramatic results almost overnight. Weed's *Evening Journal* became the unofficial press organ for the new administration.

Thurlow Weed, in Washington throughout January, took a high-profile role in promoting compromise for the president-elect, especially with moderate Republicans — his patronage appointments influenced undecided congressmen. Seward took command of the compromise movement on January 12 by making a dramatic speech to the Senate. Seizing the moment, he used his political skills to the utmost, calling for immediate passage, stating it "would preserve the Union, now and forever."

January 13 dawned with newspaper headlines across the nation trumpeting Seward's "nation-saving speech." Virtually all Democratic newspapers of the North supported it. Bennett's *Herald* trumpeted, "Seward the Savior." Moderate Republican newspapers did likewise. Raymond in the *Times* headlined "Seward Saves the Country from Disunion." Newspapers in the upper South promoted the spirit of compromise in most editorials, but the prosecession newspapers in the South like Rhett's *Charleston Mercury,* and the radical no-compromise Republican papers in the North, like Greeley's *New York Tribune,* stood opposed. Wall Street rallied.

The third, more subtle part of Seward's plan was to isolate the radicals of both North and South. The Seward compromise cut the legs out from under both groups. Radicals Republicans howled about abandonment of the Chicago Platform and warned all who would listen of the impending spread of slavery, while radical secessionists screamed the compromise was not enough, that slave-owners should be able to go anywhere in the West. Radicals, the big losers, reacted with true alarm and true anger. In the lower South, no other state joined South Carolina in secession as a "wait-and-see" attitude gripped the populace.

To repeat for emphasis, in actuality, Lincoln effectively blocked the moderate Republican effort led by Seward and Weed to secure passage of a compromise plan during the secession winter. Current offers this telling summary:

> Lincoln's party contained many men, besides himself, who were no more willing to offer territorial concessions than the Southern extremists were to receive them. But if *he* had taken a different stand, so would a number of his fellow partisans, including a few very influential ones. He probably could have carried enough of the Republicans with him to bring about the adoption of the Crittenden Compromise. Surely Seward would have favored this measure in the Senate committee of thirteen. Of the other four Republicans on that committee, at least two [Jacob Collamer and J. R. Doolittle] conceivably would have gone along with Seward and given in to Lincoln's wishes.[21]

As president-elect, there can be little doubt Henry Seward would have pushed the Seward Compromise through Congress.

At the same time President-elect Seward was implementing his plan to defeat secessionism, he announced his cabinet selections. Seward was so experienced in Washington and so connected with the country's leadership that he was able to move decisively and with great dispatch in his cabinet choices. Weed had run interference throughout the process, floating names and recording reaction, so by the end of December Henry's slate was complete. Seward's cabinet was a harmonious one, composed mostly of former Whigs. It contained a New Yorker and two Southerners. An educated guess, based on some of Seward's stated preferences, produces the following cabinet:

Secretary of State Charles Francis Adams, Sr.
Secretary of the Treasury Simon Cameron
Attorney General George W. Summers
Secretary of War John A. Gilmer
Secretary of the Navy Jacob Collamer
Secretary of the Interior Caleb B. Smith
Postmaster General John Bigelow

Seward could have reasoned in the following way: Adams, in addition to being an old friend, was a distinguished politician from the nation's most distinguished political legacy and added much luster to any cabinet; Cameron was offered the Treasury for bringing Pennsylvania's vote to Seward at the nominating convention; Summers, a judge, former Whig, and strong Virginia Unionist, was offered Attorney General for Seward wanted one Virginian in the cabinet; Gilmer was leader of Southern Unionists in the House, a former Whig, and widely regarded as a true visionary; Collamer, Republican senator from Vermont, was identified with the moderate Republican wing, favored compromise, and represented New England (a Seward stronghold); Smith was offered Interior for bringing the Indiana vote to Seward at the nominating convention; and, Bigelow, a newspaperman from New York and friend of Weed would get Postmaster General as Seward wanted a New Yorker in the cabinet.

These guesses are just that — guesses — but what is important to emphasize is that Seward announced the slate sooner rather than later and it signaled a very accommodating stance with regard to conciliation because it contained no radical Republicans and two moderate Southerners. Once he had come to appreciate the antiaristocratic, and antislaveholder reaction to the radical secessionists (almost all of whom were slaveholders), Seward moved forcefully to exploit it. Also of importance, Seward, unlike Lincoln, did not spend the entire winter making cabinet selections. He focused his attention on his plan to save the nation from war, because that was the paramount issue.

As an aside, one can argue that Abraham Lincoln's cabinet selection process consumed too much of his very limited "quality time" during the secession winter. In the end, Lincoln's cabinet was both geographically and politically balanced, with half former Whigs and half former Democrats. They were all senior politicians and all thought they were better than the man who had appointed them, "every member ... was better known, better educated, and more experienced in public life." Goodwin so ingeniously calls them a "team of rivals," summarizing, "these powerful competitors who had originally disdained Lincoln became colleagues who helped steer the country through its darkest days."[22]

However, it is important to note in the early, critical weeks of the Lincoln administration, when the nation teetered on the brink of war, his cabinet was incapable of working together or of offering him unbiased advice or support. John Nicolay, writing years after the war, offered this telling comment about Lincoln's cabinet at the outset: "It must be remembered, too, that during the month of March, 1861, Lincoln did not know the men who composed his Cabinet. Neither, on the other hand, did they know him"[23]— a "team" that acted anything but at the nation's most defining moment.

Abraham Lincoln's selection process not only took too long, but it did not produce the desired result, as least not initially. His was a cabinet full of crosscurrents and bitter political rivalries, a cabinet loaded with political intrigue, indeed, a cabinet incapable of working together. David Donald summed it up perfectly: "In this disorderly way Lincoln picked his closest advisers. The selection process ensured the cabinet would never be harmonious or loyal to the President. During the winter of 1860–61 while Lincoln was constructing his cabinet, the country was falling to pieces."[24] Henry Seward, and his harmonious cabinet of political centrists, could have made a difference.

After announcing his cabinet in early January, Henry Seward launched the last part of his plan — isolate the radical Southerners. John Gilmer, newly appointed secretary of war and a favorite of Seward and Weed, was made point man with the South and led the effort. He used the Seward Compromise, working its way through the Congress, as the centerpiece of his appeal to lower South moderates. "Gilmer's stature resulted in part from the simple fact that people liked him.... Gilmer had a remarkable ability to turn potential rivals into friends [much like Henry Seward] ... Seward ... saw John A. Gilmer as the southerner best suited to help reverse the secession movement."[25] Gilmer was widely respected in the House of Representatives and was regarded favorably by many in the lower South. Gilmer began a tour through the lower South to meet with moderates, now dubbed "cooperationists" by the hard-line radicals, in an effort to stave off immediate secession. Weed, in Washington, was handing out political patronage to many lower South moderates in a carefully coordinated effort with Gilmer.

Passage of the Seward Compromise undoubtedly would have slowed the secession movement in the lower South. But could the Seward Compromise have strengthened moderates in the lower South enough to defeat secession? Could Gilmer isolate the radicals quickly enough? South Carolina had seceded and Mississippi, Florida, and Alabama were very close in early January. Emotions ran high and secession did have real momentum.

The rapid movement toward secession in the lower South after Lincoln's election is replete with personalities, chance occurrences, indeed luck (either good or bad depending on one's point of view) impacting the eventual outcome. An example of a chance occurrence, on November 9, 1860, struck in the city of Charleston. South Carolina patriarchs assembled in legislative session at Columbia were divided on whether to push for immediate secession or wait for a convention of lower South states to be scheduled a few weeks hence. The Separatists (the hotheads demanding immediate withdrawal) wanted no parts of a convention in a few weeks— they demanded action now. But they were losing ground to the more conservative "wait and see" types, dubbed nationalists, as the legislature initially sought delay. The key issue was whether Georgia or some other lower South state would join South Carolina so the state would not have to go it alone; the Separatists had no firm commitment from any other state and thus their argument for immediate withdrawal was weakened substantially.

As chance would have it, the new Charleston and Savannah Railroad, a track connecting the two major coastal cities of the respective states, under construction for years, had been completed just days before the ninth. On that afternoon the first train from Savannah pulled into Charleston carrying a few dozen prominent Georgians to celebrate the opening of the line. After a glorious banquet, with lavish food and ample liquor, Robert Gourdin, one of the leaders of South Carolina's Separatists, who had planned a large rally to support immediate secession for this very night, asked two of the Georgians, Francis Bartow and Henry Rootes Jackson, to speak to his rally. Gourdin carefully chose the Georgians, picking ones who supported his cause, and they delivered rousing speeches not only urging immediate secession but, with stunning audacity, pledging Georgia's support to stand by the South Carolinians "to fight to the death for southern honor."[26] The crowd erupted, the city turned crazy. The next day, the excited Charleston Separatists, feeling they now had a firm commitment from Georgia (even though Bartow and Jackson could not begin to speak for the state), returned to Columbia with the news. They now pressed their demands for immediate secession with unbending furor and eventually succeeded in getting the legislature to relent and call an immediate secession convention, which they did for December 17. Had the railroad been completed just days later (or even earlier), this spark by the Georgians may not have fueled the secession fire at the precise moment it was needed by the Separatists.

While it is impossible to know for certain, if an election in the lower South had been held for or against withdrawing from the Union in early January, after announcement of the Seward Compromise, it appears the most likely scenario would have been defeat for withdrawal. Even in South Carolina, without the chance event described above (and other occurrences, too), the vote would have been close. Freehling's recent volume analyzes the lower South's road to self-destruction in fascinating detail, noting the happenstance of history, but he emphasizes, "chance leads to destiny only when beneficiaries of luck seize advantage of their good fortune."[27] Thus, the seizing of advantage, and the precise timing of events, adds an intriguing twist to history's what-if scenarios.

But what about President-elect Henry Seward and the incomparable Thurlow Weed using their political experience to alter chance? Savannah, with its heavy Irish population, would have been fertile ground for Seward and Weed. No two in the nation knew the Irish better; Seward had for years championed the rights of immigrants and as governor of New York had reached out to the Irish in countless ways. Weed would have dispatched agents to Savannah, Irish men from New York no doubt, and enticed them to counter the Charleston hotheads with promises of business for the railroad and port; he would have played his "Irish card" early on. So anything would have been possible with Seward and Weed in charge. These two politicians were very different from virtually any others in the nation — their political moves could have produced very different results. Even today, Savannah hosts a huge St. Patrick's Day celebration, second only to New York City in size and scope.

The reaction in the upper South and the border states to the Seward Compromise produced the desired result. Unionists and antisecession Democrats, now with an acceptable compromise working its way through the Congress, came together and formed the new Union Party. It commanded substantial majorities in Virginia, Maryland, Delaware, North Carolina, Kentucky, and Tennessee. Tennessee and North Carolina had voted against calling conventions to consider secession so their legislatures, the sitting elected bodies in those states, would surely endorse the Seward Compromise. Virginia, where a convention had been called and deliberations were under way, was dominated by Unionists. Unionist leaders such as George Summers, John Baldwin, and James Barbour rallied supporters in Virginia to the point where endorsement of the Seward Compromise was all but assured. Maryland, Delaware, and Kentucky would surely follow their sister states to the south. The great borderland would swing to firm support of the Union.

The new Union Party's rise to political dominance placed many former Whigs in leadership positions; Weed (and Seward) knew many of them personally. The strategy to shift to a Union Party not only took the sting of "Black Republican" out of the equation, but it gave all who opposed secession a new banner on which to rally. Lower South Cooperationists had been strengthened by the results in the upper South. Radical secessionists saw the momentum swing against them and began planning more extreme measures. Seward began consolidating support in the North likewise — moderate Republicans were joining with moderate Democrats to champion the Union Party. The visionary Seward, already anticipating the 1864 presidential election, saw the potential for a party of political moderates, North and South, much like the Whig Party of old, which could command a substantial majority across the land.

As Weed continued dispensing patronage, the new political office-holders began taking places in their respective communities, essentially putting moderates in public job after public job in the North. In the South, placing Union Party office-holders in each and every community was more acceptable than placing "Black Republicans" there, but problems remained with stiffening resistance from radical secessionists, especially in some parts of the lower South. So Weed countered with promises of government contracts to his old colleagues in the South, providing a carrot to all who would support the new party. Every moderate could look for "rewards" for continued support.

As Freehling so aptly demonstrates, chance occurrences or even a slightly different timing of some interaction could have pushed secessionism into a different channel. Weed had a real possibility to do so with his "rewards." But most radical secessionists would have reacted to Weed with true outrage; they would not have bought the "Union Party" label. Some would have prepared for armed resistance.

Again to emphasize, Seward's reasoning for cultivating the upper South was twofold. First and foremost, two-thirds of white Southerners lived in the upper South, and the vast majority of these whites did *not* favor immediate secession. Seward and Weed realized this better than most other politicians. They reasoned if the lower South seceded or if armed resistance to the new party taking control occurred, a military solution with two-thirds of Southerners in the Union, combined with the huge majority of Northerners in support, would have a much greater chance of being successful. Second, Seward thought the best chance for keeping the nation from disintegrating lay in having upper South Unionists, men who often had family, friends, and business associates in the lower South, lead the effort to convince their brethren there to reject immediate secession.

> But the entire tenor of all his [Seward's] utterances, private as well as public, his treatment of the Confederate Commissioners, and, especially, his desire to evacuate Sumter, show that he cherished the Border, not as an essential military asset, but as a bridge over which the lower South could be brought back to the Union.[28]

Seward's new secretary of war, John Gilmer, a slaveholder himself, was the perfect choice to interact with lower South Cooperationists. With the Seward Compromise receiving growing support in the Congress, Gilmer now took the legs out from under the radical Southern appeal for immediate secession as he continued his tour through the lower South. Understanding the minority status of the slaveholder and the undemocratic procedures they were using to promote immediate secession better than most, he pressed forward the call to defeat immediate secession. Gilmer boldly challenged radical Southern secessionists to give compromise a chance, and this so strengthened the Cooperationists they were able to delay votes on immediate secession.

Of course, it is impossible to document with any certainty what would have happened in a hypothetical Seward Compromise scenario. But a "united South" versus a "united North" cannot be supported with data from that era; there was much division in both sections. Barton concluded straightforwardly, "those historians are wholly wrong who suppose all people in the North opposed slavery and that all southern people favored it. There were many pro-slavery men in the North, and there was a very considerable anti-slavery sentiment in the South."[29] Freehling provides a graphic exclamation point, noting the candidate favored by secessionists, again John Breckinridge, received fewer than half the Southern vote, concluding, "the presidential election results demonstrated that secessionists faced towering obstacles."[30]

The North was dominated by the cultured, sophisticated cities of the East (Boston, New York, Philadelphia) where commerce, trade, and finance ruled. Interest in a protective tariff was high and political stability was demanded to foster economic growth. The western parts of New York and Pennsylvania were dominated by mining, manufacturers, small shops, and tradesmen. Maine, Vermont, and New Hampshire were less developed, more rural, with small populations eking out an existence in harsh environs. The rapidly growing Northwest was dominated by land issues, free land for new arrivals, and demand for state-funded internal improvements to spur economic development. Opposition to slavery cut across all of these segments, but dominated in none.

Additionally, in the North there were pockets of pro–Southern (and proslavery) sentiment, especially in the all-important metropolis of New York City. As the secession crisis intensified, Mayor Fernando Wood proposed making New York a wholly independent "free city" whereby it could continue to provide finance, commerce, and trade to both North and South. New York was intricately tied to the South as "Southern planters regularly traveled to New York to purchase luxury items, [marry] into New York's leading merchant families, [and vacation] at Saratoga." But more important to New York's financial magnates than purchases of goods, marriage, or vacationing was the breadth and depth of Southern business in which they were heavily involved. "New

York dominated every single phase of the cotton trade from plantation to market," and that included slavery.[31] The North cannot be easily categorized.

The South had multiple segments as well. The Gulf States had lately become dominated by "King Cotton," which fostered large plantations with large numbers of slaves. But the numbers of big plantations, even in the lower South, was not large. Throughout the South, resentment between rich plantation owners and poorer white nonslaveholders (a very large majority) caused political tensions to rise during the antebellum period. On the Eastern Seaboard of Maryland, Virginia, North Carolina, South Carolina, and Georgia, high-brow culture dominated, but the central and western parts of those states were dominated by plainer, middle Americans. Long-simmering political differences, involving representation in state legislatures and taxation as well as "culture," between the eastern and central/western parts of these states were exacerbated by the secession crisis. The antiaristocratic (and antislaveholder) political movement that sprang up after South Carolina seceded was partly a result of these old animosities. Parts of Mississippi and Alabama had large "white belts" where interest in slavery was minimal, Tennessee and Kentucky had a more western than Southern flavor. Arkansas was more rural and western, too. Texas, an entity unto itself, was clearly western; Florida was predominantly undeveloped swampland. Slavery cut across all of these states in vastly different ways.

Furthermore, in the South, as Freehling so convincingly demonstrates, the secession movement was not monolithic; it was very weak in the upper South with its primary support in the "black belts," most of which were on the Eastern Seaboard or in the lower South — it was a movement supported by only a minority of Southerners. Antisecession and/or pro–Union sentiment was strong in virtually every state of the lower South, as mentioned for a time there were even nationalists in South Carolina. In Mississippi, between one-fourth and one-third opposed secession. In Alabama, 39 percent of the delegates to the secession convention voted against the ordinance. In Georgia 45 percent voted against secession. And in Louisiana almost 46 percent voted against secession.[32] And all of these votes occurred without a Seward Compromise.

As previously mentioned, hundreds of thousands of Southerners fought in Union blue. Freehling offers the most compelling statistics:

> Southern blacks supplied close to 150,000 Union soldiers and sailors.... Border South whites added 200,000 and Confederate state whites 100,000 soldiers to Union troop strength. The resulting total of 450,000 Southerners who wore Union blue, half as many as the 900,000 Southerners who wore Confederate gray, replaced every one of the Federals' 350,000 slain men and supplied 100,000 more men besides — a number greater than the usual size of Robert E. Lee's main Confederate army.[33]

Clearly, there can be no "united South" based on these statistics.

Seward came to understand these intra-South divisions because of his wide range of interactions with Southerners. Seward, throughout his career, had carefully cultivated Southern gentlemen — he was a friend of Jefferson Davis, he was an intimate of many former Southern Whigs, he was even invited to "Southern" events (the dinner given by Senator Gwin noted earlier an example). He had become the consummate peacemaker between Northern and Southern politicians during the contentious 1850s: "In June, 1858, he negotiated peace between Senators Davis, of Mississippi, and Chandler, of Michigan, and between Gwin, of California, and Wilson, of Massachusetts. In the latter instance a challenge [a duel] had been sent."[34] Henry Seward, Washington's foremost conciliator, would exploit this facet of his background to the fullest as president-elect. Seward, at his best in face-to-face encounters (he was an unmatched raconteur as noted), would have scheduled dinner after dinner during the winter months — and since he was president-elect, even his strongest opponents would have felt compelled to accept an invitation.

Seward was a shrewd politician, Weed even more so. Again, their plan to save the Union was to secure the upper South firm to the Union with unending patronage and financial support, draft the Seward Compromise and push it through Congress, and then isolate Northern and Southern extremists. And by having upper South moderates convince lower South moderates that immediate secession was a mistake, that their interests could be better protected in the Union with the Seward Compromise than without, was pure genius. Seward and Weed read and understood the words of George Summers and William Holden and William Brownlow, influential Southern moderates who condemned the "slavery aristocracy" and the "slave oligarchs." Exploiting these intra-South differences led Seward to believe the Union spirit could eventually dominate even in the lower South.

Freehling summarizes:

> Slaves drained north to south, with the institution eliminated from the North and diluted in the northernmost South. As the southernmost South belatedly became the Old South ... the northernmost South became ambiguously southern. That ambiguity created the potential, still latent in prewar times, for a war of Southerners against Southerners.[35]

President-elect Seward felt that, given time, the radical secessionists would be defeated throughout the South. And if a military confrontation occurred with some hotheads in the lower South, he would have an overwhelming advantage if the entire North and fully two-thirds of Southerners were on his side.

An example of intra-South differences where a wrong personality in the right place had a negative impact on containing secession can be found in

Alexander Stephens. Sickly from birth, he stood nearly six feet tall but weighed only ninety-five pounds. He suffered constantly from numerous aches and pains, shivered uncontrollably at times, and often was seen wrapped in woolen blankets. His parents had died early on, leaving him an orphan, and like Lincoln he had had a difficult childhood that left him at times, also like Lincoln, gloomy, supersensitive, and pretty much a loner. But Stephens, again like Lincoln, was a brilliant politician and spellbinding orator, and he had risen early in Georgia politics, becoming one of its ablest and most well-known statesmen. It was on his shoulders the Cooperationists of Georgia leaned in November 1860. During the weeks following Lincoln's election, the Georgia legislature set up a series of debates regarding secession. Stephens was one of the conservative leaders seeking delay.

After a masterful speech in which he emphasized that a Democratic Congress would control the Lincoln administration (budget, appointments), he called for issuing an ultimatum demanding immediate repeal of fugitive slave laws to the new administration, then argued the territorial issue was moot (for slaveholders were not tempted to migrate to any of the western territories, as previously discussed) and suggested a year's delay in secession was necessary to see if such an ultimatum would do the trick in protecting Southern interest. Much wiser, he cautioned, to seek redress within the Union than to break it up. The Separatists were put on the defensive by Stephens's triumph, many Georgians feeling "disunion might be the corpse, unless and until the president and/or his party deployed an overt act against slavery."[36]

Following rebuttal by Separatists over the next few days, an election to choose delegates to a convention was scheduled for January 2. The campaign began immediately. But the gloomy Stephens, ever the neurotic loner, retreated to his study at his mansion and took virtually no part in the campaign for delegates. The Separatists out-spoke, out-campaigned, and out-organized the Cooperationists. "The leaderless movement stalled, drifted, wandered" and a significant opportunity was lost to find a workable solution to immediate secession. Enough Republicans likely would have bought the idea of a national settlement based on removal of fugitive slave laws (as Stephens outlined in his speech), because it would have sidestepped the thornier territorial expansion issue. And "for this missed opportunity, Stephen's peculiar personality must shoulder part of the blame."[37]

By early February John Gilmer was having real success in the lower South as immediate secession had been stalled in each and every state (with the exception of seceded South Carolina). While the situation was still very fluid, his campaign-like tour received growing fanfare as Weed contacted his old Whig friends there, who were now mostly Cooperationists, and arranged "friendly" crowds to welcome Gilmer at every stop. Weed also contacted his colleagues in the press and they saw that appropriate coverage was given to

Gilmer's speeches. Gilmer suffered some real abuse, however, as radical secessionists boldly threatened him, but he found many in the lower South warming to the Seward Compromise as it came nearer and nearer to passage in the Congress. Also, he found some plantation owners, conservative former Whigs like himself, speaking out against immediate secession.

Gilmer sent the president-elect telegram after telegram reporting on his trip. Seward determined it was time to move more aggressively to bolster

The dining room in Seward's Washington home where so many contentious issues were resolved over "good brandy and good cigars." As president, Seward would have turned the White House into a giant reception center using his grace and charm to persuade wavering politicians (Seward House, Auburn, New York).

support for unionism in the lower South as the Cooperationists seemed to be gaining ground. Leaders of the emerging Union Party were invited to Seward's house on February 22 for a birthday party honoring George Washington. Seward delivered a significant coup for lower South moderates by announcing his choice for ambassador to Great Britain, the most sought-after diplomatic post in the nation. Herschel V. Johnson of Georgia was his choice. It was electrifying news and widely reported in the press. Southerners of all political persuasions sensed Seward's seriousness of purpose to assuage the South and defeat secessionism. Johnson, vice-presidential candidate on the Douglas ticket in the recent election, was a moderate Democrat closely identified with lower South interests.

In addition, Weed coordinated an effort to influence the powerful New York City financial elites (many of whom were also Democrats) with promises of economic opportunities for the city in a Seward administration. They responded with real interest — and real money. Seward made it clear to all he was going to form a "national administration," one to foster unionism as its *sine qua non*. His administration would welcome all moderates and all those supporting the Union — a welcomed message for the financial elites as they sought political stability above all else. The moderate Northern press supported progress in every editorial and reported that the vote on the Seward Compromise was now scheduled for late February in both the House and Senate.

And indeed Weed, the nation's master political boss, was everywhere. Now armed with the authority and the prestige of being the president-elect's "right hand," anything was possible for the right price. Weed increased his activities with lower South moderates. As the congressional vote approached, Weed moved, with Seward's approval, to trump secessionism in the lower South. He made special arrangements for shipping cotton from Mobile and sugar from New Orleans to Europe — in exchange for loyalty to the Union. With Secretary of State-designate Adams, he coordinated other offers of prestigious (and lucrative) ambassadorships for key lower South leaders— in exchange for loyalty to the Union. He secured loans from New York bankers at favorable interest rates to increase opportunities in manufacturing and commerce for lower South businessmen — in exchange for loyalty to the Union. Weed loved the wheeling and dealing aspect of politics; he loved the challenge of beating his political opponents. The possibilities became endless as he gained power.

And then, on February 28, the Seward Compromise was passed in both houses of Congress by wider-than-expected margins. Radical Republicans, such as Zachariah Chandler and Ben Wade, and radical secessionists, like Robert Toombs and Henry S. Foote, led the opposition, but in the end they lost their argument as the moderates held sway. Now the center of the secessionists' appeal had suddenly disappeared, for slavery would be protected where it already existed and slaves could be taken to the New Mexico Territory (if anyone was foolish enough to go). Seward then challenged Rhett and Yancey and the other fire-eaters to cease their disloyal activities. He portrayed them as enemies of American democracy. "The tale of the southern house divided, when told in lockstep with intertwined tales of the American house divided, highlights underappreciated gems of Civil War lore."[38] President-elect Seward had a real chance to defeat secession in the lower South by adroitly using John Gilmer and by turning Weed loose to wheel and deal to shore up Unionism.

While Seward always sought to stay above the fray (he did not relish the deal-making aspect of politics) and Weed could be too tough (once bought, he demanded unceasing loyalty), who better than Seward and Weed, with the power of the presidency in their quiver, to solve the sectional crisis? In this what-if scenario, we cannot overlook the truly astonishing range of elements in the national fabric Seward and Weed held sway over, assuming they were in control of the White House. They would have:

- Pushed a compromise plan through Congress;
- created a new Union Party of political centrists using political rewards;
- influenced business and finance to political advantage;
- managed public opinion by adroitly employing their "friendly" press; and,
- isolated radicals in both North and South by playing to majority sentiment.

A final digression is necessary to discuss the emerging Union Party of political centrists. It was a huge motivator for Seward and Weed. What they saw, in both the North and the South, was the substantial majority of voters it could attract (not the 39 percent the Republicans received in the 1860 election), and they saw themselves as the leaders of a truly national party (not the primarily sectional Republican Party). Their long-awaited opportunity to create a new party that could dominate the electorate across the land for years to come, with themselves at the top of the political pyramid, was at hand. So too was the opportunity to trump the dreaded radical Republicans, and the despised Southern "fire-eaters" as well.

The new Union Party was gaining everywhere, but especially in the great borderland as moderates from all political parties joined forces to oppose the slavocracy. The elections in Virginia were scheduled for May, and in Tennessee and North Carolina for August. These were viewed as watershed events for the new Union Party and for secessionists as well, for as these mid–South states chose Union, the border South states to the north would quickly follow suit.

The Richmond Whig confidently predicted, "retribution, swift and sure, will overtake the faithless dynasty [the secessionists] which now abuses the confidence of Virginia ... a clear majority of sixty thousand votes in the State will be shown in the Congressional elections in May against the secessionists." The Virginia election thus loomed as an event of first importance.[39]

In Tennessee, the election to choose a new legislature, congressional representatives, and governor was scheduled for August. The incumbent governor, Isham G. Harris, a staunch secessionist, was sure to be defeated as "Tennessee Unionists moved rapidly to build a new party after winning their handsome victory in the convention election of February 9. They displayed unprecedented bipartisanship." The *Nashville Republican Banner* blasted, "Let us unite on good will and well known and well tried Union men, irrespective of all other considerations. The parties of last year and the past are literally dead." Tennessee Union men were coming together toward the common goal of keeping Tennessee from seceding. In the process, they sought to form a new dominant party: "conclusive evidence indicates that leading Union Democrats and Whigs in Tennessee were 'co-operating' together 'for future good.'"[40]

In North Carolina congressional elections were scheduled for August also. Union Whigs and Union Democrats were overwhelmed by their victories in the convention election. They felt sure the momentum would carry over to the congressional election later and the new Union Party would then dominate the state.

> Their success in the convention election of February 28 persuaded Union Whigs to maintain a warm welcome for Union Democrats in the emerging Union party. Former U.S. Senator George E. Badger, a Union Whig, marveled that he and two Union Democratic running mates won a landslide victory as convention delegates in normally Democratic Wake County, with Badger leading the ticket.... In Orange County, directly west of Raleigh, long an arena for close two-party competition, a bipartisan Union ticket swept to victory by a four-to-one margin, the "most lopsided" election there since political parties organized in the 1830s.[41]

Unionism had won everywhere in the upper South; secessionism had been defeated soundly.

Henry Seward was in the midst of the Union Party movement, encouraged by many leading citizens. A typical letter to Seward is that of Thomas Fitnan, one of Washington's most prominent men, dated February 19.

> All old party platforms are now either breaking down or (are) being swallowed up in the universal desire of the people to save the republic from dissolution, and a new one, constructed upon Union principles *per se* will inevitably spring up after the 4th of March. *It is for you to take the lead or not in the movement.* If you decide in the affirmative, the extreme men of the

North and South will have to be thrown off and made subordinate to the
centre, or conservative Union party. *I do not hesitate to say, that no public
man in this or any other country, has ever been placed in a better position that
you are now, either for weal or woe of the human race.*[42]

As president-elect Henry Seward would not have lost his "better position."

In actuality Seward had responded to these appeals in many ways. He
had confidentially told Unionists he would support the Crittenden Compromise or something like it, he had promoted Union-saving schemes with
Northern Democrats and Constitutional Unionists (the Douglas and Crittenden meetings), and he had encouraged conciliation with his Republican colleagues to the point where one radical Republican senator blasted, "God damn
you Seward, you've betrayed your principles and your party; we've followed
your lead long enough." Seward had distanced himself from the radical wing
of the Republican Party because he opposed their aims and methods per se,
and because he felt the radicals would destroy his beloved Union if left to
their own devices. It is unclear whether Seward ever discussed the Union
Party concept with Lincoln, although it is known Lincoln felt a Union Party
could cause real problems for the Republican Party. Many contemporaries
who debated the pros and cons of a Union Party felt it would develop with
or without Abraham Lincoln, whom they saw as merely a rising star during
the secession winter.

In the North, Seward was pushing the new Union Party no doubt. Thousands of Republicans had signed petitions urging compromise. New Jersey,
Pennsylvania, Ohio, Indiana, and Illinois were moving toward the new party.
Union men were supplanting radical Republicans in Massachusetts and elsewhere in New England. Northern Democrats and Constitutional Unionists
from everywhere were coming forward to support a Union Party. The *New
York Times* noted that "the question pending is one as to whether Mr. Lincoln shall become the head of the great 'Union Party' of the country, or
whether a party upon that issue shall be permitted to grow up in hostility to
his Administration." By late February talk was rampant about the Union
Party and whether it could supersede the Republican Party. This talk focused
on how to isolate the radical Republicans, clearly a Seward objective, and
who would replace them.

The *New York Herald,* the hugely influential, pro–Democratic paper of
New York (also friendly to Seward), stated "over a million Union loving citizens in the States of Virginia, Kentucky, Tennessee, Missouri, Maryland,
and Delaware, will rally in their places [the radical Republicans], to the support of the government which will assume the reins of power next week." The
Herald predicted a new party would rise and "the architect of this 'great Union
party' was the incoming secretary of state, William H. Seward."[43] Seward,
throughout the secession winter, had promoted the Union Party in the upper

South (as previously documented) to counter secessionism. He had promoted it in the North to counter radical Republicans. He came to understand the connection between creating a Union Party and isolating the radicals, so as the well-informed Washington correspondent James E. Harvey noted, Seward "was starting out afresh for a Union Party."[44] As president-elect, there can be little doubt as to his course.

A final supportive comment regarding Seward's motives is from Lord Lyons, the British ambassador to the United States (a close friend of Seward's) in his early March report to London,

> Mr. Seward's real view of the state of the country appears to be that if blood-shed can be avoided until the new government is installed, the seceding States will in no long time return to the Confederation. He seems to think that in a few months the evils and hardships produced by secession will become intolerably grievous to the Southern States, that they will be completely reassured as to the intentions of the Administration, and that the Conservative element which is now kept under the surface by violent pressure of the Secessionists will emerge with irresistible force.... He then hopes to place himself at the head of a strong Union party, having extensive ramifications both in the North and in the South, to make "Union" or "Disunion" not "Freedom" or "Slavery" the watchword of political parties.[45]

Inauguration day, March 4, 1861, came with Seward making a stirring speech where he asked all to give peace a chance. It made pointed comments to citizens in the lower South stating compromise had been achieved and it was time to calm down. By late spring the now–President Seward, using all the powers at his disposal to reach out to moderates in the lower South, had slowed secession — but it was not dead, especially not in the black belts of the lower South. Thurlow Weed, with the president's full backing, had set up Union Party organizations in each and every state of the Union, with the exception of seceded South Carolina, and the new party was gaining some ground, but very grudgingly in many areas. Some armed conflict had occurred in Alabama and Mississippi between Union Party officials and secessionists, several citizens were dead. As summer rolled along, radical Southern secessionist challenged the federal government ever more boldly. Excited young men from the lower South began to flock to South Carolina in response to the state's call for assistance. Tensions began to rise alarmingly.

Seward made several important moves to prepare for possible military activity. On June 1, he appointed Robert E. Lee commander of the U.S. Army, ordering him to increase the size of the army and prepare it for possible action. The next day he ordered several Navy warships in foreign ports to return home at once. For two months he had been discussing the range of options available with regard to South Carolina with his cabinet; all now supported increasing the readiness of the armed forces. He began to consult with governors on a regular basis. Weed was assigned to coordinate activities with the press. Congress was not in session, but as he had been corresponding with congressional leaders weekly since his inauguration, the President now asked them to come to Washington for formal talks.

In early May, Gen. Winfield Scott had sent Seward a letter announcing his retirement and recommending Lee in the strongest possible terms. Lee, a popular and highly respected officer, accepted command and moved with great dispatch to put in place plans for possible action by the military. No officer in the U.S. Army was more adept with organizational skills. Recruiting offices were set up in many major cities, the state militias of Virginia and North Carolina were called into service to guard the border with South Carolina, and major training centers were established in Baltimore, Philadelphia, and Richmond—cities easily accessible by rail and water, also close to the nation's capital.

September witnessed the beginning of the end for radical secessionists. Congress had convened in special session early in the month to authorize an increase in the nation's military forces and passed a resolution calling for South Carolina to nullify its secession ordinance. The South Carolinians refused, set up armed camps on their border with North Carolina, and began interactions with European governments seeking recognition of their "new government." Compromise seemed out of the question for the "hotheads" in Charleston and Columbia.

On October 1, 1861, General Robert E. Lee led the U.S. Army into South Carolina. Brushing aside the border guards, the 30,000 well-trained and well-equipped infantry, supported by artillery and 5,000 cavalry, pushed on toward Charleston. Lee had established an enormous supply depot at Lumberton, North Carolina, and thousands of wagons followed the army's advance. At Florence, the South Carolinians and radical secessionist from other states had constructed huge breastworks and congregated to make a stand — almost 20,000 young men assembled, ill-equipped, ill-prepared for combat, many in partying mode. Lee had organized his army into three infantry corps, commanded by James Longstreet, William T. Sherman, and Thomas J. Jackson, and the cavalry into two brigades under the command of J.E.B. Stuart and Philip H. Sheridan.

After two days of probing the defenses with skirmishers and cavalry patrols, Lee launched his assault. Jackson's corps had been sent on a flanking movement, with Sherman and Longstreet engaged in a frontal attack. As the South Carolinians fell back, giving ground to superior numbers, Jackson swept in from the west. A rout ensued with the young, undisciplined boys scattering everywhere. Over one-half of the secessionists surrendered, with several thousand casualties. Lee's army suffered minimal losses. A stray artillery shell hit the South Carolinian command post, killing many prominent leaders of the revolt.

On October 9, a surrender ceremony was held in Latta, a small railroad town just south of the North Carolina border. Lee then divided his victorious army, sending Longstreet to occupy Charleston and Columbia, Jackson to guard the supply depot at Lumberton, and Sherman to return to Washington. Lee accompanied Longstreet, with Stuart in the van, to Charleston, Sheridan rode on to Columbia with part of the infantry corp. Many of the Charleston squires had sons killed or captured in the Battle of Florence — they now fled to Europe. Slaves by the thousands were fleeing the large plantations; army personnel turned their attention to the issue. General Lee returned to Washington just before Christmas to a hero's welcome.

By early spring 1862 Seward, with the secession crisis moving toward resolution, now turned his visionary mind toward creating a new economic prosperity for the nation and to the issue of eliminating slavery. The radicals, in both North and South, had been overcome by events and were in complete disarray. Seward had proposed building two transcontinental railroads in a November speech, one North and one South, with the southern terminus in Richmond; Virginians were ecstatic. Secretary of State Adams was in Canada beginning discussions regarding a mutual trade pact — and possibly much more. Building new highways, opening rivers to navigation, and chartering feeder line railroads all were hot topics of conversation in just about every state, North and South. On January 2, 1862, Seward had delivered a speech to a joint session of Congress where he had outlined his vision of the nation's Manifest Destiny. He had excited the entire nation. New lands were to be opened in the western territories for all, immigration was blossoming again, the coming spring promised vigorous economic activity.

The army had begun to set up camps for slaves in South Carolina shortly after the Battle of Florence and by Thanksgiving Week real progress had been made. Early spring found President Seward, ever the visionary, holding preliminary discussions with congressional leaders regarding legislation to implement compensated emancipation, financed by the federal government. He floated the idea of a Homestead Act for Freedmen whereby freed slaves would be offered free land in the West. Army officers were breaking up large plantations in South Carolina, surveying the land, and laying out plots on which they intended to settle slaves, Seward began discussing legislation to legalize the effort.

For sure, radical Southern secessionists would continue to resist, perhaps to the point of armed conflict again, but then Seward had, as Freehling noted, Southerners fighting Southerners— and the vast majority of Northerners lined up behind him. During the secession winter, Henry had written his wife, Frances, "mad men North and mad men South, are working together to produce a dissolution of the Union, by civil war."[46] So he knew who the bad guys were. Seward had stopped secession by capturing the support of a majority of Southerners, by promoting a compromise on slavery and rallying moderate Northerners to support it, and by skillfully isolating the radicals in both North and South. And if military confrontation was again necessary, he was ready to authorize whatever.

Could the simplistic scenario outlined above have played out? The odds are remote, but the point is that a President Seward, the nation's foremost political visionary, had endless possibilities as head of state. Seward's visionary nature cannot be underestimated. Here was the man who had reformed prisons, put education in the hands of local officials, who championed the

The Auburn funeral of William Henry Seward, October 13, 1872. Dignitaries from across the nation attended. Thurlow Weed was in tears (Seward House, Auburn, New York).

rights of Irish immigrants, whose "higher law" and "irrepressible conflict" speeches had captured the nation's attention, who acquired Alaska for the incredible sum of two cents per acre, who proposed an association with Canada, and on and on. Also, it must be repeated that Seward was the only American political leader who had gone to Europe to study their successful programs to eliminate slavery. And, of course, the remarkable, if not "lily white" political talents of Thurlow Weed would have redefined mover and shaker.

Once again, the distinguished American historian James Ford Rhodes, "[Seward] had a great hold on the Northern people, their faith in him was unbounded." A President Seward would have justified that faith many times over.

We end with three comments regarding William Henry Seward: two from early twentieth-century authors, men who had interacted with many of Seward's contemporaries firsthand, and one from an historian who has produced the most recent work regarding Lincoln and his advisors. While some modern historians have reinterpreted the opinions of the early legends, we must recognize that those close to the war, and to actual participants, had a view that time had not yet diminished.

First, Seward biographer Frederic Bancroft writing in 1900:

> Jefferson Davis most resembled him in his talent for directing the thoughts and influencing the action of a whole section. But neither Davis nor any other contemporary, except Clay, [Henry] could rival Seward in his genius for politics and the wide range of his abilities.... His senatorial career is probably the best illustration in American history of how far the politician may go toward reform, and how much the reformer must bend to practical policies, in order to attain position and power and accomplish results that contemporaries and history regard as great.[47]

Second, Edward Everett Hale, writing in 1910:

> Of all the statesmen of his day, there is no one whose politics and principles lead more directly to our own. As one follows his life, one is constantly thinking how modern he is. If he could come back to his beloved country a hundred years after the days when he took his first steps in politics, he would find himself quite in touch with the present dominant motives of public life: The placing of politics in the hands of the people and the preservation and development by the state of all its possibilities and resources.[48]

Finally, this thought from Doris Kearns Goodwin as she captures the visionary Seward: As Seward understood better than Lincoln, Manifest Destiny was in the air. "Our population," Seward predicted, "is determined to roll its resistless waves to the icy barriers of the north, and to encounter Oriental civilizations on the shores of the Pacific."[49]

Gravesite of William Henry Seward, Fort Hill Cemetery, Auburn (Seward House, Auburn, New York).

"*Did it ever occur to you that the great political problem which has vexed the political theorists and philosophers is simply this — how to prevent the government from falling into the hands of knaves and fools? In all ages and in all countries that is the question they have been trying to solve — for the most part with very indifferent success.... Look at the proceedings of any party convention under this, the best government in the world, and see how close they run to that danger every time they meet.*" — William Henry Seward, the last political comment of his life, fall 1872.[50]

APPENDIX: THE 1860 PRESIDENTIAL ELECTION

An analysis of the state-by-state vote in the North, comparing the total vote for Lincoln with the total vote for all three opponents combined, produces the following changes in the official final Electoral College vote.

State	Lincoln (%)	Electoral Vote	Combined Opponents (%)	Electoral Vote
California	39,173 (31%)		79,667 (69%)	-4
Connecticut	43,792 (56%)	6	33,454 (44%)	
Illinois	172,161 (51%)	11	167,532 (49%)	
Indiana	139,033 (51%)	13	133,110(49%)	
Iowa	70,409 (55%)	4	57,922 (45%)	
Maine	62,811 (64%)	8	35,107 (36%)	
Massachusetts	106,533 (63%)	13	62,642 (37%)	
Michigan	88,480 (57%)	6	66,267 (43%)	
Minnesota	22,069 (63%)	4	12,730 (37%)	
New Hampshire	37,519 (57%)	5	28,434 (43%)	
New Jersey	58,324 (48%)		62,810 (52%)	-4
New York	362,646 (54%)	35	312,510 (46%)	
Ohio	231,610 (52%)	23	210,831 (48%)	
Oregon	5,270 (37%)		9,140 (63%)	-3
Pennsylvania	268,030 (56%)	27	208,412 (44%)	
Rhode Island	12,224 (61%)	4	7,707 (39%)	
Vermont	33,808 (76%)	5	10,732 (24%)	
Wisconsin	86,110 (57%)	5	66,070 (43%)	
Total	**1,840,022 (54%)**	**169**	**1,565,068 (46%)**	**-11**

The table verifies the conclusion drawn by John Nicolay after the war that had all opposition been concentrated on a fusion ticket, only in New Jersey, California, and Oregon would there have been any change in the Electoral College vote, just eleven fewer. Lincoln would still have had a majority of thirty-five in the Electoral College, Seward also had he been the Republican candidate.[1] Thus, the Republican Party would have won in the Electoral College no matter how the votes were aligned. The other important point to reiterate is in a four-way race, the candidate with the most popular votes out of the four in any given state takes all of the Electoral College votes for that state. Thus, while Illinois and Indiana look very close in the above chart when all opposition votes are combined against Lincoln, in actuality, he beat Douglas (his nearest competitor) handily in the four-way race, by 12,000 votes in Illinois and 23,000 in Indiana.[2] Some have argued Seward was too weak in Indiana and Illinois and would have lost those states in the election (unlikely with Weed in control of a Seward campaign), but even if he did lose them, he still would have won in the Electoral College vote. In the 1860 Presidential Election, the Republican juggernaut was in full swing.

Results of the 1860 Presidential Election

Party — Candidate	Popular Vote (%)	Electoral College Vote (%)
Southern Democrat — Breckinridge	849,781 (18%)	72 (24%)
Northern Democrat — Douglas	1,376,957 (29%)	12 (4%)
Constitutional Union — Bell	588,879 (13%)	39 (13%)
Republican — Lincoln	1,866,452 (40%)	180 (59%)

CHAPTER NOTES

Introduction

1. Joshua W. Shenk, *Lincoln's Melancholy* (Boston: Houghton Mifflin, 2005), 4.

2. David M. Potter, *Lincoln and His Party in the Secession Crisis* (New Haven: Yale University Press, 1962), 315.

3. Richard N. Current, *The Lincoln Nobody Knows* (New York: McGraw, 1958), preface.

4. Daniel W. Crofts, *Reluctant Confederates* (Chapel Hill: University of North Carolina Press, 1989).

5. David H. Donald, *Lincoln* (New York: Simon and Schuster, 1995), 176.

6. Doris Kearns Goodwin, *Team of Rivals: The Political Genius of Abraham Lincoln* (New York: Simon and Schuster, 2005).

7. William W. Freehling, *The Road to Disunion*, vol. 2 (New York: Oxford University Press, 2007).

8. Renewed interest in the secession crisis—just how the nation got itself into such a war—is evidenced by two recent works: Nelson D. Lankford, *Cry Havoc!* (New York: Viking Press, 2007); and Russell McClintock, *Lincoln and the Decision for War* (Chapel Hill: University of North Carolina Press, 2008). Both are cited in this work.

9. Drew Gilpin Faust, *This Republic of Suffering* (New York: Alfred A Knopf, 2008), 30.

10. Gabor S. Boritt, *Why the Civil War Came* (New York: Oxford University Press, 1996), 20.

11. Don E. Fehrenbacher, *The Changing Image of Lincoln in American Historiography* (London: Oxford University Press, 1968), 3–4.

12. Goodwin, *Team of Rivals*, xix.

Chapter 1

1. William E. Barringer, *Lincoln's Rise to Power* (Boston: Little, Brown and Co., 1937), 209.

2. Frederic Bancroft, *The Life of William H. Seward,* vol. 1 (New York: Harper and Brothers, 1900), 525.

3. Goodwin, *Team of Rivals*, 12–13.

4. William E. Barton, *President Lincoln,* vol. 1 (Indianapolis: Bobbs-Merrill, 1933), 84.

5. James M. McPherson, *Battle Cry of Freedom* (New York: Oxford University Press, 1988), 219.

6. Mark E. Neely Jr., *The Last Best Hope on Earth* (Cambridge: Harvard University Press, 1993), 57.

7. Goodwin, *Team of Rivals*, 215.

8. Bancroft, *Life of William H. Seward*, 1:522.

9. Thurlow Weed Barnes, *Memoir of Thurlow Weed* (Boston, 1884), 272.

10. *Atlas and Argus*, Albany, N.Y., May 19, 1860, as cited in Goodwin, *Team of Rivals*, 13.

11. William H. Seward to home, Seward, *Seward at Washington ... 1846–1861*, 395, as cited in Goodwin, *Team of Rivals*, 215–16.

12. Telegram from Preston King, William M. Evarts, and Richard M. Blatchford to Seward, May 18, 1860, William Henry Seward Papers, Department of Rare Books and Special Collections, University of Rochester, Rochester, N.Y. (hereafter Seward Papers), as cited in Goodwin, *Team of Rivals*, 16.

13. Bancroft, *Life of William H. Seward*, 1:532–33.

14. Barnes, *Memoir of Thurlow Weed*, 269.

15. Barringer, *Lincoln's Rise to Power*, 209.

16. Ibid., 227.

17. William W. Freehling, *The Road to Disunion*, vol. 2 (New York: Oxford University Press, 2007), 329.

18. Barringer, *Lincoln's Rise to Power*, 212.

19. Bancroft, *Life of William H. Seward*, 1:537.

20. Glyndon G. Van Deusen, *Thurlow Weed: Wizard of the Lobby* (Boston: Little, Brown, 1947), 248–49.

21. Barnes, *Memoir of Thurlow Weed*, 292.

22. Van Deusen, *Thurlow Weed*, 253.

23. Bancroft, *Life of William H. Seward*, 1:541.

24. Ibid., 1:538–39.

25. Ibid., 1:540.

26. Barton, *President Lincoln*, 1:103.

27. Entry of May, 19, 1860, in the *Diary of Edward Bates, 1859–1866*, as cited in Goodwin, *Team of Rivals*, 252.

28. Barton, *President Lincoln*, 1:85.

29. Goodwin, *Team of Rivals*, 254.

30. Lawrence M. Denton, *A Southern Star for Maryland* (Baltimore: Publishing Concepts, 1995), 14.

31. Edward Everett Hale Jr., *William H. Seward* (Philadelphia, 1910), 259.

32. John M. Taylor, *William Henry Seward* (New York: Brassey's, 1991), 120.

33. Glyndon G. Van Deusen, *William Henry Seward* (New York: Oxford University Press, 1967), 230–31.

34. Taylor, *William Henry Seward*, 122.

35. Goodwin, *Team of Rivals*, 269–70.

36. Donald, *Lincoln*, 110.

37. *Chicago Press and Tribune*, September 24, 1860, as cited in Goodwin, *Team of Rivals*, 268–69.

38. Van Deusen, *William Henry Seward*, 235.

39. Ibid., 232.

40. William E. Gienapp, "Who Voted for Lincoln," 50–97, as cited in Donald, *Lincoln*, 254–55.

41. John S. Wright, *Lincoln and the Politics of Slavery* (Reno: University of Nevada Press, 1970), 115.

42. Ollinger Crenshaw, *The Slave States in the Presidential Election of 1860* (Gloucester, Peter Smith, 1969), 61.

43. Freehling, *Reintegration of American History*, 226.

44. Bancroft, *Life of William H. Seward*, 546.

Chapter 2

1. Donald, *Lincoln*, 38.

2. Ibid., 48.

3. McPherson, *Battle Cry of Freedom*, 227.

4. Donald, *Lincoln*, 206

5. Abraham Lincoln, *The Collected Works of Abraham Lincoln*, ed. Roy P. Basler (New Brunswick, N.J.: Rutgers University Press, 1953–55), as cited in Donald, *Lincoln*, 233–35.

6. Ibid., 237–41.

7. Michael Burlingame, *The Inner World of Abraham Lincoln* (Urbana: University of Illinois Press, 1994), 9.

8. Webb Garrison, *The Lincoln No One Knows* (Nashville: Rutledge Hill Press, 1993), 40.

9. Donald, *Lincoln*, 238.

10. Garrison, *The Lincoln No One Knows*, 227.

11. Current, *The Lincoln Nobody Knows*, 7.

12. Hale, *William H. Seward*, 261.

13. Barton, *President Lincoln*, 1:102.

14. Crofts, *Reluctant Confederates*, xix.

15. Donald, *Lincoln*, 285.

16. Garrison, *The Lincoln No One Knows*, 23–25, above two quotes.

17. Shenk, *Lincoln's Melancholy*, 216.

18. William H. Herndon to Jesse W. Weik, July 10, 1886, as cited in Donald, *Lincoln*, 163.

19. Henry C. Whitney, *Life on the Circuit*, ed. Paul M. Angle, as cited in Donald, *Lincoln*, 164.

20. Current, *The Lincoln Nobody Knows*, 12.

21. Jason Emerson, *The Madness of Mary Lincoln* (Carbondale: Southern Illinois University Press, 2007), 5.

22. Burlingame, *The Inner World of Abraham Lincoln*, 285. Burlingame presents a most interesting analysis of Mary Todd Lincoln in his chapter titled, "The Lincoln Marriage."

23. Shenk, *Lincoln's Melancholy*, 224.

24. Current, *The Lincoln Nobody Knows*, 12.

25. Jay Winik, "Revising Mr. Lincoln," *The American Enterprise*, March 2003, 27.

26. Burlingame, *The Inner World of Abraham Lincoln*, 318. The reader interested in psychological factors that may have impacted Lincoln should read Burlingame, and other sources noted in his work.

27. Major L. Wilson, "The Repressible Conflict: Seward's Concept of Progress and the Free-Soil Movement," *Journal of Southern History* (1971): 552.

28. Van Deusen, *Thurlow Weed*, 213.

29. Bancroft, *Life of William H. Seward*, 1:523.

30. Ibid., 1:523.

31. Barringer, *Lincoln's Rise to Power*, 226.

32. Barton, *President Lincoln*, 1:202.

33. Taylor, *William Henry Seward*, 25.

34. Goodwin, *Team of Rivals*, 74.

35. Van Deusen, *Thurlow Weed*, 69.

36. Taylor, *William Henry Seward*, 44.

37. Goodwin, *Team of Rivals*, 81.

38. Autobiography of Thurlow Weed, ed., Weed, 466–67; Frederick W. Seward, *Reminiscences of a War-Time Statesman and Diplomat* (New York: G.P. Putnam's Sons, 1916), 45, 88, as cited in Goodwin, *Team of Rivals*, 80–81.

39. Van Deusen, *Thurlow Weed*, 212–13.

40. Ibid., 213.

41. Ibid., 167.

42. Goodwin, *Team of Rivals*, 134.

43. Van Deusen, *Thurlow Weed*, 175.

44. George E. Baker, ed., *The Works of William H. Seward*, vol. 1 (New York: Redfield Press, 1853), 65–75, as cited in Taylor, *William Henry Seward*, 85.

45. Thurlow Weed to William Henry Seward, March 14, 1850, William Henry Seward Papers, as cited in Goodwin, *Team of Rivals*, 148.

46. Van Deusen, *Thurlow Weed*, 167.

47. Ibid., 178–79.

48. Barton, *President Lincoln*, 1:204.

49. One of the best essays on this subject is William E. Gienapp, "The Political System and the Coming of the Civil War," in *Why the Civil War Came*, ed. Boritt.

50. Taylor, *William Henry Seward*, 61.

51. Van Deusen, *Thurlow Weed*, 218.

52. Weed's term "free thinkers" was referring to the radical liberals of his day— Greeley among them but including William Lloyd Garrison, Joshua Giddings, and some of the radical Republicans.

53. Taylor, *William Henry Seward*, 94.

54. Ibid., 97.

55. Bancroft, *Life of William H. Seward*, 2:83.

56. Taylor, *William Henry Seward*, 102.

57. Van Deusen, *Thurlow Weed*, 206.

58. Van Deusen, *William H. Seward*, 177, as cited in Taylor, *William Henry Seward*, 100.

59. Daniel W. Crofts, "William Henry Seward," in *The Encyclopedia of U.S. Political History*, to be published in the *Congressional Quarterly*, vol. 3, ed. William Shade.

60. Bancroft, *William H. Seward*, 1:458–61, as cited in Taylor, *William Henry Seward*, 106–7.

61. Wilson, "The Repressible Conflict," 533–34.

62. Van Deusen, *William Henry Seward*, 194, as cited in Goodwin, *Team of Rivals*, 192.

63. Taylor, *William Henry Seward*, 113.

64. Burton J. Hendrick, *Lincoln's War Cabinet* (Boston: Little, Brown, 1946), 8, as cited in Taylor, *William Henry Seward*, 117.

65. William Henry Seward, "The Admission of Kansas," February 29, 1860, pamphlet by the *New York Tribune*, as cited in Taylor, *William Henry Seward*, 116.

66. Goodwin, *Team of Rivals*, 214.

67. Barton, *President Lincoln*, 1:204.

68. Bancroft, *Life of William H. Seward*, 2:78.

69. Ibid., 2:82.

70. Gerry Van der Heuvel, *Crowns of Thorns and Glory* (New York: E. P. Dutton, 1988), 75, as cited in Taylor, *William Henry Seward*, 91.

71. Bancroft, *Life of William H. Seward*, 2:83.

72. Gamaliel Bradford, *Union Portraits* (Boston: Houghton Mifflin, 1916), 202, as cited in Taylor, *William Henry Seward*, 90.

73. Barton, *President Lincoln*, 1:204.

Chapter 3

1. David H. Donald, *Lincoln Reconsidered* (New York: Knopf, 1956), 57.

2. Henry J. Raymond, *The Life and Public Services of Abraham Lincoln* (New York, 1865), 120.

3. Reprinted from the *New York Independent*, March 19, 1868, 12, in Moses Coit Tyler, "One of Mr. Lincoln's Old Friends," *Journal of Illinois State Historical Society* 29 (January 1936): 256, as cited in Burlingame, *Inner World of Abraham Lincoln*, 249.

4. Donald, *Lincoln*, 285.

5. Bancroft, *Life of William H. Seward*, 1:545.

6. Thurlow Weed Papers, Department of Rare Books and Special Collections, University of Rochester, Rochester, N.Y. (hereafter Weed Papers).

7. Ibid.

8. Earl S. Miers, ed., *Lincoln Day by Day*, vol. 2, *1849–1860* (Washington, D.C.: Lincoln Bicentennial Commission, 1960), 296–97.

9. Weed Papers.

10. Henry Adams, *Letters of Henry Adams*, 2 vols., ed. Worthington C. Ford (Boston: Houghton Mifflin, 1930–38), 1: 62.

11. Van Deusen, *William Henry Seward*, 239.

12. Barnes, *Memoirs of Thurlow Weed*, 308.

13. Van Deusen, *Thurlow Weed*, 266.

14. Bancroft, *Life of William H. Seward*, 2:26–27.

15. Crofts, *Reluctant Confederates*, 219–20.

16. A new work, Russell McClintock, *Lincoln and the Decision for War* (Chapel Hill: The University of North Carolina Press, 2008) offers an excellent analysis of Douglas and Crittenden during the secession winter.

17. Miers, *Lincoln Day by Day*, 2:300.

18. Van Deusen, *Thurlow Weed*, 267.

19. Taylor, *William Henry Seward*, 128.

20. Bancroft, *Life of William H. Seward*, 2:7.

21. Chuck Leddy, "New York City's Secession Crisis," *Civil War Times*, January 2007, 35.

22. Van Deusen, *William Henry Seward*, 242.

23. Crofts, *Reluctant Confederates*, 219.

24. Weed Papers.

25. McClintock, *Lincoln and the Decision for War*, 110–13.

26. Weed Papers.

27. Crofts, *Reluctant Confederates*, 219.

28. Donald, *Lincoln*, 260.

29. Crofts, *Reluctant Confederates*, 234.

30. Potter, *Lincoln and His Party in the Secession Crisis*, 293.

31. McClintock, *Lincoln and the Decision for War*, 103.

32. Ibid., 295.

33. Martin Duberman, *Charles Francis Adams, 1807–1886* (Boston: Houghton Mifflin, 1961), 239–40.

34. Potter, *Lincoln and His Party in the Secession Crisis*, 133.

35. Donald, *Lincoln*, 268.

36. Crofts, *Reluctant Confederates*, 217.

37. Rhodes, *History of the United States from 1850 to 1877*, 3:261.

38. Albert D. Kirwan, *John J. Crittenden: The Struggle for the Union* (Lexington: University of Kentucky Press, 1962), 401.

39. *Congressional Globe*, 36th Cong., 2d sess., A77, 580–83, A170, as cited in Crofts, *Reluctant Confederates*, 124–25.

40. Crofts, *Reluctant Confederates*, 223.

41. Ibid., 111–12.

42. Duberman, *Charles Francis Adams*, 235.

43. Lincoln, *Collected Works of Abraham Lincoln*, 1: 150–51.

44. McClintock, *Lincoln and the Decision for War*, 119–20.

45. Potter, *Lincoln and His Party in the Secession Crisis*, 135.

46. Letter to the editor dated January 22, 1861, in *Nashville Weekly Patriot*, January 28, 1861, as cited in Crofts, *Reluctant Confederates*, 93.

47. Potter, *Lincoln and His Party in the Secession Crisis*, 282.

48. Randle and Donald, *The Civil War and Reconstruction* (Boston: D. C. Heath and Company, 1961), 244.

49. Laura A. White, *Robert Barnwell Rhett: Father of Secession* (New York: Century Co., 1931), 192.

50. Van Deusen, *William Henry Seward*, 247.

51. Goodwin, *Team of Rivals*, 298.

52. Kirwan, *John J. Crittenden*, 396–97.

53. Donald, *Lincoln*, 269.

54. Rhodes, *History of the United States from 1850 to 1877*, 3:261.

55. *Alexandria Gazette*, January 24, 1861, as cited in Crofts, *Reluctant Confederates*, 116.

56. For a detailed analysis of various compromise proposals, see Crofts, *Reluctant Confederates*.

57. Washburne to Lincoln, January 7, 1861, and Lincoln to Hale, January 11, 1861, in Lincoln, *Collected Works of Abraham Lincoln*, 4:172, both letters cited in Crofts, *Reluctant Confederates*, 232–33.

58. Seward Papers.

59. Potter, *Lincoln and His Party in the Secession Crisis*, 285.

60. William Henry Seward, January 12, 1861, *Congressional Globe*, 36th Cong., 2nd sess.

61. *Chicago Tribune*, January 17, 1861, as cited in Goodwin, *Team of Rivals*, 300.

62. Van Deusen, *William Henry Seward*, 244.

63. Ibid., 246–47.

64. John G. Nicolay and John Hay, *Abra-*

ham Lincoln: A History (New York: The Century Co., 1917), 364.

65. Bancroft, *Life of William H. Seward*, 2:16.

66. Seward Papers.

67. Bancroft, *Life of William H. Seward*, 2:18.

68. Seward Papers.

69. Lincoln, *The Collected Works of Abraham Lincoln*, 176.

70. Potter, *Lincoln and His Party in the Secession Crisis*, 308.

71. Ibid., 307.

72. Ibid., 304.

73. "A Table Talk with Seward," clipping from the *Philadelphia Times*, as cited in Crofts, *Reluctant Confederates*, 205.

74. Potter, *Lincoln and His Party in the Secession Crisis*, 306.

75. Seward Papers.

76. Weed Papers.

77. Burlingame, *Inner World of Abraham Lincoln*, 155.

78. *Congressional Globe*, 36th cong., 2d sess., 36:2, 690–91; Hatton to William B. Campbell, January 24, 31, 1861, as cited in Crofts, *Reluctant Confederates*, 207.

79. Barton, *President Lincoln*, 1: 130.

80. Crofts, *Reluctant Confederates*, 206.

81. Leddy, "New York City's Secession Crisis," 35.

82. Potter, *Lincoln and His Party in the Secession Crisis*, 119.

83. Weed Papers.

84. Seward Papers.

85. Barringer, *A House Dividing: Lincoln as President Elect* (Springfield: Abraham Lincoln Association, 1945), 49.

86. Reddy, "New York City's Secession Crisis," 32–37.

87. Miers, ed., *Lincoln Day by Day*, 3:7–8.

88. *New York Times*, January 25, 1861; *Boston Advertiser*, January 31, 1861; *Philadelphia North American*, January 24, 26, 29, 1861; *National Intelligencer*, February 4, 1861; *Baltimore Clipper*, quoted in *Salisbury* (N.C.) *Carolina Watchman*, February 4, 1861; Seward to Lincoln, January 27, 1861, *Lincoln Papers*, as cited in Crofts, *Reluctant Confederates*, 206–7.

89. Kirwan, *John J. Crittenden*, 403.

90. Henry Adams to Charles Francis Adams Jr., February 5, 1861, in Adams, *Letters of Henry Adams*, ed. J.C. Levinson et al., 1:227–29; *Louisville Daily Journal*, February 9, 1861; *Congressional Globe*, 36; 2, A108, A137, A104; Robert Hatton to his wife, Jan-

uary 30, 1861, in Drake, *Hatton*, 323, as cited in Crofts, *Reluctant Confederates*, 239.

91. James A. Hamilton and other New York Republicans to Lincoln, January 29, 1861, *Lincoln Papers*, as cited in Crofts, *Reluctant Confederates*, 242.

92. Nicolay and Hay, *Abraham Lincoln*, 366.

93. McClintock, *Lincoln and the Decision for War*, 133.

Chapter 4

1. Long, *The Civil War Day by Day* (New York: Da Capo Press, 1971) 32–33.

2. McClintock, *Lincoln and the Decision for War*, 178.

3. Seward Papers.

4. Lincoln, *The Collected Works of Abraham Lincoln*, 173.

5. Crofts, *Reluctant Confederates*, 132.

6. Ford, ed., *Letters of Henry Adams*, 83.

7. Barton, *President Lincoln*, 1:133.

8. Weed Papers.

9. Potter, *Lincoln and His Party in the Secession Crisis*, 132.

10. Van Deusen, *Thurlow Weed*, 268.

11. Potter, *Lincoln and His Party in the Secession Crisis*, 283.

12. John Letcher to James D. Davidson, February 11, 1861, as cited in Crofts, *Reluctant Confederates*, 207.

13. Ford, ed., *Letters of Henry Adams*, 87.

14. Kirwan, *John J. Crittenden*, 400–401.

15. Crofts, *Reluctant Confederates*, 243–44.

16. Bancroft, *Life of William H. Seward*, 2:536.

17. Barton, *President Lincoln*, 1:175.

18. Sandburg, *Abraham Lincoln: The War Years* (New York: Harcourt, Brace and Company, 1939), 46–48.

19. Goodwin, *Team of Rivals*, 308.

20. Bancroft, *Life of William H. Seward*, 2:536.

21. *New York Times*, February 12, 1861, as cited in Crofts, *Reluctant Confederates*, 240.

22. Seward Papers.

23. Crofts, *Reluctant Confederates*, 227.

24. Ibid., 228.

25. Barringer, *A House Dividing*, 164–65.

26. Lincoln, *Collected Works of Abraham Lincoln*, 4:193, as cited in Donald, *Lincoln*, 275.

27. Sandburg, *Abraham Lincoln: The War Years*, 58–65.

28. Stampp, *And the War Came* (New Orleans: Louisiana State University Press, 1950), 196.

29. Potter, *Lincoln and His Party in the Secession Crisis*, 317.

30. Ibid., 317.

31. Charles Francis Adams, diary entries of February 16, 19, 1861, as cited in Crofts, *Reluctant Confederates*, 243.

32. Seward, *Reminiscences of a War-Time Statesman*, (New York: G. P. Putnam's Sons, 1916), 139.

33. Seward Papers.

34. Ibid.

35. Ibid.

36. Donald, *Lincoln*, 279–80.

37. Seward, *Reminiscences of a War-Time Statesman and Diplomat*, 147.

38. Crofts, *Reluctant Confederates*, 245–47.

39. Stampp, *And the War Came*, 196–97.

40. Crofts, *Reluctant Confederates*, 243.

41. Sandburg, *Abraham Lincoln: The War Years*, 96–97.

42. George Fort Milton, *The Eve of Conflict: Stephen A. Douglas and the Needless War* (Boston: Houghton Mifflin, 1934), 545, as cited in Donald, *Lincoln*, 280.

43. Seward to Lincoln, February 24, 1861, as cited in Crofts, *Reluctant Confederates*, 247.

44. Henry Adams, "Great Secession Winter," 683, as cited in Crofts, *Reluctant Confederates*, 247.

45. Crofts, *Reluctant Confederates*, 251.

46. Barringer, *A House Dividing*, 319.

47. *North Carolina Semi-Weekly Standard*, March 9, 13, 16, 1861, as cited in Crofts, *Reluctant Confederates*, 157–59.

48. Andrew Johnson to Sam Milligan, January 13, 1861, Johnson to John Trimble, January 13, 1861, both in *Johnson Papers*, 4:160–65; *Weekly Knoxville Whig*, January 12, 19, 1861, as cited in Crofts, *Reluctant Confederates*, 159.

49. Stampp, *And the War Came*, 182.

50. Weed Papers.

51. Donald, *Lincoln*, 281.

52. Van Deusen, *William Henry Seward*, 253.

53. Potter, *Lincoln and His Party in the Secession Crisis*, 314.

54. Donald, *Lincoln*, 257.

Chapter 5

1. Charles Francis Adams, diary entry of February 27, 1861, as cited in Crofts, *Reluctant Confederates*, 250–51.

2. Gideon Welles, *Diary of Gideon Welles, Secretary of the Navy Under Lincoln and Johnson*, 3 vols., ed. Howard K. Beale and Alan W. Brownsword (New York: W. W. Norton, 1960) 2:391, as cited in Donald, *Lincoln*, 281–82.

3. Barringer, *A House Dividing*, 322.

4. Sincere Friend to William Henry Seward, April 5, 1861, Seward Papers; Frederick L. Roberts to William Henry Seward, March 18, 1861, Seward Papers; and Edwards Pierrepont to William Evarts, January 5, 1861 (emphasis added), collection of John M. Taylor, as cited in Taylor, *William Henry Seward*, 138–39.

5. Lincoln, *Collected Works of Abraham Lincoln*, 4:273, as cited in Donald, *Lincoln*, 282.

6. Crofts, *Reluctant Confederates*, 254.

7. Nicolay and Hay, *Abraham Lincoln: A History*, 3:371.

8. Barringer, *A House Dividing*, 322–23.

9. Scott to Seward, March 3, 1861, in *Lincoln Papers*, ed. David C. Mearns, 2:456–57, as cited in Crofts, *Reluctant Confederates*, 271.

10. Collections of Seward House, Auburn, New York (hereafter Seward Collections).

11. *Baltimore Exchange* in *Wheeling Daily Intelligencer*, March 12, 1861, as cited in Crofts, *Reluctant Confederates*, 254.

12. William H. Herndon, *Life of Lincoln* (New York: Da Capo Press, 1930), 400.

13. Nicolay and Hay, *Abraham Lincoln*, 3:371.

14. Seward, *Seward at Washington*, 518, as cited in Donald, *Lincoln*, 282.

15. Crofts, *Reluctant Confederates*, 254–55. Crofts also points out it was Dr. Patrick Sowle in "Conciliatory Republicans" who first pointed out the "well-hidden cause-and-effect relationship between Seward's resignation, the revision of the Inaugural Address, and Seward's change of heart."

16. Potter, *Lincoln and His Party in the Secession Crisis*, 324–29.

17. Donald, *Lincoln*, 285.

18. Charles Francis Adams, diary, March 10, 1861, Massachusetts Historical Society, as cited in Donald, *Lincoln*, 285.

19. Villard, *Memoirs*, 1:156, as cited in Donald, *Lincoln*, 286.

20. Henry Wilson to William Henry Seward, May 20, 1867, as cited in Donald, *Lincoln*, 285.

21. John G. Nicolay to O. M. Hatch, March 7, 1861, Hatch Mss., Illinois State Historical Society, Springfield, as cited in Donald, *Lincoln*, 285.

22. Freehling's new volume of *The Road to Disunion* is a must read for any serious student of the secession crisis.

23. T. A. R. Nelson to William G. Brownlow, March 13, 1861, in *National Intelligencer*, March 25, 1861; "Special," March 17, 1861, in *Baltimore American*, March 18, 1861, both cited in Crofts, *Reluctant Confederates*, 262.

24. Seward Collections.

25. Seward Papers.

26. *New York Times*, March 11, 1861; Joseph Segar to Simon Cameron, March 26, 1861, both cited in Crofts, *Reluctant Confederates*, 278.

27. *Congressional Globe*, 36th Congress, Special Senate sess., 1436–39, as cited in Crofts, *Reluctant Confederates*, 261.

28. Gilmer to Seward, March 7, 8, 12, Seward Papers, excerpted in Bancroft, *Seward*, 2: 545–48; Gilmer to Seward, March 9, 1861, Lincoln Papers, as cited in Crofts, *Reluctant Confederates*, 258.

29. William Ernest Smith, *The Francis Preston Blair Family in Politics* (New York: Macmillan, 1933), 2:9–10, as cited in Donald, *Lincoln*, 286.

30. Crofts, *Reluctant Confederates*, 259.

31. Georgia Lee Tatum, *Disloyalty in the Confederacy* (Chapel Hill: University of North Carolina Press, 1934), 4.

32. Denton, *A Southern Star for Maryland*, 8.

33. Crofts, Reluctant Confederates, 262–63.

34. James E. Harvey to Henry C. Carey, undated (early 1861), Henry C. Carey Papers, Edward Carey Gardiner Collection, Historical Society of Pennsylvania, Philadelphia; Martin J. Crawford to Robert Toombs, March 6, 1861, quoted in Bancroft, *Seward*, 2:108–10, as cited in Crofts, *Reluctant Confederates*, 271.

35. Crofts, *Reluctant Confederates*, 274.

36. Weed Papers.

37. Seward Papers.

38. Ibid.

39. Van Deusen, *William Henry Seward*, 278.

40. Long, *The Civil War Day by Day*, 49.

41. Nicolay and Hay, *Abraham Lincoln: A History*, 3:385.

42. Donald, *Lincoln*, 287.

43. Potter, *Lincoln and His Party in the Secession Crisis*, 340.

44. Mearns, ed., *Lincoln Papers*, 2:483–84; James Ford Rhodes, *History of the United States from the Compromise of 1850* (New York: Macmillan, 1906), 3:333, as cited in Donald, *Lincoln*, 287.

45. Nicolay and Hay, *Abraham Lincoln: A History*, 3:408.

46. William Russell, *My Diary North and South* (Boston, 1863), 17, as cited in Taylor, *William Henry Seward*, 143.

47. Long, *The Civil War Day by Day*, 50.

48. Sandburg, *Abraham Lincoln: The War Years*, 157.

49. Crofts, *Reluctant Confederates*, 275.

50. George W. Summers to James C. Welling, March 19, 1861, copy in Blair Family Papers, Library of Congress, as cited in Crofts, *Reluctant Confederates*, 276.

51. Seward Papers.

52. Crofts, *Reluctant Confederates*, 283–84.

53. Donald, *Lincoln*, 288.

54. *National Intelligencer*, March 21, 1861; *New York Times*, March 21, 1861, both cited in Crofts, *Reluctant Confederates*, 286.

55. *New York Herald*, January–April 1861, as cited in Crofts, *Reluctant Confederates*, 292.

56. Potter, *Lincoln and His Party in the Secession Crisis*, 329–31.

57. George W. Summers to James C. Welling, March 19, 1861, as cited in Crofts, *Reluctant Confederates*, 289.

58. Weed Papers.

59. Potter, *Lincoln and His Party in the Secession Crisis*, 341–42.

60. Nicolay and Hay, *Abraham Lincoln: A History*, 3:394, as cited in Donald, *Lincoln*, 288.

61. Nicolay and Hay, *Abraham Lincoln: A History*, 3:381.

62. McClintock, *Lincoln and the Decision for War*, 229–31.

63. Donald, *Lincoln*, 288.

64. Crofts, *Reluctant Confederates*, 298.

65. Long, *The Civil War Day by Day*, 51.

66. Crofts, *Reluctant Confederates*, 291–93.

67. Allan Nevins, *The War for the Union*, vol. I, *The Improvised War, 1861–1862* (New York: Scribner's Sons, 1959), 58, as cited in Donald, *Lincoln*, 289.

Chapter 6

1. Taylor, *William Henry Seward*, 150.
2. Van Deusen, *William Henry Seward*, 280.
3. Charles Francis Adams, diary, March 28, 31, 1861, as cited in Van Deusen, *William Henry Seward*, 281.
4. Richard. N. Current, *Lincoln and the First Shot* (Prospect Heights, IL: Waveland Press, Inc., 1990), 90.
5. Crenshaw, *Slave States in the Presidential Election of 1860*, 99.
6. Crofts, *Reluctant Confederates*, 299–300.
7. "Some Thoughts for the President's Consideration," April 1, 1861, Lincoln Papers (four quotes from Seward's paper).
8. Van Deusen, *William Henry Seward*, 282–83.
9. Donald, *Lincoln*, 290.
10. Crofts, *Reluctant Confederates*, 300–301.
11. Angle, ed., *Herndon's Lincoln*, 414, as cited in Burlingame, *Inner World of Abraham Lincoln*, 194.
12. Current, *Lincoln and the First Shot*, 87.
13. McClintock, *Lincoln and the Decision for War*, 246–47.
14. Seward, *Reminiscences of a War-time Statesman and Diplomat*, 148, as cited in Goodwin, *Team of Rivals*, 344.
15. Allan B. Magruder, "A Piece of Secret History: President Lincoln and the Virginia Convention of 1861," *Atlantic Monthly* 35 (1875): 438–45, as cited in Crofts, *Reluctant Confederates*, 301.
16. Nicolay and Hay, *Abraham Lincoln: A History*, 4: 65.
17. Seward Papers.
18. Reese, ed., *Virginia Convention*, 3:203, 205, 209, 325–26, 333–34, 343–45, as cited in Crofts, *Reluctant Confederates*, 309.
19. Miers, *Lincoln Day by Day*, 2:33.
20. A very good analysis of this affair can be found in Crofts, *Reluctant Confederates*, 301–6.
21. Magruder, "A Piece of Secret History."
22. Current, *The Lincoln Nobody Knows*, 120–21.
23. Ibid., 118.
24. McClintock, *Lincoln and the Decision for War*, 244–45.
25. Crofts, *Reluctant Confederates*, 308.
26. Potter, *Lincoln and His Party in the Secession Crisis*, 363.

27. Ibid., 363–64.
28. Current, *Lincoln and the First Shot*, 68–69.
29. Ibid., 119.
30. Ibid., 106.
31. Daniel W. Crofts, "James E. Harvey and the Secession Crisis," *Pennsylvania Magazine of History and Biography* 103, no. 2 (April 1979). Crofts gives a full account of this episode.
32. Van Deusen, *William Henry Seward*, 285.
33. Current, *Lincoln and the First Shot*, 115.
34. Potter, *Lincoln and His Party in the Secession Crisis*, 349.
35. Current, *Lincoln and the First Shot*, 114.
36. Long, *The Civil War Day by Day*, 55.
37. Crofts, *Reluctant Confederates*, 311.
38. Current, *Lincoln and the First Shot*, 120–21.
39. Sandburg, *Abraham Lincoln: The War Years*, 200–201.
40. Carl Sandburg, *Abraham Lincoln: The War Years*, 1:206, as cited in Taylor, *William Henry Seward*, 157.
41. Gilmer to Seward, April 12, 1861, as cited in Crofts, *Reluctant Confederates*, 311.
42. Current, *The Lincoln Nobody Knows*, 118.
43. Van Deusen, *William Henry Seward*, 286.
44. Long, *The Civil War Day by Day*, 56–60.
45. Current, *The Lincoln Nobody Knows*, 123.
46. Current, *Lincoln and the First Shot*, 159.
47. Crofts, *Reluctant Confederates*, 312.
48. Basler, *The Lincoln Legend*, (Boston: Houghton Mifflin, 1935), 332.
49. Burlingame, *Inner World of Abraham Lincoln*, 201.
50. Alexander H. H. Stuart to Seward, April 15, 1861 (telegram), as cited in Crofts, *Reluctant Confederates*, 313.
51. Reese, ed., *Virginia Convention*, 3: 749–50, 759–64, as cited in Crofts, *Reluctant Confederates*, 313.
52. Craven, *Coming of the Civil War*, 437.
53. Reese, ed., *Virginia Convention*, 4: 21–23, 70, 122–23, 144–45, as cited in Crofts, *Reluctant Confederates*, 315.
54. Reese, ed., *Virginia Convention*, 4:16, as cited in Nelson D. Lankford, *Cry Havoc* (New York: Viking Press, 2007), 119.

55. John Minor Botts, *The Great Rebellion: Its Secret History, Rise, Progress, and Disastrous Failure* (New York: Harpers & Brothers, 1866), 206, as cited in Crofts, *Reluctant Confederates*, 322.

56. For a most interesting review of the secret meeting, see Lankford, *Cry Havoc,* chap. 9.

57. Crofts, *Reluctant Confederates,* 323.

58. Ibid., 326–30.

59. Randall and Donald, *The Civil War and Reconstruction,* 177–78.

60. *North Carolina Semi-Weekly Standard*, April 24, May 8, 1861, as cited in Crofts, *Reluctant Confederates,* 333.

61. Horace Maynard to Edward Bates, April 18 (?), 1861, General Records of the Department of Justice, Record Group 60, National Archives, as cited in Crofts, *Reluctant Confederates,* 334.

62. John Bell, speech of April 23, 1861, in *Nashville Republican Banner,* May 10, 1861, as cited in Crofts, *Reluctant Confederates,* 334–35.

63. *North Carolina Semi-Weekly Standard*, April 20, 1861, as cited in Crofts, *Reluctant Confederates,* 335.

64. John Minor Botts, *The Great Rebellion: Its Secret History, Rise, Progress, and Disastrous Failure,* 205–6, as cited in Crofts, *Reluctant Confederates,* 335.

65. Jonathan Worth to Springs Oak Co., May 13, 1861, as cited in Crofts, *Reluctant Confederates,* 336.

66. Bruce S. Greenawalt, ed., "Unionists in Rockbridge County: The Correspondence of James Dorman Davidson Concerning the Virginia Secession Convention of 1861," *Virginia Magazine of History and Biography* 73 (1965): 100–101, as cited in Crofts, *Reluctant Confederates,* 336.

67. John A. Gilmer to William H. Seward, April 21, 1861, as cited in Crofts, *Reluctant Confederates,* 340.

68. Seward Papers.

69. Van Deusen, *William Henry Seward,* 286–87.

70. Potter, *Lincoln and His Party in the Secession Crisis,* 375.

71. Statement by George P. Goff, enclosed to John G. Nicolay, Washington, February 9, 1899, Nicolay Mss., Library of Congress, as cited in Burlingame, *Inner World of Abraham Lincoln,* 104.

72. Randall and Donald, *The Civil War and Reconstruction,* 188–89.

Epilogue

1. Current, *Lincoln and the First Shot,* 21–22.

2. Rhodes, *History of the United States from 1850 to 1877,* 3:260.

3. Henry Adams to Charles Francis Adams Jr., December 9, 1861, as cited in Goodwin, *Team of Rivals,* 12.

4. Stephens to _____, November 25, 1860, as cited in McPherson, *Battle Cry of Freedom,* 238.

5. Bancroft, *Life of William H. Seward,* 1:528.

6. Freehling, *The Reintegration of American History,* 140.

7. James G. Randall, *Lincoln the Liberal Statesman* (New York: Dodd, 1947), 3.

8. Freehling, *The Road to Disunion,* 2:143.

9. Richard L. Watson, Jr., "Thurlow Weed, Political Boss," *New York History* 22 (October 1941): 415, as cited in Goodwin, *Team of Rivals,* 15.

10. Van Deusen, *William Henry Seward,* 257–58.

11. Goodwin, *Team of Rivals,* 192.

12. Freehling, *The Road to Disunion,* 2:340–41.

13. *Alexandria Gazette,* December 24, 1860; *Richmond Whig,* January 4, 1861; Shanks, *Secession Movement in Virginia,* 131, 164; Frederick Fein Siegel, *A New South in the Old: Sotweed and Soil in the Development of Danville, Virginia,* 235–41, as cited in Crofts, *Reluctant Confederates,* 106–7.

14. Underwood in *Wilmington Delaware Republican,* October 17, 1859, as cited in Freehling, *The Road to Disunion,* 2:330.

15. Duberman, *Charles Francis Adams,* 225.

16. Craven, *The Coming of the Civil War,* 429.

17. Goodwin, *Team of Rivals,* 267.

18. Crofts, *Reluctant Confederates,* 90.

19. Ibid., 197.

20. Bancroft, *Life of William H. Seward,* 37.

21. Current, *The Lincoln Nobody Knows,* 94.

22. Goodwin, *Team of Rivals,* xvi.

23. Nicolay and Hay, *Abraham Lincoln,* 3:443.

24. Donald, *Lincoln,* 267.

25. Crofts, *Reluctant Confederates,* 34–36.

26. Freehling, *The Road to Disunion,* 2:400–410.

27. Ibid., 410.

28. Potter, *Lincoln and His Party in the Secession Crisis*, 284.

29. Barton, *President Lincoln*, 1:68.

30. Freehling, *The Road to Disunion*, 2:339.

31. Leddy, "New York City's Secession Crisis," 35.

32. Denton, *A Southern Star for Maryland*, 4–5.

33. William W. Freehling, *The South versus the South: How Anti-Confederate Southerners Shaped the Course of the Civil War* (Oxford: Oxford University Press, 2001), xiii.

34. Bancroft, *Life of William Henry Seward*, 2:82.

35. Freehling, *The South versus the South*, 17.

36. Ibid., 2:437.

37. Ibid., 2:442.

38. Ibid., xiii. The reader interested in this intriguing question is referred to Freehling's captivating work.

39. *Richmond Whig*, February 13, 1861, as cited in Crofts, *Reluctant Confederates*, 263.

40. *Nashville Republican Banner*, March 31, 1861, as cited in Crofts, *Reluctant Confederates*, 265–66.

41. Robert C. Kenzer, "Portrait of a Southern Community, 1849–1881: Family, Kinship, and Neighborhood in Orange County, North Carolina," Ph.D. diss., Harvard University, Cambridge, 1982, 94, as cited in Crofts, *Reluctant Confederates*, 266.

42. Bancoft, *Life of William Henry Seward*, 2:537.

43. *New York Herald*, February 28 and March 1, 1861, as cited in Crofts, *Reluctant Confederates*, 269–70.

44. Crofts, *Reluctant Confederates*, 270–71.

45. Lyons to Lord John Russell, February 4, 1861, as cited in Crofts, *Reluctant Confederates*, 272.

46. Potter, *Lincoln and His Party in the Secession Crisis*, 272.

47. Bancroft, *Life of William Henry Seward*, 2:90.

48. Hale, *William H. Seward*, 373.

49. Goodwin, *Team of Rivals*, 122.

50. Van Deusen, *William Henry Seward*, 563.

Appendix

1. J. G. Randall and David Donald, *The Civil War and Reconstruction* (Boston: D. C. Heath, 1961), 134.

2. A more complete analysis of the 1860 presidential election can be found in Denton, *A Southern Star for Maryland*, chapter 2.

Bibliography

Primary Sources

Collections of Seward House, Auburn, N.Y.

William Henry Seward Papers, Department of Rare Books and Special Collections, University of Rochester, Rochester, N.Y.

Thurlow Weed Papers, Department of Rare Books and Special Collections, University of Rochester, Rochester, N.Y.

Published Primary and Secondary Sources

Abbott, Philip. "The Lincoln Propositions and the Spirit of Secession." *Studies in American Political Development* 10 (Spring 1996).

Adams, Henry. *Letters of Henry Adams.* Ed. Worthington C. Ford. 2 vols. Boston: Houghton Mifflin, 1930–38.

Angle, Paul M. *Lincoln, 1854–1861. Being the Day-to-day Activities of Abraham Lincoln from January 1, 1854 to March 4, 1861.* Springfield, 1933.

Baker, George E., ed. *The Works of William H. Seward.* Vol. 1. New York: Redfield Press, 1853.

Bancroft, Frederic. *The Life of William H. Seward.* 2 vols. New York: Harper and Brothers, 1900.

Barnes, Thurlow Weed. *Memoir of Thurlow Weed.* Boston, 1884.

Barringer, William. *A House Dividing: Lincoln as President Elect.* Springfield, Ill.: Abraham Lincoln Association, 1945.

_____. *Lincoln's Rise to Power.* Boston: Little, Brown, 1937.

_____. *President Lincoln.* Vol. 1. Indianapolis: Bobbs-Merrill, 1933.

Basler, Roy P. *The Lincoln Legend.* Boston, Houghton Mifflin, 1935.

Boritt, Gabor S. *The Historian's Lincoln.* Chicago: 1988.

_____, ed. *Lincoln the War President.* New York: Oxford University Press, 1992.

_____, ed. *Why the Civil War Came.* New York: Oxford University Press, 1996.

Botts, John Minor. *The Great Rebellion: Its Secret History, Rise, Progress, and Disastrous Failure.* New York: Harper and Brothers, 1866.

Bradford, Gamaliel. *Union Portraits.* Boston: Houghton Mifflin, 1916.

Brown, Francis. *Raymond of the Times.* New York: W.W. Norton, 1951.

Burlingame, Michael. *The Inner World of Abraham Lincoln.* Urbana: University of Illinois Press, 1994.

Burnham, Walter Dean. *Critical Elections and the Mainsprings of American Politics.* New York: Norton, 1970.

Carter, Dan T. *When the War Was Over*. Baton Rouge: Louisiana State University Press, 1985.

Catton, Bruce. *The Coming Fury*. New York: Doubleday, 1961.

_____. *Reflections on the Civil War*. New York: Doubleday, 1981.

Chadwick, Bruce. *1858*. Naperville: Sourcebooks, 2008.

Craven, Avery O. *The Coming of the Civil War*. Chicago: University of Chicago Press, 1957.

_____. "The Price of Union." *Journal of Southern History* 18 (1952).

Crawford, S. W. *The Genesis of the Civil War: The Story of Sumter, 1860–61*. New York, 1887.

Crenshaw, Ollinger. *The Slave States in the Presidential Election of 1860*. Gloucester: Peter Smith, 1969.

Crofts, Daniel W. "James E. Harvey and the Secession Crisis." *Pennsylvania Magazine of History and Biography* 103, no. 2 (April 1979).

_____. *Reluctant Confederates*. Chapel Hill: University of North Carolina Press, 1989.

_____. "William Henry Seward." In *The Encyclopedia of U.S. Political History*, to be published in the *Congressional Quarterly*, vol. 3, ed. William Shade.

Current, Richard N. *Lincoln and the First Shot*. Prospect Heights, Ill.: Waveland Press, 1990.

_____. *The Lincoln Nobody Knows*. New York: McGraw, 1958.

Denton, Lawrence M. *A Southern Star for Maryland*. Baltimore: Publishing Concepts, 1995.

DiLorenzo, Thomas J. *The Real Lincoln*. New York: Three Rivers Press, 2002.

Donald, David H. *Lincoln*. New York: Simon and Schuster, 1995.

_____. *Lincoln Reconsidered*. New York: Knopf, 1956.

Duberman, Martin. *Charles Francis Adams, 1807–1886*. Boston: Houghton Mifflin, 1961.

Emerson, Jason. *The Madness of Mary Lincoln*. Carbondale: Southern Illinois University Press, 2007.

Faust, Drew Gilpin. *This Republic of Suffering*. New York: Knopf, 2008.

Fehrenbacher, Don E. *The Changing Image of Lincoln in American Historiography*. London: Oxford University Press, 1968.

Freehling, William W. *The Reintegration of American History*. New York: Oxford University Press, 1994.

_____. *The Road to Disunion*. Vol. 2. New York: Oxford University Press, 2007.

_____. *The South versus the South: How Anti-Confederate Southerners Shaped the Course of the Civil War*. Oxford: Oxford University Press, 2001.

Garrison, Webb. *The Lincoln No One Knows*. Nashville: Rutledge Hill Press, 1993.

Goodwin, Doris Kearns. *Team of Rivals: The Political Genius of Abraham Lincoln*. New York: Simon and Schuster, 2005.

Graebner, Norman A., ed. *Politics and the Crisis of 1860*. Urbana: University of Illinois Press, 1961.

Greenawalt, Bruce S., ed. "Unionists in Rockbridge County: The Correspondence of James Dorman Davidson Concerning the Virginia Secession Convention of 1861." *Virginia Magazine of History and Biography* 73 (1965).

Hale, Edward Everett, Jr. *William H. Seward*. Philadelphia: G.W. Jacobs, 1910.

Harris, William C. "The Southern Unionist Critique of the Civil War." *CWH* 31 (1985).

Hendrick, Burton J. *Lincoln's War Cabinet*. Boston: Little, Brown, 1946.

Herndon, William H. *Life of Lincoln*. New York: Da Capo Press, 1930.

Kenzer, Robert C. "Portrait of a Southern Community, 1849–1881: Family, Kinship, and Neighborhood in Orange County, North Carolina." Ph.D. diss., Harvard University, Cambridge, 1982.

Kirwan, Albert D. *John J. Crittenden: The Struggle for the Union*. Lexington: University of Kentucky Press, 1962.

Klement, Frank L. *Lincoln's Critics*. Shippensburg, PA: White Mane, 1999.
Kruman, Marc W. *Parties and Politics in North Carolina, 1836–1865*. Baton Rouge: Louisiana State University Press, 1983.
Lankford, Nelson D. *Cry Havoc!* New York: Viking Press, 2007.
Leddy, Chuck. "New York City's Secession Crisis." *Civil War Times,* January 2007.
Levinson et al., eds. *Letters of Henry Adams,* 3 vols. Cambridge: Belknap Press of Harvard University Press, 1982.
Lincoln, Abraham. *The Collected Works of Abraham Lincoln*. Ed. Roy P. Basler. New Brunswick, N.J.: Rutgers University Press, 1953–55.
Long, E. B. *The Civil War Day by Day*. New York: Da Capo Press, 1971.
Magruder, Allan B. "A Piece of Secret History: President Lincoln and the Virginia Convention of 1861." *Atlantic Monthly* 35 (1875).
McClintock, Russell. *Lincoln and the Decision for War*. Chapel Hill: University of North Carolina Press, 2008.
McPherson, James M. *Battle Cry of Freedom*. New York: Oxford University Press, 1988.
_____. *Drawn with the Sword*. New York: Oxford University Press, 1996.
Miers, Earl S., ed. *Lincoln Day by Day*. Vol. 2, *1849–1860*. Washington, D.C.: Lincoln Bicentennial Commission, 1960.
Milton, George Fort. *The Eve of Conflict: Stephen A. Douglas and the Needless War*. Boston: Houghton Mifflin, 1934.
Morison, Samuel E., and Henry S. Commager. *The Growth of the American Republic*. Vol. 1. New York: Oxford University Press, 1962.
Neely, Mark E., Jr. *The Last Best Hope on Earth*. Cambridge: Harvard University Press, 1993.
Nevins, Allan. *The War for the Union*. Vol. 1, *The Improvised War, 1861–1862*. New York: Scribner's Sons, 1959.
Nicolay, John G., and John Hay. *Abraham Lincoln: A History*. New York: Century Co., 1917.
Potter, David M. *Lincoln and His Party in the Secession Crisis*. New Haven: Yale University Press, 1962.
Randall, J. G., and David Donald. *The Civil War and Reconstruction*. Boston: D. C. Heath, 1961.
Randall, James G. *Lincoln the Liberal Statesman*. New York: Dodd, 1947.
Raymond, Henry J. *The Life and Public Services of Abraham Lincoln*. New York, 1865.
_____, ed. "Excerpts from the Journal of Henry J. Raymond." *Scribner's Monthly* (November 1879; January 1880; March 1880.)
Rhodes, James Ford. *History of the United States from 1850 to 1877*. Vol. 3, *The Compromise of 1850*. New York: Macmillan, 1906.
Russell, William. *My Diary North and South*. Boston, 1863.
Sandburg, Carl. *Abraham Lincoln: The War Years*. New York: Harcourt, Brace, 1939.
Seward, Frederick W. *Reminiscences of a War-Time Statesman and Diplomat*. New York: G. P. Putnam's Sons, 1916.
Shanks, Henry T. *Secession Movement in Virginia. 1847–1861*. Richmond: Garrett and Massie, 1934.
Shenk, Joshua W. *Lincoln's Melancholy*. Boston: Houghton Mifflin, 2005.
Smith, William Ernest. *The Francis Preston Blair Family in Politics*. New York: Macmillan, 1933.
Soule, Patrick M. "The Conciliatory Republicans during the Winter of Secession." Ph.D. diss., Duke University, Durham, N.C., 1963.
Stampp, Kenneth W. *And the War Came*. New Orleans: Louisiana State University Press, 1950.
Striner, Richard. *Father Abraham*. New York: Oxford University Press, 2006.

Tatum, Georgia Lee. *Disloyalty in the Confederacy*. Chapel Hill: University of North Carolina Press, 1934.

Taylor, John M. *William Henry Seward*. New York: Brassey's, 1991.

Tyler, Moses Coit. "One of Mr. Lincoln's Old Friends." *Journal of Illinois State Historical Society* 29 (January 1936).

Van der Heuvel, Gerry. *Crowns of Thorns and Glory*. New York: E. P. Dutton, 1988.

Van Deusen, Glyndon G. *Thurlow Weed: Wizard of the Lobby*. Boston: Little, Brown, 1947.

_____*William Henry Seward*. New York: Oxford University Press, 1967.

Warren, Robert P. *The Legacy of the Civil War*. Lincoln: University of Nebraska Press, 1961.

Watson, Richard L., Jr. "Thurlow Weed, Political Boss." *New York History* 22 (October 1941).

Welles, Gideon. *Diary of Gideon Welles, Secretary of the Navy Under Lincoln and Johnson*. Ed. Beale, Howard K., and Alan W. Brownsword. 3 vols. New York: W. W. Norton, 1960.

White, Laura A. *Robert Barnwell Rhett: Father of Secession*. New York: Century Co., 1931.

Williams, Harry T. *Lincoln and the Radicals*. Madison: University of Wisconsin Press, 1941.

Wilson, Major L. "The Repressible Conflict: Seward's Concept of Progress and the Free-Soil Movement." *Journal of Southern History* (1971).

Winik, Jay. *April 1865*. New York: Perennial, 2002.

_____. "Revising Mr. Lincoln." *The American Enterprise*, March 2003.

Wright, John S. *Lincoln and the Politics of Slavery*. Reno: University of Nevada Press, 1970.

Wright, William C. *The Secession Movement in the Middle Atlantic States*. Rutherford, N.J.: Fairleigh Dickinson University Press, 1973.

INDEX

Numbers in *bold italics* indicate pages with photographs.